Now the news in detail

A Guide to Broadcast Journalism in Australia

Murray Masterton and
Roger Patching

Deakin University Press

Published and distributed by Deakin
University Press, Victoria, Australia, 3217
First published 1986, Second edition 1990
© Murray Masterton and Roger Patching
1986, 1990

Designed and typeset by Deakin University
Book Production Unit

Front Cover devised by Rona Abbott

Printed by Brown Prior Anderson Pty Ltd
Burwood, Vic 3125

National Library of Australia
Cataloguing-in-publication data

Masterton, Murray, 1929–
   Now the news in detail.

   Bibliography.
   ISBN 0 7300 1441 X

   1. Broadcast journalism. I. Patching,
Roger, 1944–   . II. Title.

070.1'9

Previous page
Photograph courtesy of Channel 10

Contents

Introduction   1

Aims
What is broadcast journalism trying to do?   5

Logistics
Where news comes from and how it is put together   23

Equipment
A brief survey of the tools of the electronic journalist   51

Words
One of the tools, but worth a whole chapter   77

Techniques 1
How to do it, mainly in radio   103

Techniques 2
Extending the how to do it to television   127

The Art of it
About interviewing, which is an art   155

Current Affairs broadcasting
The wider aspects, including documentaries   189

> **Before satellite, transistors or radio-cars**
> *Historic pictures from broadcasting's past*   follows page 208

Keeping it ethical
About the ethics of journalism, especially broadcasting   211

Know the law
Broadcasters have even more legal problems than other journalists   231

And tomorrow . . .
Some inequalities and deficiencies still to be remedied   253

Appendix 1:
Glossary   263

Appendix 2:
Australian broadcasting stations   271

Appendix 3:
Some useful and relevant reading   285

Few broadcasters, except the ABC, have any structured training for those who will staff the newsroom. More and more of today's news broadcasters come from university programs in journalism which offer understanding of journalism as a profession and practical instruction from the gathering of facts to their final presentation on air.

(Picture: Charles Sturt University, Bathurst)

1
Introduction

Writing books about the media, especially critical books, has been in vogue in Australia for several years, so any new offering must be either more up to date, more critical or different from the others. This one is different, in both approach and content. It is also more up to date, more critical and more explanatory than the first edition, published by Deakin University Press in 1986.

This is a book about broadcast journalism, not the news media as a whole or even radio and television, except as purveyors of news. It is intended to be explanatory and informational, and for those who want to be journalists, instructional.

While this is a book about broadcast journalism, there is no intention to justify journalism as practised by the broadcast media in Australia today, though much of what happens in today's journalism can be both understood and justified. Much of what media critics say about the gathering, selection and presentation of print or broadcast news is true enough, so it would be wasted effort to argue otherwise. But when there are reasons why journalists gather, select and present news the way they do, and those reasons are overlooked or misunderstood by the critics, this book may clarify the situation.

There is a further reason for yet another book about news and current affairs on air. Most existing books describing how radio and television journalists go about their daily duties are either American or British. This means they are relevant only in part in Australia, and only to experienced working journalists — those competent to translate overseas situations and descriptions to Australian equivalents. They offer little to readers who have no understanding of journalism or of the workings of broadcasting.

There are Australian-published books about how journalists work in newspapers and elsewhere in the print media. Those which have much relevance for those who work, or want to work, in broadcasting, are included in the bibliography in the appendix.

If this book gives some understanding of how and why radio and television news in Australia reaches its consumers in its present form, it will serve its major purpose. If it also gives readers an understanding of why broadcast journalists work as they do, why the news services are as they are, and some understanding of the problems as well as the advantages and prospects of broadcast journalism, then it will be meeting the authors' aims more completely. It is not a do-it-yourself text for would-be broadcast journalists: no book can be. It may serve as a text for student journalists as well as students of broadcast journalism, but anyone with aspirations to practise as a journalist needs much more.

The profession of journalism is more complex today than ever before, because the world is a more complex place and more is expected than ever before of those who report it. Broadcast journalism adds to this complexity its own ever-developing variety of techniques and skills, and its own constraints and problems. If readers who truly wish to become journalists, in print or broadcasting, gain enthusiasm and direction from this book as well as some how-to-do-it tips, then that's a bonus.

Combining radio and television journalism in the one book is logical but not always comfortable: logical because the two media share so much in aims, writing style and certain techniques; uneasy because the overlap goes only so far. Although television almost invariably goes beyond radio in its required skills, technical complexity and logistical problems, dealing with both in nearly every chapter seems the most logical approach. Those interested in radio or television, but not both, will have to be selective. Anyone who aspires to be a broadcast journalist would do well to read and absorb both.

Readers who have progressed this far are probably aware that the language of this introduction is not that normally seen in print. Because this is a book about broadcasting, it is written in a broadcasting style. The words used and the order in which they are used are as much as possible the language of the airwaves—the language of speech, not print. Print-oriented grammarians may argue that the punctuation is not what it should be. In theory they may be right, but in the spoken work punctuation is more flexible, and radio and television are the media of the spoken word.

If any colleague in journalism or journalism teaching finds in this book words or expressions they believe they originated, the authors can only say "thank you" and apologise for the lack of proper attribution. Most of the material derives from lecture notes since the authors, though both former journalists, are now teachers of journalism. The notes themselves are an amalgam of distilled personal experience in broadcast journalism and the wisdom and experience of others, drawn from their writings or sayings, and acknowledged where the source is known.

Some of the material included here first appeared in Roger Patching's series of radio training programs, prepared by Mitchellsearch for the Public Broadcasting Association of Australia. Some first appeared in Murray Masterton's profile of Australian working journalists and their backgrounds . . . *but you'll never be bored*. The sub-chapter on news criteria is from *What makes news news?*, Murray Masterton's unpublished doctoral thesis.

To other people more direct thanks are due; for instance to Rona Abbott for devising the cover and to Roy Walshe who gave the book its attractive form. The providers of photographs are acknowledged in the text.

Journalists crowd in for such memorable news conferences as that given by Don Dunstan on his resignation as premier of South Australia. The technical requirements of their cameras and recorders make the broadcasters stand out at such a gathering.

(Picture: Adelaide Advertiser)

Aims

What is a journalist and what does a journalist try to do? What is broadcast journalism and what does a broadcast journalist try to do?

None of these questions has a single answer. They are questions often asked by those who think they might like to become journalists or by others, incredulous of what they see in the newspapers or hear on the broadcast media, who ponder the type of person who might write such material.

If there is no definition of a journalist, there is considerable agreement on the attributes which make an otherwise normal person into a journalist. These attributes are not inflexible, nor is this list absolute, but those who have thought about it more or less agree that most journalists have, or should have:

- Curiosity—the desire to find out what happened and why.
- Accuracy—the ability and intelligence to get facts right.
- Clarity of thought—getting meanings right in the journalist's mind.
- Clarity of expression—being able to make a story clear to other people.
- The ability to get along with others, especially under pressure.
- A sense of fair play—the ability to report both sides.

- Trustworthiness — a matter of ethics and remaining a journalist.
- Observation — seeing more than others and seeing accurately.
- A sense of urgency — realising that news means NOW.
- A news sense — a "feeling" for what others want or need to know.

It is a journalist's job to pass information to his organisation's public as accurately, completely, concisely and understandably as possible and always in a responsible manner. The entire business of gathering, selecting and presenting news in any medium is carried out according to this dictum. The means by which it is done will vary from medium to medium and to a lesser extent from institution to institution — the techniques involved will vary much more — but the aim is always the same.

There are many working journalists, even well-respected and senior ones, who have never had occasion to pause long enough to work out for themselves what the principles of working journalists should be. They take them for granted, by instinct. Few journalists of any standing will argue this basic guideline, though there may be some who would extend it.

Why journalists do their job as they do is also easily explained. In all news media there is a continuing evolution in the techniques and equipment for news gathering and presentation. Almost daily it becomes a faster and faster process from a wider and wider area, yet the language and presentation to the public remain much the same. Many journalists — and non-journalists too — have tried to find some better way to present the news. One day there may be a breakthrough, but it hasn't happened yet. In the meantime the continuing problem for working broadcast journalists is to understand who it is they talk to and to work out how best to reach their audience.

Radio is the most universal form of mass communication. With the price of a portable "trannie" down to a few dollars — including those which can receive FM as well as AM broadcasts — listeners have cheap access to round-the-clock entertainment, news, information and views from more and more radio stations. Not only this, but in the past decade the rapidly increasing number of public broadcasting stations has meant almost everybody has the chance to become a broadcaster as well as part of an audience. But the question still remains: who are the journalists talking to?

As a medium, radio has many advantages over its "big brothers" newspapers and television. It is not nearly as expensive to establish or operate. Radio equipment is becoming both cheaper and easier to use while newspaper and television technology seems to be becoming more complex and in some cases more expensive.

Radio can take its audience instantly to the other side of the street, the city, the state, the nation or the world. It can be broadcasting from the scene of a major news event while the television crews are still unloading "live-eye" equipment and newspaper reporters are still taking their notes. It will be many more minutes before the audience can see it on television and hours before it can be read in the newspapers.

While newspapers and television are visual media, in that you see what you read or view, radio is the medium of the imagination. The mix of words and sounds in a radio program stimulates the audience into creating mental pictures, whether the program is news, current affairs or entertainment. The radio reporter is limited only by his or her power to describe and the listeners' ability to imagine.

Radio is a warm, emotional medium. It relies heavily on the warmth and feeling of the human voice — a powerful weapon. The emphasis, variety, inflection and pace of the human voice are used to maximum effect in the presentation of news and information programs on radio.

But radio also has weaknesses. It is difficult for radio to convey a large amount of information, especially if it is complex. Newspaper readers can choose the stories they want to read by scanning the pages of their daily paper and reading only what interests them. Radio and television news editors have to make this "what am I interested in?" choice for their audiences, so that for listeners or viewers the only decision is to leave the set on or turn it off.

This still doesn't answer the question: what (or who) is the audience? Radio and television stations pay organisations like McNair Anderson to confirm what kind of people and how many of them make up the audience. It wasn't always so.

In the "golden age" of radio, just before television arrived, Australia's broadcasters competed just as vigorously as today's television stations to win the largest audience — to be all things to all people. Their target audience was everyone. When television began in 1956 that mass audience of Australians quickly moved to the new medium. What had been peak listening hours became peak viewing hours, so radio was left with few listeners and little income from advertising.

Resourceful programmers soon found that although radio could no longer be all things to all people all of the time, it could very profitably be a lot of things to some of the people most of the time. Stations set out to cater specifically for one part of the total audience and to do it at times and with programs with which television could not compete.

This resourcefulness and the timely invention of the transistor allowed specialised radio to grow, so that in most cities there are many radio stations with different programs and different styles, including news styles. Stations have carved up the total audience and program to attract one or more of these specific but smaller groups. In other words, stations and their programmers set out to meet the understood interests and needs of a specific part of the listening population.

Some stations set out to attract the younger set, others the family/home-builders, others the mature and settled. The station's programming, advertising, presentation style—everything—is adjusted to meet the needs of the audience it aims to attract. So it is up to that station's news editor and staff to decide how to cater best for the people who are listening—the known audience.

It can be an ethical dilemma: how far should a journalist go to cater to the interests, rather than the perceived needs, of the audience? Should it affect news content selection or just presentation style? Should some stories be ignored, no matter how important, because audience surveys say they are not the type of material an audience wants? The effect of this on radio is apparent to anyone who tunes in. Newscasts on 2JJJ sound quite different from newscasts on parent ABC stations, even though it all comes from the same newsroom. Commercial stations have their own news formats, which means that they sound different in order to appeal to different audience groups, even though across the radio spectrum the news content may be much the same.

The audience is a bigger problem for television news editors. Surveys show that every year a larger portion of the public receives its news of the day from television. To more and more people television is the sole source of information on what is happening around the world.

Even with this responsibility in mind, how can any news editor cram everything the audience should be told into the limited minutes of a television newscast?

Not so long ago television news executives saw it as their responsibility to give their audience "the tip of the news iceberg". If viewers wanted or needed more, they could find it in the morning newspapers. That view has gone. Statistics show fewer people buy newspapers than before — or at least newspaper circulations are not increasing in proportion to population — so television now must present a comprehensive news service, including all the news people need to know as well as what they might want to know.

Radio stations, thanks to management decisions and survey confirmation, have a fair idea of the audience they aim to serve. But the business of carving up the population into selected audience segments has not really begun on television. Radio stations may know that most of the younger audience is interested in sport, the pop scene and the latest fad; more mature audiences in business and politics.

Television can not afford to carve up the audience in the same way. Like a sole newspaper in a large town, it has to serve the whole audience to earn enough money to survive, so television plans its content, including its news content, accordingly. Each newsroom includes the local, state, national and international stories it considers of greatest interest or importance for its audience. With only minor differences, all television stations seek the same audience, even the ABC.

What makes news

It is over-simplifying the answer to reduce news to its traditional five Ws: Who, What, Where, When and Why. Every good news story answers those questions and probably the How as well, but separately or together they don't become news. They are a journalist's guide to the finding and telling of a news story, but they are not the reason why it is a news story.

Nor is it much use trying to define news. There are hundreds, perhaps thousands, of definitions of news. A few of them are:

News is anything which interests or affects the public.

News is anything timely that interests a number of persons and the best news is that which has the greatest interest for the greatest number.

News is what somebody somewhere wants to suppress. Everything else is advertising (Lord Northcliffe's definition).

News is anything timely that is interesting and significant to readers in respect to their personal affairs or their relations to society (an academic definition).

News is the end result of a reporter's instinct.

News is the reporting of change (a simplified academic definition).

News is what the editor says it is (a cynical journalist's definition).

News is whatever fits into the newspaper (a cynical reader's definition).

News is what the media decide is worth reporting (a media critic's definition).

None of these definitions is adequate in all circumstances and certainly not for all journalists. Most of them contain an element of the truth but are coloured by experience, cynicism, anger, bitterness or pedantry. All are correct to some extent, which proves only that news is truly indefinable.

Yet news is certainly not as static as some of these definitions claim. What information becomes news changes as time, interests and media audiences change, but why information becomes news is much more constant.

Most journalists explain "news sense" as a hunch honed by experience; most researchers try to explain what news is by studying what is published as news. They study the content of newspapers and broadcast bulletins and derive their definitions and their newsworthiness criteria by empirical means.

In spite of the diversity of researchers and methods, the criteria which have resulted from researching why journalists write what they consider to be news and what is finally published as news show a reassuring similarity. Criteria vary in number and name. Some don't call them "criteria" at all, but categories, codes, elements, indicators, guides or signals.

Whatever they are called, comparing criteria lists and how they have been framed makes it obvious that there is a ranking in their importance.

To be news information needs three basics:
- it must be new (**Timeliness**)
- it must interest a large number of people (**Interest**)
- it must be understandable to all (**Clarity**).

These three elements are always present in all news items, so much so that they are almost self-explanatory.

Timeliness is so important that the very word "news" seems to spring from it. Information must be new, or newly available, if it is to warrant the name news. Why else do reporters try to beat the opposition by being more up to the minute with their stories. But up-to-the-minuteness is not the only kind of timeliness. A day-old story becomes newsworthy again if there are new facts to "freshen" it. And it may be so with a story that is a week old, a year old, or even many years old. The Mi Lai massacre in Viet Nam made big news even though it was not revealed for years after it occurred. As with Cabinet papers released after 30 years in secret Canberra files, the information in them may be new, and the release itself is new and thus news.

Interest seems such an obvious requirement. If the information is not interesting, how can it be considered as news? Of course not all people are interested in the same information, which is why newspapers and broadcast news services differ from city to city, country to country. There are also times when it is up to the journalists to make clear why some information should be of interest to anyone. But if there is no inherent or explainable interest in the information, it can never become news.

Clarity is an element of another type. It exists in the manner of the writing or telling rather than in the information itself. But it is still a basic element of newsworthiness, since without clarity information can not become news.

All three basic elements must be present if any information is to become news of any kind. If any one of them is absent, the information can not become news. Work it out for yourself:

Timeliness and Interest are no use without Clarity.
Timeliness and Clarity are no use without Interest.
Interest and Clarity are no use without Timeliness.

When these core requirements are present other criteria become relevant in determining how newsworthy any piece of information may be. And there are six criteria of news which are recognised by journalists world-wide as determinants of newsworthiness, regardless of national, cultural, religious or economic differences.

The sequence of dominance of these six criteria varies a little from region to region, but in the English speaking world that sequence is:

Consequence (or Significance or Importance), which indicates the number of people who will be affected by the information. It is a measure of a story's impact. Consequence is evident in stories about taxes and the cost of living, even if such stories are seldom the most enjoyable or even the most interesting. Because they are the most important it is a journalist's task to make them interesting and understandable.

A storm which kills or cripples someone and causes widespread damage is obviously of greater consequence than one which does no more than make thousands of people late for work, though it is not always reported as such, for reasons which will become obvious later. There is a certain significance in people being late, but in most people's estimation death and destruction are more significant.

Proximity: Other things being equal, an event in a reader's or listener's home town is of more interest than one in the Congo or Colombia. If you need proof, look and listen to the media in different cities to see how local affairs dominate the news content.

But distance is only one guide to proximity. In some cases a city identifies more readily with another far distant than it does with one which is physically or politically closer. Mount Gambier often has a closer affiliation with Melbourne than with its South Australian capital, Adelaide. Broken Hill in New South Wales is more attuned to South Australia than it is to Sydney, for commercial reasons. Much of the

New South Wales Riverina seems to identify more with Melbourne than it does with Sydney for the same reason.

The same thing can be said on an international scale. Australia as a whole has a closer association, because of cultural proximity, with London and New York than it does with Jakarta or Bangkok which are much closer geographically. This psychological proximity is relevant also where people are concerned. The doings of a Brisbane person in London are usually of more interest to Brisbane's media than the doings of a London person in Brisbane. Of course it depends on what they do.

Conflict may sound as though it caters, as a news category, to those who like to hear about violence. It does, but it covers a lot more as well. Many stories have great impact because they mirror the conflict which is everywhere in the world: the social, psychological, legal and even economic conflicts, as well as the physical conflicts of war and crime. Any protest, even a non-violent one, shows conflict with the establishment.

News is, as one definition claims, the reporting of change or the pressure for change, so there is conflict of some kind in almost every story, even if it is not immediately evident. Consider the differing types of conflict in strikes, demonstrations, debates of any kind (from council or parliament), the little man who takes on the system, civil and criminal court cases, sporting contests and international events where feelings are inflamed by nationalism and national aspirations.

Human Interest is a term used frequently and misused even more frequently. Essentially a Human Interest story is an item about a person or people — people everywhere love to read or hear about other people. Yet for many newsmen Human Interest is a synonym for "soft" news, an equally vague term. It is a cliche among journalists that children, dogs and universally-known people are sure-fire news items because they have Human Interest.

The legendary little Aussie battler has Human Interest as well as Conflict going for him, not because he is newsworthy as a person but because he represents something. Should he and his pet dog get into trouble with a council, or better still with a big, impersonal corporation, the story is twice as good, even if it is still not a big one.

Human Interest stories are almost always the first read in newspapers, often the most widely read though usually the least likely remembered. Despite instant international communications and interpretive reporting on everything from council rates to macro-economics, a story about something human, perhaps trivial, usually wins widest readership, as long as it's local.

Novelty is easily recognised in the adage that it's news when a man bites a dog. It is genuinely rare. It is also rare when an individual bucks a council or the government. The novelty value of an item varies from location to location, from audience to audience, thus from newsroom to newsroom.

Novelty also comes in many guises. People are always doing something new, or trying to. It is one of the most frequent ways in which publicity seekers try to manipulate the media. They recognise the interest in something that is new and different and set out to provide it, preferably with a good picture, to win a place in the news.

Prominence may play a part in a human interest story, but it is also a category on its own. Who makes news can be as important as what. Any local editor in any medium will confirm that "names make news", so it follows that the bigger the name the more certain it is to make news. In the United States the President can't sneeze without the nation being told. In Britain, and to a certain extent here, everything the Queen does is reported. Journalists may scoff but they go on reporting such things because it is obvious to them that many of their audience do not scoff.

Beneath such titled and powerful positions, prominence is a matter of scale. Every community has its prominent citizens, every state or nation its most newsworthy leaders. Sportsmen, eccentric clergy, pop stars and entertainers can win news space because of who they are, if not for what they say or do. And who is considered prominent depends on the newsroom's audience, the type of medium and its location.

After these six criteria, which journalists say apply in all news media in all countries, there are others which have more regional effect or which apply more to one type of medium than another. The other news criteria which apply most in Australia and most of the Western world are:

Suspense because almost everyone likes a mystery story. What will happen next? Who did it? Journalists don't call their reports "stories" without reason. In broadcast journalism they are often read (told) as dramas of what happened today, and they include the element of Suspense where appropriate. Sporting events keep us in suspense until we know who wins. Elections are reported as if they were sporting events for the same reason. It heightens the Suspense. Thousands of people stay up half the night to listen to a football or cricket game on the other side of the world or to an election in Australia, even though they know the result will hardly affect them at all — in the case of elections not for some months. It is the Suspense which holds their interest, so Suspense is newsworthy.

Resolution is the opposite of suspense, so it seems strange that it too should be a criterion of newsworthiness. It is the object of Resolution (also referred to as Certainty) to tie up the loose ends and make known what was not known before. It settles the vague estimates given in hurried early stories about some dramatic event and thus ends speculation and rumour.

Think of a train wreck story. The first reports say people are dead without saying how many. Later reports give varying estimates from different people of dead and injured and of the extent of the damage and how it happened. Only the final clarifying story tells it all: how many died and who they were, how many and who are injured and where they are now, and how it happened. It might also explain what is going to be done about it. If it doesn't, suspense is still involved until the matter is sorted out.

Sensation: Sensationalism is a pejorative word applied to some afternoon newspapers, but Sensation as a news criterion is not the prerogative of that kind of newspaper. There is such a thing as a sensation and when there is it makes news. Few newsrooms ignore news of crime and violence, especially if it is sensational. The fact that it is extreme makes it newsworthy, even if the crime is a minor one.

Secrecy: Australian journalists believe very strongly that anything that anyone wants kept secret is almost certainly newsworthy, and that belief has world-wide currency. This is one of the strongest news motives behind investigative journalism and is an obvious factor in a large part of Australia's political reporting.

Ethics as a criterion of news, is more difficult to understand. Journalists in an international survey rank Ethics seventh in observance, though Australians rank it lower. Those journalists claim that to be news, information must comply with the ethics of professional journalism rather than any other judgments.

Journalists and the news organisations for which they work don't consciously consider the newsworthiness criteria listed, even though they all observe all the major six. There is ample evidence that all media acknowledge by usage the other criteria as well, but they give them different weightings according to the medium and the type of publication.

Serious daily newspapers like the Age and the Sydney Morning Herald use the same criteria with almost the same weightings and differ in content mainly because of their different location and thus different audience interests. The Sydney Morning Herald and the Mirror used to publish in the same city. Their criteria weightings differed because they appealled to different audiences and thus put different values on many aspects of news content. The same can be said of the Age and the former Sun News-Pictorial in Melbourne. After the main six criteria, these papers used them differently because one is "responsible" and one was "popular". It remains to be seen into what position on the "responsible-popular" scale the merged Herald-Sun and Telegraph-Mirror eventually settle. At this time of their merging in 1990 they appeared set on a "popular" path.

It is the same with broadcasting stations, radio or television, though the difference is more marked in radio where the audience segmentation has progressed further.

Regardless of the medium or its style, a news item must be new, interesting to a lot of people and absolutely clear, and it must contain one or more of the remaining criteria of newsworthiness.

Because it has been gathered by a journalist the facts are right, though accuracy itself is not a criterion of news. Statements can be accurate without being news. Even when the information seems to be newsworthy, if it is proved to be inaccurate it loses credibility and is not news for long.

There is no prize for being first with a story, in print or in broadcast, if it turns out to be wrong. When journalists get together there is always a new story about how so-and-so or such-and-such an organisation jumped the gun to put out a story first, and got it wrong.

There is only one thing news can never be: dull. The adage that "bad news is good news" may be true in big cities with competing news services. Smaller media outlets in the country probably claim that in their context "good news is good news, too". No one anywhere ever says "dull news is good news", or even "dull news is news".

There's little point in saying "There have been no murders, bashings, thefts, fires, road accidents or rapes today." News is about events that have taken place, seldom about negative or non-events. The exceptions are when nothing happens when it was expected to happen, or when there is nothing new in an on-going story of great public interest. To keep the news from being dull, or even from seeming to be dull, most broadcast editors try to broadcast as much of any story as will interest half the broadcasting station's audience. This basis for selection allows for wide differences in content in a city with many radio stations.

The radio spectrum is so divided because each has its own audience and tries to serve that audience with its programming, including its news. Only a station originating a national news service looks on the news of the day from an Australia-wide viewpoint. Even in an efficient news network, chances are that if there is no network station in city X, news from that city will have to be supremely important to be included. It is simply a case of serving an audience by meeting its demands for news.

This is why broadcast news is different in content from that which appears in the daily newspapers and with which broadcast news is so often and wrongly compared. The broadcasters serve different audiences, so why should their news content be the same?

It is also one reason why radio news is so often in short, sharp bursts. It is an updating process for a particular audience in a particular locality. Radio news is designed to deliver as much information as most members of a particular audience want, in the full realisation that those who want more will read it in the next morning's newspapers.

The problem for radio and television journalists is that they must never be boring. Essentially radio and television are not news media. They are entertainment media. Most people listen or watch to be entertained. Being informed is coincidental, except for those people in the minority who tune in specifically for the news. The more information passed successfully to the audience being entertained, the better the job the broadcast journalist is doing.

Also, newspaper readers can choose what they want to read from a wide range of headlines across many pages. They choose what interests them as well as some of what they think may affect them. Research shows that the greater part of most newspapers goes unread by the vast majority of buyers.

There is no such choice for the broadcast news consumer. The listener tunes in for the first item and listens to what is offered in the sequence it is offered, regardless of personal interest or importance. If interest wanes the listener/watcher may turn off, psychologically if not physically, and ignore the rest of the newscast. So broadcast items are always short enough not to bore even those who are not interested.

If the news is written and presented well enough to win and hold the listener/viewer's interest it may arouse a new awareness in that person. It is a primary task of news on the broadcast media to attract and hold the interest of people in matters in which they may have not shown interest before. Certainly it creates a market for the next daily newspaper, but it also creates an audience for the broadcasting station's next newscast, which can be expected to deliver more up-to-date news on the same subject.

Most important of all, it builds an audience awareness of what is happening in the world and why, which is what good journalism in any medium is all about.

So it follows that a good news bulletin in broadcasting is made up of stories which will interest at least half of any broadcaster's audience and written so interestingly and concisely that everyone who hears it will remain interested for the brief duration of the story.

The means of expanding a story in both content and duration without losing interest are explained elsewhere in this book. These are voice reports, interview clips, recorded sound and the planned use of a variety of voices. No matter what techniques are employed, the story must always be as brief as possible commensurate with clarity and understanding.

These demands mean that some news items are easier to present on radio or television than others. Radio requires no picture other than that engendered by the words themselves in the listener's head; television's task of providing pictures is both a huge advantage and a massive impediment to accurate and balanced reporting. But it is difficult in either broadcast medium to tell accurately and interestingly the detail required in a story about a budget, an involved debate in parliament or any other story in which complex structure is involved. This is doubly difficult when the detail consists of figures: broadcasting, especially radio, finds figures hard to handle, so they must be approached with special care and more than the usual verbal fluency.

If this special care is taken there is no type of news item that cannot be told adequately on radio or television. On television, graphics and pictures can help overcome some of radio's handicaps. But financial and statistical stories are usually better done in print, where it is not so difficult to absorb the needed detail from a paper's page. A paragraph can be read more than once, if necessary. There is no second reading in broadcasting, and no slackening of speed for individual comprehension rates. If it is not understood on first hearing, it is not understood at all.

However, the printed word can not match radio for speed or television for clarity and total impact in stories of action. Who wants to read about a football or cricket match in the daily paper when they can watch it on television or hear a commentary on radio? The same applies to many other stories, too. Any story which can be told, rather than read, is ideal for broadcasting. This excludes very few.

Radio is the town crier of today, telling the interested what is happening in their world when they want to know. Television can do this live if the story is big enough. Usually television is confined to a few, fixed time newscasts because of the logistics involved, as are newspapers. So while it is usually radio that tells the story first and briefly, it is television which tells it graphically and the newspaper which fills in the details for those who still want to know more.

The media hardly compete, except within their own medium, but they certainly complement each other. In many respects tonight's television news is a great advertisement for tomorrow's newspaper.

Journalists in broadcasting accept that many of their audience with a real thirst for information will read the morning newspaper after having already heard the news on radio or television. The journalists do it themselves. This should not divert them, however, from trying to make their newscasts as complete and accurate as possible within the tight time constraints imposed. Because so much information has to be compressed into so little time in broadcasting, there are additional skills required when writing for the broadcast media.

Where does public affairs broadcasting fit into all this? If news is about facts which are new and interesting, then public affairs—current affairs if you wish—is about the opinions, comments and reaction to those same facts. The basic difference between news and current affairs is that the current affairs reporter presents more background information so that the event/announcement/decision, or whatever the facts are about, is set in context. There is no time to do this in most broadcast newsrooms preparing regular newscasts.

A news report of an event might run 45 to 60 seconds, often less. A current affairs item on the same subject might run anything from one to 10 minutes, even more if the editor of the program considers it worth more.

Broadcasting has had its effect on newspapers. Any honest editor knows that much of the news in his paper has already been seen on television or heard on radio, according to the time of day, and takes that into consideration. So newspapers are concentrating these days more on explaining the news than on breaking new stories. Of course they still have new material to publish, in spite of broadcast journalists, because they have more staff to report it, which means they have better opportunities to report and interpret local issues. For all this, as broadcast journalists continue to improve, newspapers will more and more be expected to provide the explanations, the background and finer detail. They are still the publications of record.

Broadcast news moves instantly from almost anywhere. Here a Channel 7 journalist records her report in Kiev, in the Soviet Ukraine, for transmission to Australia by satellite. It is thus immediately available to network stations across the country.

(Picture: Channel 7)

Logistics

Where news comes from and how it is put together

Where does broadcast news come from? It comes from the same places as the news for newspapers, although the method of delivery may sometimes be different, and for television there is the added problem of gathering pictures as well as words from local and remote sources.

Most people who look at or listen to any medium realise that there is news from just across the road, from the far corners of Australia or from around the world. Local, state, national and international (overseas) is the usual break-down.

Overseas news comes in word form and as still pictures to most Australian newspapers through Australian Associated Press (AAP). Most use other international news agencies as well, but in principle they all operate the same way. The sources of overseas news are the same for radio and television, except that they also receive audio clips and moving pictures.

AAP has its own staff members in some Asian locations and its own offices in London and New York. Throughout the world, however, it has access through reciprocal agreements to the reports of other major international news agencies — Reuters (with which AAP is directly associated), the American agency Associated Press (AP) and the Paris-based Agence France Press (AFP). It also has agreements, on its own or through those major agencies, with smaller regional or national news agencies and uses the services of "stringers".

A stringer is a reporter who works for a news organisation on a casual or part-time basis in an area of Australia or overseas where that organisation does not maintain a full-time staff reporter. Such a person is usually, though not necessarily, a reporter for a local paper or radio station, who offers to provide major news stories from his or her area if and when they occur.

AAP and the bigger agencies work the same way. They have their own staff in the news centres of greatest importance to them and rely on their stringers or on news from other agencies to cover the rest.

Millions of words arrive in AAP's Sydney headquarters every day from all over the world. Stories are sifted to sort out what is of greatest importance or interest to readers, listeners and viewers in Australia. They are edited as necessary and then distributed over a series of news circuits to printers and video screens in newsrooms across the country.

There are two basic news services provided by AAP across Australia; a service for newspapers and a service for radio and television. Stories on the broadcast wire are usually briefer than the newspaper versions and have been rewritten in the AAP office to meet broadcasting needs. They have been written to be heard, not to be read.

In radio and television newsrooms the AAP news flows in all day. As these newsrooms become computerised, software has been developed to do away with the noisy teleprinter. Most major radio and television newsrooms now store their AAP copy (and all other copy for that matter) on computers.

The growth of networks

When AAP first became a distributor of domestic as well as overseas news throughout Australia it replaced local news agencies and news groupings which used to do the job in various states. In some cases these were groups of newspapers with the same or overlapping ownership, or newspapers in different states but with shared deadlines — i.e. morning papers would exchange stories between states, or the Murdoch papers would exchange stories. News exchange still happens in the major newspaper groups and among radio and television network groupings.

Some news organisations in Australia have their own staff members interstate, but most rely on these reciprocal agreements with other organisations for the speedy exchange of news. Most major news groups have reporters in Canberra, but in recent years some groups have reduced their representation there. With tight economic times in the media, some organisations from different states have agreed to share reporters in the national capital. AAP still maintains a large news staff there.

In broadcasting there is "network" co-operation between stations, radio or television, so that news is passed quickly from one station to a network "sister station" elsewhere. In television the news networks are obvious. Those in radio, except for the Wesgo network of commercial stations and the ABC, are perhaps not so obvious. For instance, a report by an Adelaide radio station of a fire ravaging the Adelaide Hills will quickly be passed to affiliated stations across Australia and be heard within minutes on newscasts in Melbourne, Sydney, Brisbane and Perth and on all the smaller country radio stations which those capital city stations provide with a news service.

The network stations are linked either by what are called broadcast or radio "lines", which are high-quality telephone lines linking broadcasting studios, or increasingly are linked through the Aussat satellite. Local radio lines are usually installed by radio stations from regular news or commentary sources such as parliament, major sportsgrounds, law courts, the Industrial Commission, perhaps even the airport, or from wherever the station wishes to receive information regularly and reliably.

The procedure in a station with a report worth networking is to notify affiliate members when the report is ready, then "play it down the line" to those who wish to record it. If time is short, the originating station's actual newscast may be "played down the line" and the receiving stations record the report they want from it.

In a receiving station the system is the same as if a report was coming in by phone from one of its own reporters in the field. A tape recorder is plugged in to record the in-coming signal from the interstate station and the item recorded in ready-for-air condition. It requires only seconds — usually the writing of an appropriate localised introduction for the newsreader — to have it ready for the next news bulletin.

Television operates in much the same way, but its agency and exchange systems are more complex and expensive because of the necessity to move pictures as well as words.

There are international news agencies which specialise in television news and nothing else. The biggest of these, and the one which supplies most Australian television stations, is Visnews, based in London. As with other international news agencies, Visnews has arranged reciprocal exchanges with other agencies in the interests of better world-wide coverage. By this means the Visnews service into Australia carries television reports from NBC in the United States with news from the Americas, from Eurovision (a television news exchange group which covers most of Europe), from NHK in Japan and others.

Visnews is a co-operative — as Reuters was until a few years ago — and the Australian member of that co-operative is the ABC. That means that any Australian television news worthy of international coverage is fed back to Visnews by the ABC to be passed on to others who wish to use it.

Visnews briefly and unwillingly held a monopoly in supplying Australian television stations with a service by satellite. Now most Australian stations or networks have supply contracts with others, such as Britain's ITN news operation which cooperates with CBS in the United States, with America's other network giants NBC and ABC and with America's 24-hours-a-day Cable News Network CNN.

From film by plane to satellites

The international exchange of television news has advanced as swiftly as television itself in Australia. In the 1960s television newsfilm from other parts of the world arrived by plane. It took days for the necessary multiple film prints to be made in London or elsewhere and flown here, then hours more to clear airport customs and distribute them across the country. Receipt of the newsfilm was only marginally quicker when a single negative was flown in and multiple prints made in Australia.

Then came videotape and the expansion of the microwave or coaxial cable system across Australia. Flying in tapes meant that reports in colour could be received complete with sound tracks from the originators. The growth of the Australian electronic distribution system permitted these to be dispatched to television newsrooms across the country without having to wait for prints or internal planes. It meant a great advance in the quality of the product but only a marginal saving in time, because the originals still had to be flown from all over the world.

Satellites brought swifter delivery. Australian television brought in major news reports by satellite on an ad hoc basis for some years before arrangements were made for a regular, daily transmissions originating from Visnews in London and receivable simultaneously by stations across the country, or as far as the microwave network extended. The Australian contract for regular use of satellites for television news transmission was the first such contract in the world.

Now it seems ordinary, everyday. It is everyday. Regular news transmissions flow in to Australian television stations every day from London, from the United States and from other regular sources, with extra transmissions called up whenever some major item of news occurs.

The most recent development has been the creation of portable satellite transmission stations, enabling coverage of the news of the day from anywhere in Australia — anywhere in the world for that matter — to be beamed direct to the station. For instance, during the major flooding in western New South Wales in 1990, it was possible for the day's story to be sent by satellite from say, Nyngan or Parkes. In the early days camera crews would have had to leave the scene fairly early in the day to ensure same day coverage that night.

Before the latest advance in satellite technology it was possible to distribute coverage of western New South Wales flooding only by sending the pictures from a regional station to the nearest capital city station.

In most broadcast newsrooms however, news from overseas makes up a third or less of the content of newscasts. The overseas content varies from day to day, as does the proportion of local or national news, according to what has happened and it's relative importance.

In almost all newsrooms, whether a one-journalist newsroom in a country radio station or in AAP's Sydney office, probably the biggest newsroom in the country, the process of collecting and collating the news is much the same. Journalists are organised into staffs to report on what is happening.

The need to plan

No news organisation starts the day on the assumption that something will happen to fill the time or space. The process of gathering news is a complex combination of considered anticipation, prior knowledge and the ability to adapt to changing circumstances.

A journalist sent to cover a soccer match on Sydney's southside on Fathers Day a few years ago may have been contacted by two-way radio on route to the game, and diverted to what police described as a major "bikie brawl" at a nearby hotel. The reporter found himself in the middle of one of the major news stories of the year—the Milperra Massacre. This may sound far-fetched, but it actually happened. Usually the process is under much greater control and contains fewer surprises.

News executives begin the day with a good idea of what to expect from that day's news-gathering activities. The considered planning may not be obvious in the end product, but without it the resultant news bulletins would sound very different, probably deficient. Much of the news heard, seen or read has been expected by those who reported it and by their superiors who plan how it will be gathered, who will gather it, and how it will be used.

The news diary

All newsrooms have a diary. It's entries are reminders of all those things which working journalists know will happen, even events several months ahead—the dates of city council meetings; those of the chamber of commerce and trades and labour council; major regular dates like the Melbourne Cup or sporting grand finals. Parliamentary sittings and the sitting of courts at all levels and of government and major inquiries are noted in the diary. Even dog, cat or flower shows are noted. In most offices, a staff member is detailed to search the advertising columns as well as the news columns to make sure no future event of possible news interest is omitted.

News releases associated with upcoming events are filed in an associated "throw forward" system, so that they emerge on the appropriate day.

Take an example: A court report today says that a newsworthy case has been adjourned to a particular date. That date is entered in the diary. Today's published story and any unpublished material which may be useful for future stories are stored in the "throw forward" system. When the date comes up—usually on the day before—the information is retrieved and made available to background the reporter or reporters who will work on the story.

Individual reporters keep their own diaries about the stories they are following, especially if they have been given a particular news "round" to cover on a regular basis. They may have been told by one of their news contacts that so-and-so will issue a statement on Tuesday, so they enter it in their own diary as well as that of the newsroom.

Obviously, the bigger and better-organised the news organisation, the bigger its diary. News agencies maintain huge diaries for their own prompting—they must miss nothing the opposition agencies might have. To help newsrooms fill out their own diaries, agencies issue customers with what is called a daily news "menu", listing the major items on which reports are expected during that day.

A large amount of the news which appears, even though it may seem unexpected to the public, begins as diary items. A surprising amount begins as news handouts from public relations consultants, companies or special interest groups with reasons of their own for seeking publicity through the news media. Media newsrooms are constantly inundated with such handouts, and AAP offers a special service through which governments and major institutions can distribute their handouts to newsrooms throughout the country. Those handouts which are totally self-seeking and not considered newsworthy go straight into the wastepaper basket. The rest go to the diary.

Some of the sources of predictable news are:

Published news stories that contain information on when something more will happen, even if only indirectly related to the original story. They may be worth following up from a different, newly-revealed point of view. Often the person updating the diary need look no further than his or her own product to keep an efficient diary.

For instance, an early morning radio news item announces there will be a teachers' strike that day. Naturally, there will be checks throughout the day to see what happened: did it actually happen? How many children arrived at school? Were there disruptions in the schools? This is, of course, in addition to finding out the reasons for the strike. The original announcement of the strike might have been made a week or even a month before and been in the diary since then.

Other media have to be searched too, since the media feeds off itself for stories. Stories in this morning's newspaper or on a radio or TV station might provide story ideas for another paper or broadcasting organisation to follow up. Stealing stories originally published by someone else is unethical, sometimes illegal and always dangerous. Poaching ideas from others is accepted and encouraged.

For the same reason broadcast newsrooms monitor the bulletins of other broadcasting stations and programs like "AM", "Four Corners" or "Sunday". There are often new stories to be found in what those news-oriented programs report. Remember the long-running story for all media which began with the "Four Corners" investigation into corruption in Queensland. It lead to the Fitzgerald Royal Commission and the ramifications are still making news.

Weekly and Sunday newspapers often break major stories. They have the time to develop a story well before going to print, so their big stories often yield a plentiful harvest of follow-ups for others. The National Times was often first to tell many big stories in the eighties. Even country newspapers are worth scanning. What seems an item of only local interest in such a paper has lead to a major story of national importance when put in a wider perspective.

Advertisements, even if scanning them seems a chore. They offer surprises in the way of news items. Is that advertisement for staff the first hint of a big new industry in the area? What is behind the apparently bland public notice advising that such and such a street will be closed for a period?

Even small advertisements in the births, deaths and marriages columns or the personal ads can lead to unexpected human interest stories, often important ones.

Letters to the editor. Letters often raise for the first time matters which concern the community.

Radio talk shows and talk-back programs provide the same prolific source of new story ideas for those who monitor them. Radio hosts and the interviewees they bring to the air are creating an increasing amount of material for the news bulletins which follow and then for news in other media.

Specialist magazines and house journals. Although they cater deliberately for small audiences with specific interests, they can conceal items of much wider interest. Newsletters from all sorts of organisations, from sporting clubs, parent and teacher groups or social and political splinter groups, no matter how small or extreme in their views, should not be ignored.

In some newspapers it is an assigned duty for a staff member each day, or at least at regular intervals, to prowl the ever-growing pile of such pamphlets and magazines which flood into the newsroom, to find any stories there may be.

All these contribute principally to the diary, though in some cases monitoring and searches lead to stories which are followed up and reported immediately.

"Spot" news

There is also a system in most newsrooms for being prepared for the unpredictable in news—a sort of news early warning system. No one knows when a fire will break out, an accident will happen or a storm cause havoc. The people who know first when these things do happen are the police, ambulance, fire brigade, and state emergency services, so all news organisations keep in close touch with them.

Most of the organisations involved in the "disaster" round, as it is often called, use radio to control their operations, so newsrooms listen in to find out as quickly as possible what is happening. It is frowned on to do this too obviously. News organisations have had trouble on occasions in explaining how they could arrive at the scene of a robbery ahead of the police! Few of the organisations being reported like the idea of outsiders listening in to their radio control system, but they know it happens.

It is illegal to maintain a radio receiver locked to an emergency service frequency or frequencies, so to cover as many frequencies as possible on a rotating but continuing basis, newsrooms use scanners. These are radio receivers which scan a given range of frequencies in a matter of a few seconds and stop and listen if a signal is being transmitted on any of them. The journalist or journalists listening hear hundreds of routine, un-newsworthy messages for every one which proves useful, but when one is heard they move quickly.

Emergency service frequencies most commonly scanned are:

- Police, for accidents, crimes, appeals for help, fires, unexpected events, searches, missing persons. Police are also involved in the work of so many of the other agencies that messages frequently overlap.
- Water Police, if they have their own frequency, for similar reasons.
- Fire brigades, for fires, rescues, pumping jobs, and sometimes for demonstrations.
- Ambulance services, which tell of calls to accidents and often details about those accidents. Ambulances are called for many other reasons, and some of them may prove to be news. How many births have been reported as having taken place in the back of an ambulance, often in the most unusual places or circumstances?
- Marine Operations Centre when there is a sea rescue operation under way.
- Transport Australia, in its local form, for information on air traffic control and events in the air.

It is not usual to scan the taxi services, though they yield many news items. It is more usual to arrange with the taxi services so they contact the newsroom if anything newsworthy happens. Often during morning and afternoon "drive time" programming a taxi service will provide regular updates on traffic conditions in the major cities.

One thing must be remembered by all who monitor for such news: **nothing heard on a radio scanner should ever be published without**

careful verification. A police message may seem abundantly loud and clear, wonderfully detailed (it seldom is, for good reasons) and to be a perfect news item ready for publication. Don't do it!

Verification in this case means checking with the police, or whoever's radio service is being monitored. The message could have been wrong or misleading, or its premature publication may hinder the work of that service.

It is one thing to hear on monitored radio that an armoured car has just been stopped in the street and that police cars are rushing in its direction. It is probably true, but armoured cars may stop for many reasons other than what seems the obvious one. Check it out. Never be caught publishing what is heard; only what is known.

Stories abound of reporters "jumping the gun" and reporting as fact what was heard on a scanner, only to find they were wrong. It might have been a test message, or the reported emergency might only have been a training exercise for the emergency services.

Other regular sources which do not use radio to control their operations are on the "regular calls" list. Reporters must keep in touch with hospitals, not only to find out the condition of people hurt in accidents which are already being reported, but for all sorts of other newsworthy events in which the staff of the hospital may be involved.

Hospitals these days are regular providers of news on innovative and life-saving operations, and of stories about exciting research into deadly or threatening diseases.

And there is always the weather office. All newsrooms keep in touch by phone or by regular telex or fax messages, and not only for the regular forecasts. Weather is always news because it is something that everyone experiences, and when the weather itself makes news it is always big news. The only people who can explain what is going to happen, is happening or has happened and why, are the experts in the local meteorological office.

For news executives surveying the flow of expected news for the day, these regular sources of expected and unexpected reports are continually taken into consideration. Even so, that is only half the story. The other half is in the hands of the reporters themselves.

Contacts book

Every reporter should have a contacts book. Contacts are as important to a reporter as the diary is to the Chief of Staff. Contacts are people who know, or who should know, or know where to find out. Reporters on regular rounds often build up contacts lists which run beyond a book into a whole filing system. They enter stories as well as details about who gave the information and what is likely or possible in the future.

To start your own contacts book begin with something modest. Get a pocket-sized notebook with alphabetical listings and start from there. Enter the names and telephone numbers of your contacts right from the first reporting experience—the police sergeant who gave useful background about an accident, the local council alderman who was so willing to tell what happened, and the employer's representative who took the time to offer an explanation.

That is only the beginning. Before long it becomes clear that names mean full names, so there is no need to check elsewhere for spellings or first names. Addresses mean all addresses, so that the person can be found at work, at home, perhaps at a favourite pub or sporting club. Complete contacts books list everything useful that is, or should be known, about a person who is a useful news source.

Reporters on specific rounds make their books into mini reference systems. The council rounds reporter will have a list of all council members in detail, when they were elected, whom they represent, and where they can be found at any time. There will also be a list of most, if not all, council officials, with the same detailed information on those who are likely to provide information when it is needed.

Specialists like Laurie Oakes and Michelle Gratten would not have become such reliable authorities without their wide contacts. Their books include contacts unknown to others, even others working for the same employer. They are people they can trust and who have learned to trust them.

Radio and television journalists suffer from not being able to call on their contacts personally as often as they would like or should if the contacts are to be maintained effectively. The wise ones keep in touch as often as they can, sharing the occasional joke and telling the interesting story. With good contacts it is not a case of calling them up only when information is needed. It takes time to build a strong list of contacts. Time spent with contacts at those times when there is nothing more important to do will be repaid when the pressure is on. That is when contacts are most useful. In the reporting business, time saved is something money can't buy.

Because of the nature of their contents, contact books are strictly personal property. It is not done to pry into another journalist's contact book, regardless of the circumstances. If a novice reporter wants to know who to contact for specific information, he or she should ask, not delve into another's carefully gathered information. Most journalists will help willingly. Some will offer the use of the treasured contacts book, even if only up to a point. But it is a mistake to expect it to happen.

For this reason many broadcast newsrooms, in which staff switch from one round to another at very short notice or don't have regular rounds at all, have a common contacts book as well as individual ones. In such situations reporters should make sure they do their share in keeping that book up to date. They should reserve for their own books only those contacts with whom they have built up a relationship genuinely based on mutual trust.

Getting the right mix

Usually there is far more news available than there is time to use it, no matter how many bulletins there are during the day. Whether it is the normal news feast or the occasional news famine, the bulletin still has to be filled in the best way possible. How does the editor, or person responsible, choose which items to use and which to drop, which to repeat (almost always after a re-write) and which to replace?

There is more to compiling a radio news bulletin, and much more in putting together a television bulletin, than just shuffling the stories into some perceived descending order of audience interest.

What if every story which seems usable involves the same politician making announcements? It is conceivable that on a relatively-slow news day the regular news conference of a State Premier could bring forth four or five good stories. This is even more likely to happen in a relatively-small country centre, where the local State and Federal

Members of Parliament and the Mayor are always the major providers of news. As interesting as the Premier or other newsmaker may be, there is no way an editor can justify, or the audience tolerate, the first four stories all from the same source, even with enlivening voice reports and interviews.

One way is to ask the political reporter to summarise the state government's decisions into one composite story, but that will take time. If it is done, are the stories being given their relative importance in the bulletin? This is a particular dilemma for commercial radio stations which are locked into the 3 to 5-minute news-on-the-hour format.

What if several of the stories turn out to be the major news events of the day, not just the hour? Does the newsroom work to change them around during the next few hours, hoping to give each one its fair exposure?

It is the same problem in another guise when every story is about a disaster. There is a big accident in the city, a cruise ship goes down in a storm, an earthquake kills hundreds in the Middle East or South America, and so on.

It is hardly a balanced view of the news of the world to use four or five state political stories or four or five disaster stories to fill the news bulletin, even if that seems all that is coming into the newsroom at the time. There are times when it seems that only one part of the news machine is working. There is an inundation of industrial stories or political stories, police round stories or disasters. Too often one area dominates the news. It's as if nothing else has happened in the city, let alone the state or the whole world.

The flavour of the news on any radio station is the responsibility of the news editor and the sub-editor or person working with and for the editor. They have to decide which stories will be used in which bulletins, which will be repeated "as is" (rare nowadays) or be re-written and which will be discarded for fresh stories.

Usually the top stories stand out. Deciding which story will lead a news bulletin is probably the easiest part of the exercise, except on truly slow news days. Even so, different choices are made by different stations according to the station's known audience interests or its presentation style.

And there is always the "silly season"—that period between mid-December and mid-January—when the news-generators of the community, especially in business and politics, close for the holiday season. During this period news bulletins often contain little more than accidents, sports stories and the weather.

Experienced journalists will say they have an instinct for the order of the items in a bulletin, just as they have an instinct for what makes news. "The news orders itself," they say, but seldom offer any help to someone new to the ordeal of sub-editing suddenly faced with assembling bulletins for the midnight-to-dawn shift.

With more and more people relying on the broadcast media for their news, deciding what goes into each bulletin becomes an increasing responsibility.

Guides to a story's importance

There are really only three ways by which an audience should be able to gauge the relative importance of an item in a broadcast bulletin.

The first is one which is often overlooked. **Using an item at all**, in competition with all the other news available, gives that item a degree of importance. One of the media biases referred to by critics is the bias of omission. Those critics claim that a person who watches only television news has a world view limited to what appears in the television news. Therefore, if something is not reported in that news it didn't happen. A simplistic statement, but few can deny that there is an element of truth in it.

The second immediate judgment is **the position of the story in the bulletin**. If the item comes first, it must be important, or at least the journalist who assembled the items considered it the most important. It is natural to most listeners and viewers that the "top" stories come first or they would not be "top" stories. Journalists agree that the top story should come first, even though they might not always agree on what is "top".

An added complication is this age of cellular phones and portable satellite dishes, is that the "top" story may not always be available at the beginning of the bulletin. Sometimes the location of a story in the bulletin is dictated by its availability or by a technical constraint. Even the most up-to-date technology still imposes constraints on the preparation and movement of news.

It is not unusual for a story which "breaks" while the news bulletin is being broadcast to be included in that bulletin. In radio, journalists are expected to report "live" into news-on-the-hour bulletins from the location of the story.

The third audience guide to importance is **the story's length**. The longer the story, especially in radio and TV bulletins, the more important it is considered to be, especially if it is reported at obviously greater length than other items in the bulletin. But this can be deceptive, since some stories take longer to tell than others. It may need only one sentence to tell about a straightforward event of world significance yet a dozen sentences to make clear a complex local political or economic story.

Using this formula, a listener would assume that the most important stories are the longer ones at or near the start of the bulletin. In an ideal situation this might be so, but situations in newsrooms are seldom ideal. Like the news events themselves, the business of gathering them and presenting them on air takes place in the real world, not in a laboratory.

The unpredictability of the flow of news is only one impediment to achieving the desired balance in news bulletins. The balance will vary slightly from station to station, according to their audience. Balance invariably means getting as close as possible to the ideal mix of story content, whether in a single bulletin or in the news services over a whole day, or even several days.

At weekends, bulletins tend to be top-heavy with sport, but it is a time for sport so most audiences accept that. They do not accept a continuing top-heaviness of disasters or politics, no matter how serious those stories may be. Such top-heaviness provokes comments like: "The news is always bad—all death and disaster", or "Boring. Just politicians saying that they are right and the others always wrong".

A frequent problem comes from what is called the "running" story. It begins with a few sketchy details but will obviously develop into a major story within a few hours or days. All that is available for the first report may be two or three sentences, because that is all the reporter can gather in time for the bulletin. The Newcastle earthquake of December, 1989, is a classic example of this problem in both reporting and bulletin balance. It was seen as a top story, certainly as a potential top story, so it became the lead as soon as it was known, even though it was both short and incomplete. Such stories take prominence in the bulletin over stories which are much longer and more complete.

In such cases a journalist's instinct for what makes top news will over-ride the normal criteria for balance. The editor must be careful not to over-react to the potential of the story, otherwise he or she could lay the station open to accusations of sensational reporting. In a typical bulletin, though, this will not be the case. The stories which are most important will come first, and within reasonable limits the items which follow will be arranged in descending order of importance.

For those who have to compile bulletins, the shorter the bulletin the greater the problem of choosing what goes in. In longer bulletins it is usually easier to achieve a balanced line-up of items. Assume that the bulletin being assembled will run 15 minutes, with local, state, national and international material available; perhaps a late night round-up of the news of the day. There may be 30 or more items worthy of consideration.

First, divide the stories into two groups—those which are so important that they must be included and those of sufficient interest to be worthy of consideration. Any which don't fall into either group can be set aside. They probably won't make it.

That's the easy part. Now comes the harder part of deciding in what order these items should be presented. This is where knowledge of the station's audience plays a modest role. Most stations have an audience profile, determined by surveys, so that they know how their audience is made up and from that can determine what are their **most likely news interests**.

For instance, Australia has a large ethnic community. Melbourne is home to the largest Greek community outside Athens so its members will be interested in news from their homeland. Greek news will thus have a better chance of being included by a Melbourne station than it might elsewhere. Melbourne's Italian ethnic community is even bigger, so it is no surprise that Australia's first "narrowcasting" stations appeared there.

Narrowcasting affects the content of news as it affects the rest of a station's programming. It is designed for an audience that is so specific that is has "narrow" limits. In Melbourne one former commercial AM station changed its programming with its ownership and began broadcasting to Melbourne's Italian audience, though it broadcast in both Italian and English. Another station followed to serve Melbourne's Greek audience in the same way.

Knowing audience interest, it might be easy to decide that the latest cricket score or football result holds greater interest than a more significant story about the state of the economy.

There is a place for both, but the choice of order is up to the journalist in charge. Most radio stations make it easier by separating sports news and giving it its own segment within the news bulletin. Sport is a very important component in any newscast. It interests a lot of people, as any newspaper's sporting section will confirm. Watch people reading their papers on the way to work in a train or bus. At least half of them will turn first to the sports pages before reading what interests them on pages 1 or 3.

It is easy to fall for the "soft option" of filling a bulletin with accidents and sport. Certainly it is quickly done and will provide a certain interest for a large part of the audience, but it is done at the expense of deserving political and economic stories with more lasting significance.

In the final analysis it is a matter of a journalist's judgment. There is seldom any time or anyone else to ask. The person in charge has to choose the items and their order from what is on hand, and do it quickly.

. . . and the right balance

But there is more to balance than just getting a good content mix. There should be a balance **between active and passive stories**. There should also be a balance **between new stories and repeats**, even if the repeated stories have been updated and rewritten. It is shameful to repeat items in the same order, even if they have all been rewritten. There are always fresh items, even if only short ones, which should be included so that every bulletin has something new.

Of course, not everyone has heard every news bulletin in any morning, afternoon or evening, which is the principal reason items are repeated and why there are bulletins on radio every half hour in the early morning and late afternoon. This means that in any substantial round-up of what has happened—and in theory this is what even the shortest news bulletins should be—there is always a place for recounting the major news of the day.

Then there's **balance of location**. Most audiences are more interested in local items, or items with local significance. This does not mean they have to originate within the local community. What happens elsewhere in the state or nation, or even on the far side of the world, can have local significance. So local items should be mixed with non-local items in the interests of a balanced presentation. Major stories from elsewhere should always be given their due place. But if a story has no local significance, or interest, and can not be given such an interest by a local journalist, it has no place in any bulletin.

Many editors consider there should be a **balance in presentation** between items with voice reports or interview segments and those without. In short on-the-hour bulletins most items have tape inserts; it may well be one of the reasons they are included. Voice reports and interviews add interest, if not significance, to a story. However there are often items for which there are no taped inserts but which are so important they should be included.

This consideration is usually one of pace rather than balance. **Pace** has more to do with the manner of presentation than the content of a news bulletin, but it can affect the order in which items are presented.

Pace is determined by several things; voice report and interview inserts, duration of items, the nature and speed of the reader's voice, the change of voice which occurs with taped inserts, even the style of writing of the raw material. All play their part in giving a bulletin a character distinctive to the station and its audience.

Obviously, given ten items worthy of inclusion, it would be unbalanced presentation to put all those with taped inserts first, so that the "tail" is no more than a long newsreader presentation from the studio. Spacing the inserts through the bulletin sounds better and holds listener-interest longer.

Similarly, a bulletin which begins with three or four long items seems to drag, even if those items are important. The bulletin will hold more interest if a short but interesting item is inserted between two longer and weightier ones. The right **balance in story length** creates pace and pace retains audience interest.

Whether for pace or balance, it is also best to **mix story types** — hard factual items interspersed with human interest stories, a sports segment, perhaps a financial report and, usually at the end, the weather.

In all this, the only predictable aspect of a news bulletin should be its quality.

Pictures profits and problems

Putting all the raw materials together for a television news bulletin is not necessarily more difficult, but the logistics are more complex. Most television newscasts run half an hour (including commercials), so they are all major ones. There are certainly news updates on most capital city stations — a minute or so of news headlines is about all they manage, usually a rehash of what has already been telecast and very rarely with anything new. There is seldom much production effort in most of these.

In television the problems are doubled. Instead of working with words alone, as in radio, television also has to work with pictures, which multiplies the difficulties of determining a bulletin order without losing balance or pace. There is an order, balance and pace in picture content, too, and since in television the picture dominates, it often wins first consideration.

Television news editors, or whoever determines the shape a newscast will take, have to ensure the dominance of the picture does not extend to dominance over content. It is too easy to inject into a bulletin a story for which the pictures are good but the story insignificant, even trivial. Such inclusions are justified on the grounds that it is often the trivial, not the important, which causes discussion next day.

Animal stories, beauty contests and bizarre accidents are the television items which seem to dominate discussions at morning tea the next day. How often do those taking part in the discussions realise that they are commenting on pictures that make good television, not necessarily good television news? It seems there are television news editors who also fail to appreciate the difference.

Most television bulletins are also cut into sections by commercial breaks. In planning a bulletin's shape over a half-hour or hour, alert news editors make a virtue of necessity and **turn the commercial breaks to advantage**. The public is so accustomed to commercials at given intervals that in the past, even the ABC did not hesitate to break its news bulletins with advertisements for later programs to help in its bulletin building.

American researchers claim that the domination of commercial television in that country has meant that the attention span of many viewers is now limited to the time between commercial breaks—up to eight minutes. Whether such research has been duplicated in Australia or not, television news editors use its assumptions when planning how to get maximum attention for the items they offer. They use the commercial breaks to give viewers with a short attention span a chance to relax before asking them to absorb another series of items in which they may—perhaps should—be interested.

The steps in planning the content of a television bulletin are no different from those in radio; what is available, what are the most important items, what are the most interesting? Answering these questions should decide what gets into the bulletin, though this doesn't always happen. Many other things intrude to affect the order in which those items will be presented.

Television news researchers, even more than those working in radio, have found that most people watch a television bulletin from beginning to end. Television news is not like a newspaper, where a wide variety of material is offered, conveniently labelled by headlines. Given such a choice the average reader elects to read only about 15 per cent of what the news columns in most daily papers have to offer.

Newspaper sub-editors try to make their presented items tempting to readers by using headlines, layout techniques and a fact-packed writing style, but it has limited effectiveness. The majority of readers still choose to read only what interests them. In terms of content, those readers take in little more than if they were watching an average television newscast, and it is a content narrowed by the limits of the readers' existing interests. True news seekers, of course, read and absorb a lot more.

Those who sit down to watch television news have no such viewer choice. That has been made for them by the journalists preparing the newscast. Critics say television news can't adequately meet the needs of its varied audience. They forget that television often interests viewers in items they would never elect to read in a newspaper. Thus television is broadening public awareness of what is happening in the world. It is left to newspapers to do the job of further informing those whose interest has been newly sparked.

Knowing this doesn't help the television editor to put together a bulletin. There are items prepared by the station's own reporters, items received by AUSSAT from stations interstate and further items received in regular or special services by satellite from overseas. They are all, once their introductions have been written, in ready-for-air form, but they seldom form an ideal bulletin.

What about the items which are important enough to warrant inclusion but for which there are no pictures? The incidence of these is decreasing, thanks to the speed with which pictures can be moved around the country or the world, but they still exist. Many long and fact-filled introductions which lead to stand-ups or packages also fall into this category. They are too long to be read from the news desk. They must have pictures or imaginative graphics to enhance viewer interest.

In many cases it is the task of a studio-based journalist/ producer, with the office files, the art department or perhaps the newsroom's own artist, to provide illustration. This can come from many sources, but writing them into a story or an introduction adds more problems.

Viewers may think television news uses few **still pictures** — they are often not obvious as stills — yet it happens all the time. When they appear with the newsreader, stills used intelligently subtly add information or an explanation to what is being said. Poorly chosen stills, or worse still carelessly used ones, add nothing and can even detract from what is being said.

Stills can be 35mm slides, frozen frames of video stored electronically for instant retrieval or artwork prepared using the latest generation of sophisticated equipment owned by the studio—anything from simple lettering to complex moving vision inserts. No matter how simple or how complex, its use is wasted if it fails to add information or understanding to what is being seen and said.

Every station has its slide **library**, in addition to a library of past newsclips from which segments are used as appropriate. It pays all television journalists to know what is on hand and how to find it, and then how to use it properly.

An example, already dated: There is an item on the AAP wire from London that Prime Minister Thatcher has come under attack from the Labour leader in the House of Commons over some aspect of her policy. It is a longish lead to an item from London, delivered by satellite as a package—too long to be read without some visual amplification. The journalist has the choice of three still pictures: Thatcher, the Labour leader or the House of Commons. All three are available in the library.

It is so easy to choose one and write for another. The original story says "British Prime Minister Margaret Thatcher came under fire today" but it would be confusing for the audience to hear these words and see a still of the Labour leader. If the story is to begin with a reference to Mrs Thatcher it is her picture that should be seen. If it is to show the Labour leader then the story should be re-written to read "The British Labour Party leader " If the pictures of both have been used so frequently that another showing the House of Commons is the best choice, then the lead should say "In Britain's House of Commons today . . ."

Any **conflict between pictures and words destroys the impact** of the item immediately. It can be so distracting that the credibility of the news service suffers.

The same problem extends into almost everything a television reporter writes. It also extends into putting a bulletin together. The person responsible has to consider not only each item's content and the best possible order, but also **continuity in pictures and words** and, on top of that, the **logistics** of presenting the bulletin in the desired order. Can it be done physically with the equipment the station has available?

It is no use deciding, for the best possible reasons, that a story received from New York should be followed seconds later by another received on the same satellite feed, if there is no time for the operators to cue the second item. In most of the capital city or major stations it is possible, because they have the equipment to play items—each recorded onto a separate video cartridge—in any order. Often stations will run 30 or so seconds on two or three overseas stories together, calling it, in the jargon, an "overseas wrap", meaning a wrap-up of important overseas stories worthy of use, but not on their own, or to any length. Most stations have the equipment to do this, but not all. To help make the rapid presentation of television news more immediately understandable, news producers "key" essential words across the picture on the air. This means that information to ensure better understanding of what is being seen and heard, is prepared in a separate source and electronically worked into the main picture to remind viewers where the item is from or who is speaking. Even such simple reminders require planning. It is bad planning when the wrong name or location is seen on air and since it is done live, there is no margin for error.

Maps and diagrams also need careful planning. It is not possible to pluck a portion of a map from an atlas (copyright considerations aside) and present it on air. It is far too detailed for the audience to make quick use of the information offered. A television news map must show only what is relevant to the story. Usually it must be specially drawn by an expert.

Maps which are too complicated, too mis-shapen to be recognised quickly, or wrong, are worse than no illustration at all. Why bother to draw a map to remind viewers where Gallipoli is if the map puts it in the wrong place? (It has happened, much to the embarrassment of a capital city station).

It is the same in the preparation of diagrams, graphs or any other type of illustrative material. The journalist does not have the task of preparing such illustrations, but must carry the responsibility for making sure they show the correct information in the clearest possible way and that the words complement the illustration. The audience has only seconds to take in the illustration so the scripted words should help, not hinder the process. It is no use showing a diagram of fluctuating milk prices while the words are about dairy farmers' incomes. The two are associated, but there is conflict. Chances are the audience will take in neither, so the story will be wasted.

Seconds and segments

There is no sense trying to cram 40 minutes of material into a 30-minute newscast. It is a daily struggle for the news producer to time so accurately that a bulletin fills its given 30 minutes, especially if attention is also given to the best story order.

Each day the television station issues a log which shows the times at which each item, from shortest commercial to longest program, goes to air, complete with actual running times. That portion for the news is usually left vacant, except for the commercials. This allows the news producer to push the commercial breaks forward or back to suit the smooth running of the bulletin, but not to cut the actual content or duration of the breaks themselves.

Every television script should have an accurate running time clearly shown. The producer can thus work out to the second how long each news segment (between commercial breaks) will be. To make the total segment and commercial times fit a precise total running time, a story may have to be cut, or perhaps dropped altogether in favour of another which is slightly shorter or longer.

And then something may still go wrong during the live presentation. Video-cartridge items can be activated in the wrong sequence or the players can break down or deliver a defective signal; the inadvertent pressing of a wrong button can start the wrong picture or sound source; script pages can get out of sequence or the autocue develop a fault. Any of these mean the planned flow of the presentation is disrupted and the accurate timing destroyed. This is why producers always have on hand a couple of "iffers"—short newsreader-only items which can be dropped in if needed or discarded if they are not required. Recalculating timing on air, during the actual presentation of the news bulletin, is a nerve-wracking necessity when something goes wrong.

Television newscasts go to air at fixed times. Material from interstate via AUSSAT must arrive in sufficient time for the receiving station to see it, edit it if necessary, and write a suitable introduction. Delayed delivery—and it sometimes happens—can cause a string of further delays, which may mean that an item is not ready to play to air when required.

Bulletin planners have to bear such logistics in mind when determining the order in which their stories will appear. Smaller stations face a different problem when news from a capital city station is replayed before or after the local news service. Will the major local story appear in condensed form in the capital city bulletin and will the two conflict? This is why most regional stations prefer to have their local news first — they can give the major local story what they consider adequate coverage. What's big news in Dubbo might only be of passing interest to a Sydney audience, so why make the people of Dubbo wait until 15 or 20 minutes into the bulletin before they see their major news of the day?

Even that is not the end of the bulletin building story. Consider the commercial breaks. There are two schools of thought, both acknowledging that most viewers will watch from beginning to end, if the bulletin retains their interest. One theory holds that a bulletin should start with the best material and grade down in importance or interest to the last item — always allowing for a sports segment and the weather.   The other theory, also popular in Australia, holds that commercials break the telecast into three or four separate bulletins, so each segment should be built separately. Thus each segment, whether it is news, sport or anything else, will have its own "lead" item, its own closing item and its own material in between, preferably with some cohesion between them.

This means that although the bulletin will open with the top two or three stories of the day, the third or fourth most important item might well be held back to open the second segment of the news and another important story, possibly the major sports story, might open the third segment. The variety of choices is greatly increased, but there is still the consideration of what should go into each segment.

Research, most of it done in the United States, shows that people pay most attention to what is first or last in any television segment, whether it is news, other programming or commercials. The research was originally done to determine the effectiveness of commercial breaks — should the customer buy the first commercial or the last commercial? The results are the same for news items in a newscast, provided the stories are of more or less equal interest. It is the middle story or stories which achieve lowest viewer attention and retention.

So segments, like bulletins, begin with the most important or interesting item available. They end with another item of some significance or importance, since that item will also be well received and remembered. In between, the canny bulletin planner inserts those items with the stunning pictures or the absorbing presentation, to hold viewer interest.

It is usual for television news bulletin planners to try to find a "lightener" to end the bulletin, especially if the day has had more than its share of grim and gory stories. Bulletins often end with something which causes the viewer to smile. If two or three catastrophes are reported back to back in the valid consideration of continuity and similarity of content, then many news editors will try to find something much lighter to follow immediately. But it must be in keeping and not show bad taste or a cavalier approach to what has already been reported.

This is when it comes back to the ability of the continuity writer, usually the News Editor for the day, to make one story follow naturally from the preceding one. Such a skill is confined to journalists with a facility with words and a "feel" for both the substance of the news and the sympathy of his or her audience. Such people are rare.

All types of bulletin patterns have been tried: breaking a bulletin into clear segments for local, national and overseas news, plus weather; breaking it up into political news, other news, sport, then weather. All seem to end with the weather, for which there is a steady and demanding audience, provided it is done well.

Another approach has been to introduce different presenters, quite apart from the station's reporters, each presenting only a portion of the news, with a separate "expert" for finance, the environment, sport and yet another for weather.

Styles in television presentation are changing all the time. It is part of the station managements' continuing struggle to get more viewers than their competitors and thus win the ratings. However, there is one constant — news. Presentation gimmicks have only temporary appeal. Sooner or later, the station which presents the most credible news service and makes fewest errors in doing so, will win.

Broadcast news-gathering equipment consistently becomes smaller, lighter, yet more efficient, which means pictures and reports can be made more reliably and of better quality, but it often requires a helicopter to move news crews quickly over metropolitan traffic congestion.

(Picture: Channel 9)

Equipment

A brief survey of the tools of the broadcast journalist

This chapter looks briefly, and in general terms, at the equipment used in the news gathering process for radio and television. Although much of it looks intimidating, the good reporter will know and understand the equipment, realise its potential and recognise its limitations.

The path of sound

Radio is about changing one form of sound to another, enabling the broadcaster to communicate with his or her audience. The words of a news story are changed by a broadcaster into sound waves, which are picked up by the microphone. The electronic signal gathered by the microphone can be stored in magnetic form on audio tape, or be sent directly to the transmitter.

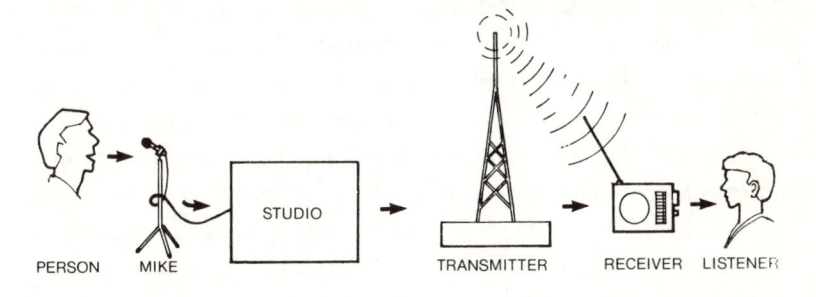

The path of sound

The transmitter sends out the signal to the receivers tuned to the appropriate frequency. The radio receiver changes the signal back into sound waves, which are picked up by the listener's ears and changed into signals to the brain, where the message is registered. The whole process takes a fraction of a second.

This path is the same for AM and FM radio, except that in FM radio there are two channels to provide stereo sound. It is basically the same with digital sound as well, since this applies to the treatment of the signal between microphone and tape and between receipt and the loudspeaker. It does not affect the path itself.

Let's start this exploration of the equipment of the broadcast journalist with that piece which comes to hand first, the **microphone** — usually referred to as the mike or mic. There are many kinds of microphones — all sensitive instruments — used to pick up voices and other sounds. They are differentiated in two main ways; by whether they need a power supply and by the pattern of their receptive sound area.

Among the microphones most commonly used in radio are rugged **dynamic** mikes which need no power supply, so there is no need to worry about batteries. These microphones generate their sound signals when the sound waves cause sensitive filaments or strips within the microphone to vibrate.

Condenser microphones need batteries, or some other source of power, to operate. Condenser mikes can be much smaller than dynamics, since they need no long fibres to vibrate to generate sound. The incoming sound causes a tiny diaphragm to vibrate, but this tiny sound is magnified within the microphone itself using power from the battery so that a stronger signal is sent down the cable to the recorder.

There is a trap with condenser microphones: because they run on batteries they have an on-off switch. It is easy to forget to turn them on. Switching off saves battery power, but forgetting to switch on again saves nothing and may cost a whole interview, even a whole story.

Each microphone type has its advocates, according to the work it is asked to do and the recording equipment to which it is attached. The most important difference between the mikes used in broadcast journalism is not their power source but their pattern of pick-up, their sensitivity to sounds from various directions. There are three pattern-types in common use: cardioid, omni-directional and uni-directional.

Cardioid is the pick-up pattern most commonly used in radio. Such microphones are given that name because their pick-up pattern is heart-shaped. They are most receptive to sounds coming from directly in front and to a certain extent from the sides, but decreasing to almost nothing for sound coming from behind. Such a pattern makes them the most useful for announcing in a studio and for interviewing almost anywhere.

Omni-directional mikes are no longer favoured by broadcast journalists, though they once were, because they tend to pick up sound equally from all directions. The disadvantage for a journalist in the field is obvious. Omni-directional mikes pick up any sound in the area: traffic, a refrigerator motor, conversations of other people. Sounds the ear may not register as loud may seem loud to the microphone and may ruin a recording. Omni-directional mikes may have had advantages for group discussions in a studio situation when there is no sound coming from elsewhere. These days, in the interests of sound quality it is normal for those taking part in a studio-based discussions to be allocated a mike each.

Uni-directional or "shotgun" mikes are used for much television news work, but much less used by radio reporters. They are sensitive to sound from directly in front and to very little else. They are much larger than other commonly-used mikes and get their name from their shape—long, sometimes very long, usually covered by a wind baffle and held by a pistol grip. They are specially useful at news conferences, since they enable the recording of questions or answers at relatively long distances and because they shut out most other sounds. They can record a speaker across a room or even further away, without that person sounding "off-mike".

They are particularly popular with television sound recordists not wanting to intrude into the picture during the so-called "door stop" TV news interview. But these mikes have handicaps, too. They are so directional that it is easy for novices to miss what they want to record simply because the mike is off target—i.e. not pointed at the right angle to pick up the required sound. This is why television sound recordists wear headphones—to ensure they are getting a satisfactory recording.

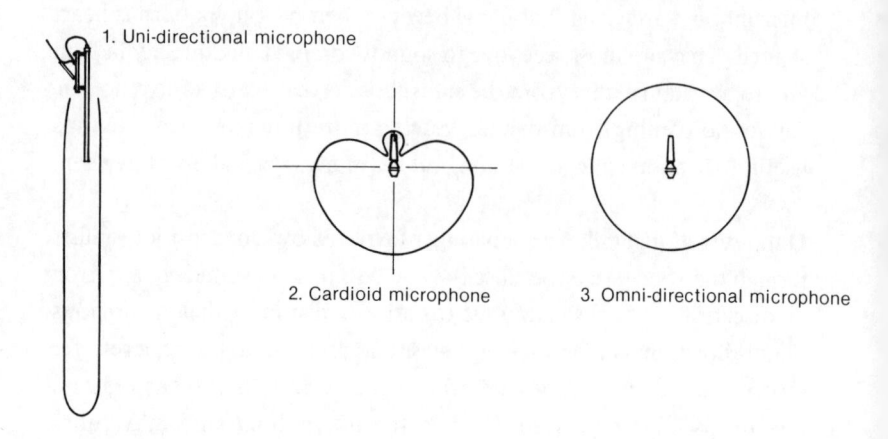

1. Uni-directional microphone

2. Cardioid microphone

3. Omni-directional microphone

The sound pattern of microphones

Television reporters don't have to worry as much about the technicalities of microphones. In most stations, certainly in the larger ones, they have sound operators (sometimes the camera operator) doing the job, so all the reporter has to do is ask the right questions. The radio journalist must keep constantly in mind the sensitivity of the mike he or she is using.

Using a mike properly is less simple than it sounds. A microphone is an ear, not necessarily more sensitive than our own—though some are—but certainly less discriminating. When we listen, our ears may well hear what a microphone hears, but our brains filter out those sounds which are not relevant to our concentration. This is how we can talk to another person on a crowded bus, filled with dozens of others doing the same thing. We can hear what someone else is saying in a factory, even when the machinery is making more noise than the voice we are trying to hear.

Not so with a microphone. It registers everything. Record in a kitchen and the microphone will pick up the high-pitched whine of the refrigerator motor. In an office it will hear the air conditioning unit you, as reporter, didn't realise was running. Most novice reporters lose at least one interview to an air conditioner early in their career, or to the wind. The microphone hears wind passing over its surface when the reporter hardly realises there is a wind blowing.

This is why most mikes for outside use have a wind-noise dampener. These wind socks, baffles or shields, are usually removable, but because they are made of easily-damaged plastic foam it is best to fit them and leave them in place. The plastic shield, though bulbous, detracts so little from the sensitivity of the mike that it is not worth the risk to keep removing it. The wind shields are such a familiar sight on television newscasts that many people might mistake them for the microphones they cover.

There's more about the proper care and handling of a microphone in the chapter on techniques, but even at this early stage here are a few don'ts.

- Don't dangle the mike from its cable — always hold the mike itself.
- Don't tap it to see if it works — it will sound like an explosion.
- Don't blow on it to check it — speaking into it is enough.
- Don't drag the mike cable around — it transmits noise to the recorder.
- Don't leave mike cables where they can be trodden on or rolled over.
- Don't bump the mike against anything — it is delicate, so be gentle.

Recording sound

Tape recorders these days are almost as universal as transistor radios. Most families have one, many have more than one. They are used to record all kinds of sounds on audio tape of one kind or another: everything from huge multi-track open reel machines to tiny mini-cassettes.

Tape recording works on the same principle as the common schoolroom experiment of a magnet creating patterns with iron filings. Audio tape consists of a strong plastic backing material which has been coated with a thin layer of particles, usually iron oxide. Other materials, such as chrome oxide, are used on more expensive and more long-lasting tapes, but for broadcast journalism work any good quality standard (ferric oxide) tape is adequate.

When tape passes through a recorder it passes across a variety of "heads". Most domestic recorders have two heads, one to record the new signal and overwrite any signal which may already be on the tape and a second to read the signal and thus play it. Better quality recorders have three heads—to erase, to record and to play, in that order.

The key requirement of good recording, apart from a good microphone and good technique, is a good recording head. The signals from the microphone are amplified within the recorder and relayed to the recording head, so that when the tape passes smoothly across it the electrical signals imparted by the head form patterns in the particles on the surface of the tape. When the same particle patterns are passed over the play head the process is reversed. The head reads the patterns, turning them into electrical impulses which are amplified in the recorder unit and emerge through a speaker as sound. The better the equipment and its operator, the closer that emerging sound is to the original sound picked up by the microphone.

On better recorders the erase head's task is to "wipe" any previous signals before recording begins so that the tape reaches the recording head in uniformly blank condition.

In a broadcasting station the whole tape is erased before use, just to make sure nothing goes wrong. This is most quickly and effectively done in a bulk eraser, a box-like unit containing a powerful magnet. Put the audio or video tape into or onto the eraser and the tape is "wiped" within a second or two.

Audio tapes do not last forever. Every time the tape passes over a head there is a loss of quality. In good equipment this is so slight it is not discernible, even to experts, until it has passed 30 or more times. Videotape ages more quickly because the heads operate in a different way. It is a good idea to keep track of the age of tapes in use, either by dating them the first time they are used, or (if you are really diligent) keeping track of the number of times they have been used.

Nor do the heads in the recorders last forever. They become clogged with dust and oxide from the tapes—low quality tapes clog heads faster than good tapes. Heads should be cleaned regularly, using a soft cloth or a cotton bud dipped in pure alcohol. There are several cleaning preparations on the market which will do the job.

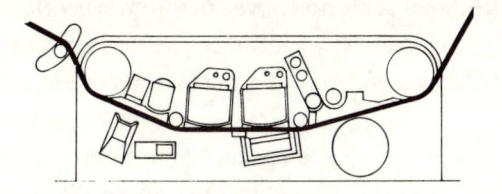

Typical tape threading for an audio recorder, in this case, a Revox B77.

1. Left-hand turntable
2. Right-hand turntable
3. Counter with reset button
4. Headblock cover
5. Splicing block with cutter
6. Power switch. On/Off
7. Speed controls 3¾ or 7½
8. Monitor switch (tape/output)
9. Monitor volume
10. Record pre-selector, left
11. Record pre-selector, right
12. Input level, left channel
13. Input level, right channel
14. Recording level indicator, left channel
15. Recording level indicator, right channel
16. Microphone input, left channel
17. Microphone input, right channel
18. Input selector, left channel
19. Input selector, right channel
20. Pause control
21. Fast rewind
22. Fast forward
23. Play
24. Stop
25. Record
26. Cue lever

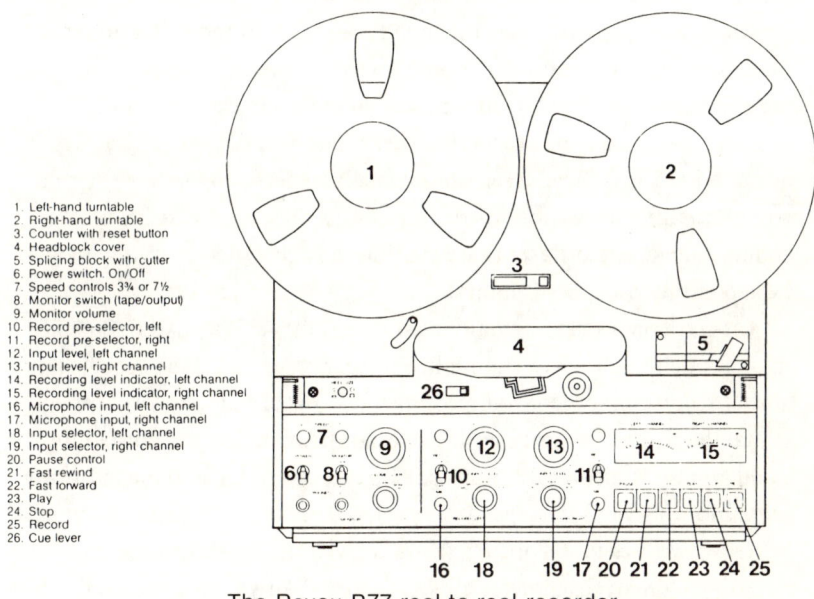

The Revox B77 reel-to-reel recorder.

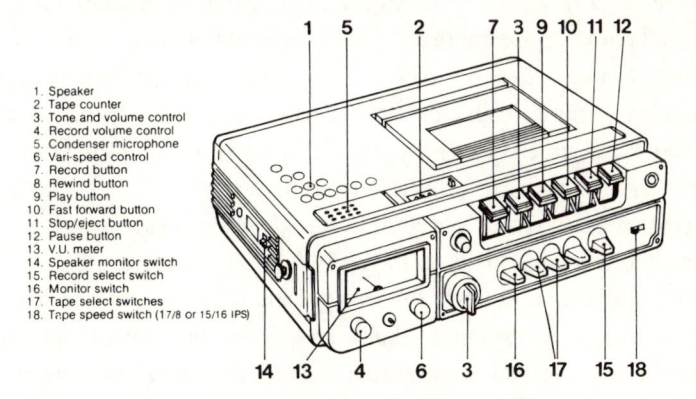

1. Speaker
2. Tape counter
3. Tone and volume control
4. Record volume control
5. Condenser microphone
6. Vari-speed control
7. Record button
8. Rewind button
9. Play button
10. Fast forward button
11. Stop/eject button
12. Pause button
13. V.U. meter
14. Speaker monitor switch
15. Record select switch
16. Monitor switch
17. Tape select switches
18. Tape speed switch (17/8 or 15/16 IPS)

A Superscope cassette recorder.

Check with someone who knows, before you try cleaning the heads of a recorder, no matter how badly they need a clean. Improper cleaning can do more damage to a recorder than improper use, and much more quickly.

There is a variety of reel-to-reel and cassette recorders in use in radio (and television) stations across Australia, so the diagram below shows only how a typical recorder works. To get the best from any equipment, read the operator's manual carefully.

Reel-to-reel recorders — both small ones used in the field and larger ones used in studio control rooms and editing suites — have multiple speed settings. Most will record at 9.5cm and 19cm each second — that's 3¾ and 7½ inches per second, (ips). Some will also record at 38cm a second (15 ips). The faster the recording speed, the better the final sound quality, since more of the tape is used to lay down the original signal. Fine music programs are traditionally recorded at 15 ips for the best possible quality of sound.

Cassette recorders normally record at only 4.75cm a second (1 7/8 ips), though some have the ability to record at half that speed. The slower recording speed is not recommended for broadcast work, though it may be useful for storage of material, provided it is recorded on a good quality machine. Always make sure material is replayed on a machine with the same speed settings. To ensure this happens, mark all tapes with their recording speed as well as the duration.

It is unwise to use longer cassette tapes than you need for the job. Most news operators use 60-minute cassettes, or even 30-minute ones (remember that a 60-minute cassette has 30 minutes on each side). Avoid using longer cassettes for news. Ninety or 120-minute cassettes usually have thinner tape which can stretch, distort or break, especially in the rugged use to which tapes are subjected in news work. Trying to repair a stretched or torn cassette tape is a terrible job.

Longer cassettes are acceptable for storing recorded material, but even then it is unwise to go beyond 90-minute cassettes.

Preparation is essential for any outside recording. Before leaving on any project a reporter must know how to use the recorder and should check that it contains well-charged batteries. Take a blank tape and a spare (and a take-up spool if you are using a reel-to-reel recorder).

Also, take along masking or plastic tape to fix the mike firmly into position beside the others at a news conference. And don't forget the windshield. A microphone stand may also be useful. Make a test recording before leaving the office.

At the assignment's location make another test recording to ensure nothing has gone wrong during the journey. This is also the time to mark on the tape its content (who or what is recorded), date, duration and recording speed.

Most people understand the basic functions of tape recorders because they are used in most homes, but to achieve professional quality requires more than basic understanding.

Press both RECORD and PLAY simultaneously to record (unless it is a "one-touch RECORD" unit). Never force down the RECORD button. It should move down easily. If it does not, check that the cassette in use has its record "tab" in place. These tabs can be broken out if a previous user wants to make sure what is on the tape will not be wiped by a new recording.

Most machines have a PAUSE control, which stops the tape while the button is depressed. Good PAUSE buttons stop and restart the tape instantly and are silent in operation. Some recorders are voice-activated, which means that once in record mode the PAUSE is applied automatically until an incoming sound triggers recording.

Professional recorders have meters so the operator can monitor most of the functions, but meters are no use unless they are understood. The most important meter is the one which shows the level (volume) of the signal being recorded. To achieve the best possible sound this level should be neither too low nor too high. If the signal is too low and has to be boosted for replay in the studio, background sounds and tape noises will also be boosted, resulting in poor quality sound. If the recorded level is too high, the sound will be distorted.

To ensure broadcast quality sound, use the meters properly. On audio equipment the meters are usually VU or "peak" meters. Both measure the level of signals being received. VU meters give an average reading of sound levels. Peak meters give a more accurate reading of the peaks (the loudest parts) of the recorded signal. Both do the required job.

There is no standard setting for all equipment or for all situations, but the best setting is when the meter moves as widely as possible across its field. It should peak into the red segment but not remain there. The signal should never be so strong that the meter needle (or lights, if it is that type of meter) reaches the extremity of the red area.

Every recording requires a different level according to the situation, background noise levels, the level of the voice or voices to be recorded, even the condition of the batteries. Always test levels before beginning a recording. Have the people involved say a few words and check the incoming sound. Raise or lower the recording level accordingly.

The same meter will also show the level of the recorded material when the recorder plays the tape.

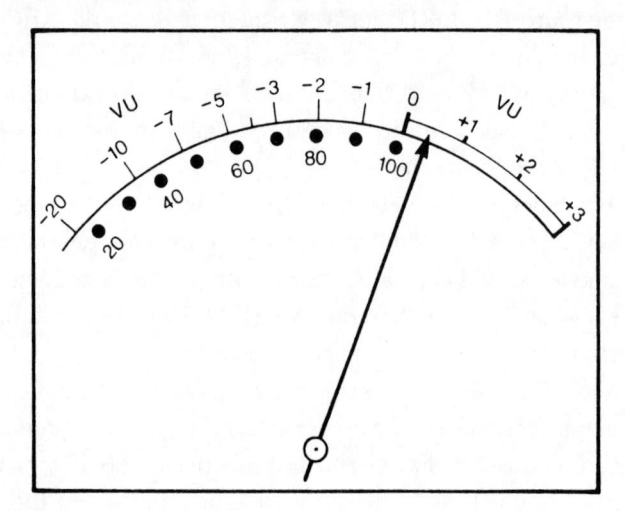

A VU meter

There is a third type of audio recorder in most radio and television newsrooms and control rooms: the cartridge machine. Cartridges, usually called "carts", are endless loops of tape of varying durations. They are used extensively in radio news production. Voice reports or segments of interviews are recorded in their edited form onto carts for use in news programs.

The advantages of a cartridge are that it starts instantly and automatically re-cues ready for re-use. All the operator has to do with a completed cartridge is press the PLAY button and it comes up with the first word.

For the same reasons carts are the obvious choice for commercials. The segments recorded on cartridges are usually short. A 27-second segment is recorded on a 30-second cartridge, so that re-cueing time is cut to a minimum, especially since it recues at high speed. In any case the cart. unit may be required for another cartridge within a few seconds.

Playing a cart. is simplicity itself: load it, press the PLAY button at the appropriate time, when the required segment has played, "kill" the sound from the cart. but allow the machine to roll on to its re-cue.

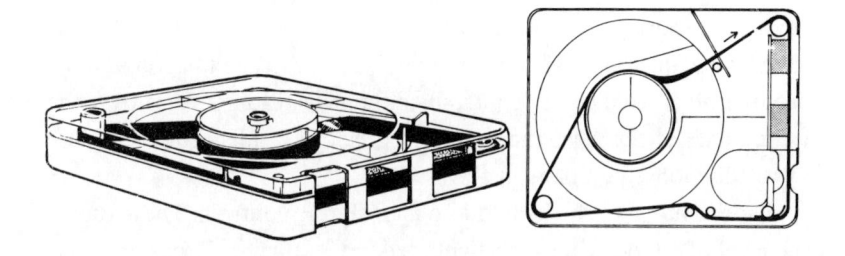

Two views of a cartridge

The studio/control area

Whether in a small station with a news staff of one, a large metropolitan newsroom, or a school or tertiary institution, radio journalists present their newscasts from a studio. Broadcasting involves the selective use of sound, produced from a sound-proofed studio using electronic equipment to produce the sounds.

Studios are sound-proofed to keep unwanted sounds out and to avoid the reflection and echoing of sound inside. Small news operations produce their news from one of their station's presentation studios; larger newsrooms have presentation studios of their own.

In a normal radio presentation studio, the presenter is surrounded by equipment—reel-to-reel units, cartridge machines, turntables, microphones, monitor speakers and the most intimidating piece of studio equipment of all, the mixer or control panel. The more sources of sound in the studio and its control room, the larger the mixer. The mixer links all the equipment and controls the quality of the signal which goes to air.

In a radio news operation with its own presentation studio, the controls are usually simpler: a small mixer (with provision to take in reports live from journalists on location), a microphone or two, cartridge machines for playing inserts and a reel-to-reel unit.

This equipment looks more intimidating than it really is. Understand what it does and it is easy to master.

The **mixer** is central to everything produced in and broadcast from the studio. The controller can switch from one source of sound to another at the touch of a button, or the closing of a fader—from the cartridge of the news theme to the reading of the headlines in the studio, from a read introduction back to the cartridge machine for a prerecorded report.

As the name implies, a mixer can mix sounds. The fashion in news production these days is to introduce the newsreader's voice over the fading bars of the news theme. Every mixer has faders for each piece of production equipment in the studio.

Faders may be either round knobs or sliding controls. They control the level of sound from a particular sound source—microphone, cartridge player, turntable, reel-to-reel or cassette tape player. Each sound source will be different in delivered level, so each has to be adjusted to the production's requirements.

Above each fader there is usually a toggle switch with settings for **program** and **cue**—program goes to air, cue does not. Before any segment goes to air, use the cue channel to set the appropriate sound level. The program setting is for actual broadcasting, or pre-recording for broadcast later.

The studio is also equipped with **monitor** speakers and with headphones, to let the operator hear what is happening. As soon as a fader for one of the studio microphones is opened (turned on), the monitor cuts out automatically, to avoid feed-back. This is why most broadcasters check their output through headphones.

Audio editing equipment is for either cutting (physically cutting up and rejoining the tape) or dubbing (joining segments electronically).

Cutting means just that: literally cutting up a taped interview and reassembling the pieces in the required order. It is still a popular method with those who use reel-to-reel tape, though most like to cut a dub of the original, so the original is still available in the event of a mistake, or should a re-edit be necessary.

Dubbing means electronically transferring required segments from the original recording to another tape in a selected order. In the case of news material this usually means transferring to a cartridge.

Reporters in the field usually use cassette recorders, though some (especially on the ABC) still prefer reel-to-reel. The quality of reel-to-reel recording is better than that from a cassette, though this often depends on the ability of the operator. Reel-to-reel equipment is more expensive and cumbersome, but it is still preferred by those making programs where sound quality is of great importance.

If the original recording is made on a reel-to-reel machine, it will probably be edited by **physical cutting**. This is done by selecting the required segments, their order, then splicing them together to achieve a coherent and shorter end product. Once a reel-to-reel tape has been cut edited it is unwise to use it again for recording. At every spot where an edit has been made — where the two pieces of tape have been spliced together — there is a fraction of an inch of tape that is unusable. If re-recorded this will create a sound drop-out. That loss of sound for a fraction of a second is very noticeable when replayed.

Cut editing is impossible with material recorded on a cassette, because of its small size and slow recording speed. Physical editing is hardly an option in editing short news clips. It comes into its own in the production of longer segments where quality is more important, such as magazine programs, current affairs and documentaries.

Many stations will not broadcast from cassette, even if that is how the original recording was made. They used to claim, with justification, that the quality was not good enough, especially after it had been dubbed to reel-to-reel or cartridge. Since then the quality of cassette recording has improved, but there is still the problem of control. The cassette's slower tape speed means lack of precision in stopping, starting, and thus editing. So stations which now accept material recorded on a cassette edit it to cartridge before playing it to air.

For news editors this slight loss of quality is hardly a problem, since it is still better than material delivered over telephone lines, by cellular phones or from news cars by two-way radio. So cassettes can get by phones or from news cars by two-way radio. So cassettes can get by in news, but not in current affairs or documentary productions.

Cassette recorders used in radio news are little different from those used in the home, except they are of higher quality and are used in conjuction with a high-quality microphone. Reel-to-reel recorders are less common. Those most used in broadcasting are in two categories — portables for field work and studio editing models. In operation they are all the same. Most major manufacturers have built models for broadcast use in the field, but in the studio there are only a few makes in general use. The best-known are Revox, Cuemaster, Tascam and Otari.

The advantages of these specialist machines is their precision and versatility, especially in editing. They have three heads, where most domestic and field models have two, and the heads are accessible. They have counters which are far more accurate, so that specific places on long tapes can be found quickly. They have a "fast start" facility, which means they start recording or playing instantly, without wow — few cassette players can equal such performance, although it can be partially imitated by using the pause function.

Most important of all for editing, they have a "cue" facility. This frees the tape from the capstans, so it can be inched back and forth by hand ("rocking and rolling") so that it is possible to find exactly where a sound begins or ends.

Dub editing requires two or more machines, for news work usually only two. One plays the original, the other records the end product. If any mixing is to be done, two or more players must be connected through the mixer (panel) to the recording unit.

The telephone is so commonplace in today's world that for most people it is hardly a tool of trade. For the broadcast journalist, especially the radio journalist, it is probably the greatest news-gathering tool since the pencil. Journalists would be lost without it.

A telephone permits quick and wide news coverage, but like most tools is only as good as those who use it. Phones bridge time and distance, so there are few stories which can't be covered, at least at the basic level. But the sound quality of that report will always be deficient, and the content still depends on the ability of the journalist.

Radio and television news services, servants to the clock, could not exist without the telephone. News flows in over the phones because people call in with information, all of which has to be checked. Such a flood of information is so common that many stations reserve a number for people to phone in, and have other numbers on which newsroom staff can phone out.

All this apparently easy gathering of news by phone has problems. There have been instances when the phone has been the reason for accidental distortion, simply because the reporter mis-heard or misunderstood what was said. The phone also enables misguided members of the public to use its anonymity to pass deliberately misleading reports, even hoaxes.

Cellular phones have added a new dimension to the news-gathering process. The reporter no longer has to be near a public phone to keep in touch with the office.

Recorder phones are essential devices in all news-gathering organisations. The recorder phone has a number of uses from recording reports from journalists in the field to interviews with newsmakers without the reporter leaving the newsroom.

There are several models in use across Australia, so reporters should familiarise themselves with the unit in their particular newsroom.

For a journalist with a recorder phone, no newsmaker with a telephone is out of range. This has proved valuable to radio. In recent years, particularly in the United States, enterprising journalists have telephoned terrorists who have taken over embassies or other buildings and interviewed them by telephone. There was no other way to talk to them. A newspaper reporter can only report next morning what was said on the radio. The television reporter is handicapped without pictures, although television news is more and more using phone excerpts or parts of radio interviews as part of news reports.

Recording Pictures

Equipment for television is more complex and expensive, though in principle it works in much the same way; impulses on tape are put on by recorders and read by the play-back video tape machines. In television, except for the making of special documentaries, film is a thing of the past, though it was from the cinema that television inherited the concept of news in pictures. Its first news pictures were gathered on film.

Cameras: When television began in Britain and the United States, the pictures came from studio cameras. Because television cameras were then so cumbersome, almost anything outside the studio had to be recorded on film, which then had to be processed, edited and scripted, before it could be played into the television system. In spite of the delay film took little of the "liveness" out of television and widened its scope. Film introduced the viewers to "see it happen" news.

In those early years television newsfilm was mute; there was no sound on the film shot in the field, or even later after it was edited. Synchronous sound-recording equipment existed—the movie producers had used it for years—but it was far too bulky and costly for day to day news work. So the silent film, after processing, was edited into as complete a picture story as the film editor could manage and then scripted by a television journalist. This script was then read, live, as the film was broadcast.

Not that there was much newsfilm in early television bulletins. When television began in the United States the main network stations were controlled by public companies already in the radio business, and outside the major networks by a variety of business interests. Those who came from radio did not yet consider news an important part of programming and many of those who came to television management from elsewhere thought it expensive and undesirable: compared with entertainment, news yielded little revenue. So news was confined to ten minutes each night or less, and most of that was read live, without many pictures.

It did not take television long to include more news on film, copying the style of the cinema newsreels. As television grew, television news grew and newsmen with big reputations moved from radio to compete on the new medium. The invention of a sound-on-film camera of a size that could be used in the field revolutionised television news as much in its day as electronic news gathering and satellites have done since.

The Bach-Auricon, an American camera, made the recording of sound and picture simultaneously an everyday event, even though the camera was very heavy by today's standards. The amplifier had to be carried and operated separately, and the quality of the optical sound track left a lot to be desired. Previously the German Arriflex had been without peer as a camera for news work, even though it was heavy and noisy in operation. But a "blimped" Arriflex appeared—the entire camera was encased in a noise-insulating shield so that the sound of its operation could not reach the microphones—and soon re-established Arriflex as the best camera in the business.

But "Arris", beloved of cameramen, were expensive, so only the major stations could afford to risk them in day-to-day news situations.

When the less expensive but just as versatile CP-16 camera (from Cinema Products in the United States) arrived, every station could afford to produce quality newsfilm, with synchronous sound. Like the Arriflex, it recorded sound on a narrow "stripe" of magnetic tape on the edge of the 16mm film, which enabled news crews to get good quality sound and pictures. But film, even though vastly improved in picture and sound quality, still suffered as a news medium from time delays. It had to be moved physically from where it was shot in the field to the film processor. Processing took anything from 30 minutes up, according to the amount, type of film, the size and efficiency of the processor. Only then could the editing begin.

Sound-on-film, known as SOF, added new editing problems, because the sound was recorded 28 frames (26 for optical sound tracks) ahead of the picture so it would replay smoothly and not be subjected to the frame-by-frame jerk involved in projection.

No wonder when videotape arrived it was so welcomed by the television companies. The first public demonstration of videotape in the United States, where it was invented, took place within days of television beginning in Australia in November 1956. The first videotape recorders were anything but portable. They were huge studio-based machines used to record whole programs for the major television studios. Initially that was their value—to record programs made at convenient times and to play them when required.

Videotape had to progress a long way before it challenged film in news work. As well as being so big, the early machines had very limited editing.

Most had none. When editing was introduced it was slow and expensive — nothing like the speed of cutting a strip of film. So while the rest of the station changed to videotape, newsrooms continued to use film.

All this added to the cost of news production. Film rose rapidly in price. Processing continued to be expensive, especially when maintained for news alone. Newsrooms still had to have film cameras even after no one else was using them.

Not that videotape equipment was cheap. The first portable camera and recorder cost almost as much as four sound-on-film cameras, but tape was cheap and could be re-used. Since then the price of electronic equipment has come down as the price of film cameras has risen, and quick and easy tape editing is now possible.

Film can still produce better, sharper pictures, but economics are increasingly on the side of videotape. Film cameras are a rare sight in television newsrooms these days, reserved for outback documentaries or very special projects. The once busy film processors within television stations are idle or discarded, since what film is shot is now processed commercially.

Television news editors refer to ENG (electronic news gathering) with a familiarity that suggests it has been around since television began, yet it is only one development in a rapidly developing business. In the past few years news has become television's experimental area.

Electronic news gathering is a three-word name for a process which may use varieties of different equipment, but all of them begin with a television camera. Americans and Europeans developed video cameras, but the Japanese miniaturised them and made them versatile tools for gathering news.

A television camera uses a picture tube or charge coupled devices (CCDs) instead of film to capture the light rays which are resolved through the lens. The tubes or CCDs convert the light rays into electronic signals by means of an electron gun, which scans the base of the picture tube 25 times a second, turning the light rays into 625 lines of television picture (525 lines in the American television system).

The flow of electronic impulses produced is taped in the recorder unit, now small enough to be included within the camera. There are many kinds of recorder and about the only thing they have in common is that they record electronic impulses on videotape. When video recording began the tapes were on bulky reels and were two inches wide. This "quad" tape is still widely used for recording within studio buildings. It is considered by many the most reliable and the best quality, but it is too bulky for field work.

Then came narrower tapes: one-inch on reels, then ¾-inch and ½ inch in cassettes — still the most widely used form for news editing and replay — and even 8mm, which is slightly more than ¼ inch. The most popular format for video news work in Australia is the Betacam SP which uses 12mm tape, referred to as half-inch, in a cassette. A few use M-2s, a Panasonic system with 12mm tape in a different type of cassette. Less expensive Super VHS (S-VHS) and hi-band Video-8 equipment is increasingly popular with camera news crews, especially in smaller stations, but the editing is done on higher standard systems.

Videodisks are also in expanding use in television stations, though not widely for news. For the storage of visual information videodisks are superior to anything else so far devised because they offer immediate random access, just as a compact disk does in audio recording. This is not so with a reel or cassette of tape. For news, most stations still use tape, and regardless of its width or format, the tape is the same. It is a wider version of audio-recording tape.

Inside each recorder of any format, from the modestly-priced VHS or Beta to expensive professional equipment, the electronic signals are put onto the tape by recording heads. Instead of the tape being drawn steadily over a stationary head, as in audio recorders, the heads in video recorders spin at high speed. By this means the heads make helical sweeps across the tape as it moves around a rotating drum.

In addition to the picture signals, the tape also records the sound and the synchronisation (sync.) control information, so that replay equipment can start reading each picture at the right place and maintain sync. with the recorder.

Electronic picture recording for news took less than a decade to replace film, and even less time in other aspects of television. Equipment now in use may be replaced just as effectively, and possibly as quickly, by equipment using cassettes of even narrower videotape, by a digital recording system or by another yet to be devised.

Once the required pictures have been taken in the field, complete with such sound as the journalist wants to record at the scene, the tape, or the signal from the tape, is returned to the studio for editing. Pictures are not usually shot in the sequence in which they are to be screened, nor at the precise duration required. This is why editing is necessary. The pictures, and if necessary the commentary recorded with them, have to be rearranged in order to tell the story in the best possible way.

Editing units are basically a videotape player and a recorder, so set up that sequences from the original are played in a chosen order and length onto the recorder to form a complete visual story. To do this without the picture becoming ragged and breaking up every time one shot is edited to another, editing equipment must be hyper-critically accurate in its scanning, which means it is more expensive than the recorders which provide the raw material. As with other electronic equipment, prices have come down.

In most major television stations the editing equipment provides frame counters — a term carried over from the editing of film — so that those doing the editing can choose the precise frame (scanned picture) on which they wish a shot to begin or end. In some cases this can be entered into the editor as if it were a computer, so that when all the choices have been made the editing — the actual assembling of the final product — will go ahead automatically. Smaller stations have less versatile editing equipment, but in essence it operates the same way. In educational institutions few editing units have frame counters, so the selected shots or sequences are assembled one by one until the edited product is complete.

On all editing equipment pictures can be replaced without destroying existing sound or vice versa. On videotape (not on film) pictures and sound are recorded at the same point. There is no frame-count difference to confuse the editor.

In most television stations the edited news tapes, in the form of cassettes carrying tape can be played directly to air as part of the news service. Some stations take the extra step of editing news items onto the video cartridge recorder, or VCR. This expensive unit prepares and plays video cartridges in the same way that audio carts are made and played in a radio station. Each cartridge—a squarish box carrying a precisely measured amount of "quad" (2-inch) videotape—records one story, in its edited form, complete with all pictures and sound required. It is dubbed from the edited news tape. The cartridges are then loaded into the machine and programmed to play in the desired order. When the "start" button is pressed, replay begins instantly. After replay the cartridge automatically re-cues.

VCR equipment is much more valuable for presentation of television commercials, which are repeated more often than any news tape, but some stations use them for news as well, for error-proof presentation.

All this is only part of the equipment arsenal of most stations. There is a whole array of equipment employed in getting the signal from the field, wherever it is, to the television studios for broadcasting. "Link" equipment moves pictures and sound over relatively short line-of-sight distances. It is used when reports are put to air live from golf courses, football grounds, significant news events, or dramatic events like fires which last long enough for the equipment to get there before the event is over.

The picture from the camera or cameras in the field can be transmitted directly back to the television station, for immediate use or recording, by means of a portable transmitter. One make is known as a Golden Rod. From the top of a news car, or from a convenient building if the car is not tall enough to provide line-of-sight, the transmitter is aimed at the station's receiving dish. It may be more practical to aim at a dish mounted on the transmitting mast or even to aim at a helicopter receiver (two-step link), which can operate as a relay point. The picture is usually recorded in the field as well, as a safeguard.

By these means the news editor in the studio can see what is happening in the field as it happens. This means events which occur at news time can be included live and un-edited, which can cause problems of content control. The director in the field is **responsible** for transmitting to the studio the best pictures available, which means making fast decisions with no second chances. For news work this means two cameras, at the most three, linked to a control panel. For a golf championship or a motor race it could mean more than a dozen, though in such circumstances the director and camera crews have the benefit of some rehearsal. Rarely does a reporter have the time or opportunity for a dry run.

Even though most television stations in major cities have helicopters, their principal use is to move news staff to and from events without the time delays caused by crowded highways and traffic jams. On some occasions the helicopter becomes a platform for a camera, and an ideal platform it is, too, for rescues at sea or from cliff faces, when there is no other means of getting a camera into position. Editors have learned not to overdo the helicopter filming: an eye in the sky is an unnatural viewpoint to be employed sparingly. But a helicopter relay is often the only way to move signals from the field to the television station. Even when there is no necessity for any such live transmission, the helicopter can return the news tape to the station for editing much more quickly than any other transport.

Moving pictures across the nation or across the world uses bigger and more powerful equipment of the same type. The microwave paths which cross Australia on dish-bearing towers, each within line-of-sight of the next, are only larger versions of the car-top transmitter used in the field. Coaxial cables are another means of moving a television signal. Both have been largely supplanted in moving television pictures across Australia by the use of Aussat.

Satellites are in operation no more than more distant versions of helicopter relay points, though they are becoming more and more complex. When satellites arrived television newsmen were freed from the impact-killing delays of having to wait two or three days for pictures of major events to arrive by plane from the other side of the world.

The very first communication satellite was a balloon called Echo 1, launched in 1960. It was gas-filled and its aluminium surface was carried high into the stratosphere to act as a reflector for beamed signals. Telstar was the first communication satellite to orbit the earth, and although a great improvement on the balloon, it had serious handicaps. It was difficult to track, had such a low orbit that it was never within range for very long, and delivered a very weak reflected signal, but it proved that signals could be relayed over long distances from stations in space.

It was the British science fiction author Arthur C. Clarke, writing in 1945, who suggested that satellites for communication should be placed in geosynchronous orbits, which means they should be set at the exact height to orbit in the same time as the earth turns. This means the satellites are stationary to transmitting and receiving stations which must be aimed at them. Today's communications satellites, by which news items can be passed from one side of the world to the other in a fraction of a second, are all in geosynchronous orbits. The far-sighted author was so right that communications scientists have suggested that "geosychronous" satellites should be renamed Clarke satellites, to honour the man who virtually invented them and made modern communications possible.

Stationary satellites mean that once the earth stations are pointed in the right direction, no tracking is necessary. It also means that those earth stations need not be so large, since the satellites are much more than reflectors. They capture the up-path signal, amplify it, and retransmit it on its down-path, sometimes on a new frequency. Although the building and launching of satellites costs a lot of money, the vast amount of traffic that can be passed through them during their years in space makes them the cheapest, most reliable and now the highest quality means of moving programs around the world.

The reliability of stationary satellites has allowed portable units for world-wide connections through a satellite to become almost commonplace. In addition to the daily coverage of major world events countries, networks or even individual stations can mount their own coverage by satellite of one-off specials, like the Prime Minister overseas or the latest on the Middle East crisis from Australian reporters in the region.

Thanks to smaller and less expensive connections, the whole world is on Australia's daily news agenda.

With space shuttle services available to repair and even restore satellites so that their period of usefulness can be extended, this cost should continue to come down, or at least not go up, as the information age advances.

There is another essential tool for the broadcast journalist, even though few outside the world of journalism would recognise it as a tool—language. It is all very well to be able to type, on a typewriter or a video display terminal. It is what is typed that matters, and that demands a competence with language. Without a facility with words, all the latest electronic equipment and the pictorial messages it can disseminate are a waste of time. For all the potency of pictures, there is not one news item in a hundred, maybe in a thousand, which does not need words as well to impart its information accurately and briefly.

Reporters in broadcast newsrooms write their stories into word-processing computers. Through these terminals material can be sent and received from other stations and from AAP, Australia's international and national news agency.

(Picture: Masterton, at 3AW)

Words

One of the tools, but worth a whole chapter

Before looking at the peculiar needs of the broadcast media in language, style and the use of words, lets see how other forms of communication differ from the mass media.

There are major differences between essays written as part of a school or higher education course, letters written to a friend, telephone conversations, what appears in a daily newspaper and what is heard on radio or television. What they have in common is that they are all forms of communication with specific objectives, all achieved in different ways.

An essay is, or should be, a coherent exposition of a series of facts leading to a logical conclusion. A letter to a friend is more often than not a collection of thoughts, not necessarily in logical order. A telephone or face-to-face conversation is usually the random verbalising of a string of thoughts as they come to mind (face-to-face conversation has the advantage of non-verbal communication to enhance the messages received by the listener).

The forms used in the mass media vary. As a simple test, read aloud the front page of a broadsheet newspaper for about five minutes. You will read two, perhaps three, stories of reasonable length, or more if they are shorter items. Five minutes is the duration of a commercial radio station's longer news on the hour. Most run somewhere between three and five minutes, with or without commercials.

Journalists involved in the production of these bulletins have only that amount of time to bring their listeners up to date with what has happened around the world in the last few hours. Obviously, items on radio—and television for that matter—have to be shorter than they appear in a broadsheet newspaper. The same news items in tabloid newspapers are often compressed to not much longer than broadcast length.

The most important difference between print and broadcast news writing is that if a newspaper reader doesn't understand something in print he or she can read it again, and again if necessary, until the meaning is clear. Not so on radio and television. There is one chance, and only one, to have the information understood. Television has its pictures to help make things clear to the viewer, but radio has only words—what is said and how it is said.

If the story is not written well enough to be understood first time, the listener can't slip back a paragraph and hear it again. It means waiting for the next newscast, at best half an hour or an hour away, and then only if the item is repeated.

The problem is further complicated on radio because most people listen while doing something else. Newspapers need the full attention of readers, and most viewers stop whatever else they are doing to watch television. Radio has to compete for listener attention with diversions like ironing, children playing, someone else talking, the clamour of family breakfast, or in the case of drive-time newscasts, the traffic.

To survive this sort of competition, news on radio must be attention-grabbing, as complete and as informative as necessary, yet in as few words as practicable.

Strange though it may seem, it requires a better command of language to write briefly than it does to write at length. Broadcasting's brevity means its journalists must put together their stories using the most precise and appropriate words in the most fluent and easily understood order.

Broadcast style is meant to be heard, not read; it is writing for the ear, not the eye. If it sounds easy, it is because the newscasts are well written. Good broadcast writing always sounds natural. Most novices find it is not as easy as it sounds when they come to try it.

Writing for the ear must at the same time be in good English yet sound right, and correct grammar does not always sound easy on the ear.

For most people, information is much more efficiently absorbed by the eye than the ear. The eye can take in 250 words a minute for even the most modest readers. Speak that quickly and no one will understand you. Speed readers claim they can read a thousand words a minute or more, with reasonable retention. No such speed-up is possible in broadcasting. Its delivery must be that of everyday speech, and if it is to be understood at first hearing it must be in the language of everyday speech at the speed of everyday speech.

For this reason broadcast journalists try to write as they speak (always assuming that they speak well), using language sparingly, with a regard for the meaning of words. It is a technique that often comes hard to those who have spent years writing for a newspaper, but a good journalist can learn to handle both styles and change from print to broadcast style at will.

Just as newspapers have devised type faces and column widths to aid the swift reading and easy comprehension of words on a printed page, so broadcasting has devised a style of writing which makes for the best possible comprehension by the listener.

In many ways getting broadcast style right is far more important than how the words are delivered to a microphone. There was a time when radio station managers wanted all their newsreaders to have "ABC voices"—"frightfully" precise in the pronunciation of every syllable. This is no longer so even in the ABC, because few Australians speak that way. For news purposes, any voice which is clear and easily understood, which does not mispronounce words and which reads copy intelligently—especially the intelligent reading—can be made suitable. This can't happen unless the copy is properly written in the first place.

1 Write the way you speak.

People seldom write to each other, they talk. The great majority of the information we receive as ordinary people each day, even as students or academics, is transmitted verbally, not in print. Broadcast journalists telling people the news of the hour, or of the day, should write as if speaking to them, personally, because although the newscast may be heard by thousands of people it is usually one person to a radio and not many more to each television set. In broadcasting the journalist is *telling* a story, not writing it. Many people who speak fluently and clearly are tempted, by the very act of putting it in writing, to become formal and artificial.

2 Be brief, but not too brief

Think about what is happening to meaning when a story is being cut down to broadcast length. Brevity serves no purpose if clarity is lost. If the story takes too many words to tell, that's poor writing; too few, that's useless.

The best of concise writing comes from precision in the use of words. It is the reporter on the job who must decide what is worth including in the story. To get started, think: "What is the guts of the story?" and begin with what springs spontaneously to mind. It won't always be a complete lead, but it will serve to get started. Then ask: "How much of this story will interest or affect at least half the audience?" and when that much is written, stop.

Then make sure it is in the right style, using the best possible words, and that what is written is unmistakably clear, informative and self-contained.

Often, being brief is a case of not wasting words — not a problem peculiar to broadcasting. Make one word do the work of two or three. Why say "will hold a conference with" when "will confer with" says the same thing? There are many word-wasting phrases in everyday speech which the careless writer may pick up. For instance the politicians' favourite "at this point in time" means "now". "In the ordinary course of events" is another example of officialese. Try "usually".

Be a miser with words and use the simplest to make yourself clear.

3 Write it your way

Don't parrot other people's copy in words or structure. It's very easily done when re-writing from a newspaper or from a public relations handout. It is both lazy and ineffective to re-write someone else's copy line-by-line or paragraph-by-paragraph, changing only the tenses and perhaps word order to comply with broadcast style.

The necessity to *tell* stories requires that the whole approach to broadcast writing be different from print. There is no rigid inverted pyramid construction, nor any other strict formula for the structure of a news story in broadcasting as there is in print. *Telling* is like a narrative or a conversation. It progresses from its beginning to its end with few rules (except those of grammar) but with such clarity that even when the briefest of stories is told the listener need ask no questions.

If there is a word for this type of story construction it is "linear", though it is so variable it can hardly be called a formula. For all this, clarity and the need to be newsworthy demand that most stories begin with the significant facts.

When a re-write for broadcast is necessary, and it usually is, the best method is to read the original material often enough to know its content. Then turn it face down and tell it onto the typewriter in your own words, as if *telling* the story to a person who has paused at your side. Remember the questions "What is the guts of . . .; How much of . . ." and get that much information in. Then refer again to the original to check names, figures and other essentials, but not until the writing is complete. Check again after editing. There is no excuse for clumsy, avoidable errors of fact.

4 Use straightforward language in simple sentences.

Broadcast journalism is not restricted to one-syllable words, nor to the maximum 25-word sentences favoured by print. The maxim is plain: use simple language in simple sentences.

If you don't know what plain language is, listen to people speaking. They use quite a versatile vocabulary but they use it in a straightforward way. The sentences are simple, without inversions, and usually in word orders which need little or no punctuation when written down. Listening to people speak is fun — not eavesdropping, which is listening for the content, but ear-noting, which is listening for the words and the manner of their use. Try it.

Simple sentences are a matter of structure, not just of avoiding long words, though you should do that too. Using simple language does not excuse inaccuracy or over-simplification. If there is a right word — a precise word — use it. If the context doesn't make the meaning of the word clear, and it usually does, then re-write until it does. If this can't be done, spend a few more words to explain the precise word's meaning. Common sense is your best guide.

5 Don't clutter sentences with facts.

Write as if you were *telling* the story to someone else. It is not a case of one fact one sentence so much as one idea one sentence, and even this is not absolute. Two or more logically associated ideas — but not half a dozen — can fit naturally into one sentence. A clutter of facts can not be taken in aurally without risking confusion and lack of comprehension.

"And" and "but" are not banned in broadcasting, even at the start of a sentence, because they occur in everyday speech, but they should be used in that position rarely and with care. Don't use them to cram more information into a sentence unless that information is relevant and cannot be written more fluently in the next. It may be very well for a newspaper to cram as many essential facts as possible into the lead paragraph; readers can take their time to absorb its content. Listeners can't. Besides, people don't speak that way, so for broadcasting it is wrong.

Nor are adjectives banned in broadcasting, especially when they are precise and appropriate. But don't exaggerate. If you use exaggerated descriptions of events you lower the credibility of what you write. News writers should not use adjectives carelessly. Words like "brilliant", "famous" and "well-known" are unnecessary. Brilliance is a matter of opinion (or measurable brightness) and if a person is famous or well-known is it hardly necessary to say so.

This is where something should be said about sentence length. Newspapers seem to like sentences of no more than 25 words. People don't speak in sentences like that, even though they can read them easily. They speak in sentences which vary from one or two words to 40 or 50. Some spoken sentences are never finished, as you will find if you try "people-listening". The best broadcast news writing uses sentences at their natural length, which means they will vary from a very short half-dozen words to a very long 35 or 40. Fifty is definitely too many.

6 Make the lead lead.

Start a story, no matter what it is about, in such a manner that people want to hear more. Unlike a newspaper introduction, the first sentences in broadcasting need not be filled with essential facts, since people will keep listening once their interest is won. It is important to include some of the essentials of the story at the start. A newspaper lead usually tries to cram in as many of journalism's five Ws as possible; two or three may do in a broadcast lead. In broadcasting the first sentence must tell people what the story is about, in substance or in mood. In radio, even more than in television, the lead must also be a lead-in.

Listeners tune in to stories they think will interest them, so give some hint in the first sentence that the story is worth hearing, without blurting out key facts in the first few words. Listeners need "tune-in time" of three or four words to concentrate their attention if they are to absorb the facts, so give them these three or four words as a sort of "subject cue" before delivering the hard facts. This is why so many broadcast news stories begin "In Canberra today. . .", or something similar, since that tells anyone who wants to hear it that the story is about federal politics. Others may begin: "Cricket. . . (pause). . . in the match between. . ." Again it is giving time for people to hear the word "cricket" so that those interested can start paying special attention.

Not every story needs such a blatant signal to its contents, but all broadcasting stories need a lead-in rather than launching straight into the facts. If you begin a story with "Fred Smith said today the world will end on Tuesday at 9a.m.", the audience attracted by the words "world will end" will mentally be asking "who said so?" That information has been missed.

If the story has drama, pathos or humour, this will attract attention in the lead-in, but be careful with mood leads. They should be used sparingly and very well, since it often means leaving the punchline to the end—a style for practised wordsmiths, not for novices.

After getting the lead right, take the listeners or viewers through the facts of the story in their most logical and fluent order. Clear broadcast writing demands that the facts always be set out in the most easily absorbed order.

It pays to repeat key words, especially if they have been mentioned in the lead. When quoting some other publication or a news release, or perhaps something someone said, first make sure the source is clearly attributed, and if the reference is more than two paragraphs, repeat the source. Repeat it again if the item is a long one, so the audience is in no doubt about where it came from. Other key elements often worth repeating are names, locations, titles and times. Repeat whatever is necessary to make the meaning and the source unmistakably clear.

7 Write the way you speak.

This is important enough to warrant repetition. It is difficult to listen to yourself, so listen to others. People speak in basic subject-verb-object sentences without inversions, so broadcast copy should be written that way. Many school essays — and some newspaper reports — start with an "-ing" word. This is a sure sign of a sentence inversion, which means an unimportant phrase or clause is being put first. People don't speak that way because it confuses the listener. There is nothing wrong with words ending in "-ing" in their right place, but in speech they don't occur at the start of a sentence.

You never hear people say, "Having bought the fish and chips, I went home." It is correct enough grammatically, but not right for broadcasting. Most speakers would say, "I bought some fish and chips and went home," or if the chronology was important they might say, "I went home after I bought the fish and chips." Neither the second nor third versions require the comma in the middle, a sure sign of more natural speech.

If you listen you will find people speak in simple, un-inverted sentences. The subject comes first, then the verb and finally the object — not quite "the cat sat on the mat", but equally straightforward.

8 Get the facts right.

A reminder — changing from print to the simpler style of radio or television and trimming some of a story's details is no excuse for relaxing on accuracy. Facts are sacred for journalists, regardless of the medium.

9 Names are always important.

The style for the presentation of names varies from medium to medium, even from one newsroom to another, but the need to get them right does not. There are house styles (styles specified by the editor or management of a particular institution) for names which must be learned to satisfy employers. The most usual style in broadcasting (though not in print) is to use given names, or at least one such name, rather than initials, and positions rather than the formal Mr, Mrs, Miss or Ms. This is because it flows more naturally to say "Town Clerk John Smith" than to say "The Town Clerk, Mr John (or J) Smith". It also requires no punctuation, which makes for more fluent reading.

There are obviously times when this guideline need not apply. When the person referred to is well known there is no need to use a given name at all: for instance, "Prime Minister Hawke" — who needs reminding that his name is Bob? At the other end of the significance scale, sometimes a person's name is important to the story and the position involved is incidental. Perhaps the title or position-description is too long to be handled in place of Mr or Mrs and it is more easily understood to put the name first: for instance, "Fred Smith, acting secretary of the Little Umptington Junior Basketball Association". Or the two can be integrated, as in "Acting secretary Fred Smith of the Little Umptington Basketball Association, said today. . ."

No matter which form is used, avoid starting a lead with a key name. It may be missed, or mis-heard.

10 Attribution comes before what was said or done.

Listen to people speak and you will never hear "he said" tacked on the end of a sentence. Who said it or who did it invariably comes first, no matter how strong the statement or dramatic the action. In broadcast style this is a rule, not a guideline. It is a significant difference between writing for broadcast and writing for print and it is based on the way people speak.

Consider: "It will be hot in Perth tomorrow, the weather bureau said." Rubbish! Speech pattern demands: "The weather office says it will be hot in Perth tomorrow."

Try a more dramatic but hypothetical announcement. Australia has declared war on New Zealand for some reason and this has been announced by the Prime Minister in Parliament. Under its banner headline "War" a newspaper's first paragraph might well be: "Australia is at war with New Zealand,' Prime Minister Hawke said in Parliament this afternoon."

Broadcast style demands: "Prime Minister Hawke told Parliament a few minutes ago Australia is at war with New Zealand."

In both cases the broadcast style is clearer and more fluent. No matter how shocking the statement or the action, the attribution comes first. If you don't believe people speak that way, listen.

11 Be careful with contractions and pronouns.

This is a case where common sense overrides the instruction to write as you speak. Contractions like "isn't" and "don't", "we'll" and "they're" certainly represent the way we speak, but to many people they are difficult or confusing to read, simply because that is not the normal way we see them in print. This may well be the case with the person who will read your copy in front of the microphone.

Broadcasting stations sometimes impose their own rules for the writing of contractions for on-air reading. Some newsreaders also express their own preferences. Many prefer to see the words in the form in which they normally appear in print; "it is" rather than "it's" — even though "it's" is not uncommon — "we will" rather than "we'll". When they read the words in these forms they speak them as colloquial English so that they come across as "it's" and "we'll". Few readers quibble about "don't" since it occurs often enough in print.

Possessives are very useful words in contracting a story. They sound natural in speech but should be written only when their appearance and meaning are both absolutely clear. And remember to put the apostrophes in the right places. A wrongly used apostrophe can upset the smooth reading of even a good presenter in the same way that a spelling mistake can cause an unexpected pause.

Personal pronouns are contractions of a sort and there is no rule restricting their use as long as it is absolutely clear to whom the "he", "she" or "they" refers. If there is any ambiguity, or if the original mention of the name was too far back in the story to be recalled instantly, use the name again or use some other method of clear identification.

12 Don't try to be too smart.

In terms of language this means taking special care with your choice of words. Unnecessarily long words, colloquialisms, officialese, cliches and superlatives are all signs of either a desire to impress or an inability to write properly and accurately, or both.

Avoid polysyllabic words unless there is no shorter word with the same meaning. There usually is. Any good book on the use of English will provide a long list of better word choices: fire for conflagration, bruises for abrasions, buy for purchase. But if the right and accurate word is a long one, use it. Just make sure that the context makes its meaning clear.

There are several reasons for avoiding colloquialisms. Many of them verge on slang, which means their precise meanings, if they have them, are not known to enough people for a writer to be sure they will be understood. Who knows exactly what the term "with it" means today, or ever meant. There are hundreds more examples of colloquialisms, though some of them are more properly slang or jargon. The term "colloquialism" means, according to the dictionary, "as people speak", but too often it represents only the speech of the moment or perhaps of one locality. Either way it is too narrow to be used in a newscast.

Some words which were once slang have progressed to wider colloquial usage and are now established in the language. They become established because enough people use the word with the same meaning so it can become acceptable. "Jet" is an example of this. Look it up in almost any dictionary and see that the first meanings given are "hard black lignite" and "stream of water or gas". This is why the first aeroplanes which used this means of propulsion were called "jet-propelled aircraft", then "jet planes", now just "jets". Although it is not yet listed in the dictionaries as a verb — to jet — it is used so frequently that no doubt the listing will come soon, even if labelled "colloquial".

There are plenty of examples of words coming into general usage by extension of meaning, by analogy or by the corruption of trade names. Think about words like "fridge" (or it is more correctly "frig"?). Does it come from "refrigerator" or from the trade name "Frigidaire"? Either way "frig" seems the right spelling, but because that already has another meaning, the best thing to do is use the whole word "refrigerator" and avoid trouble. It is the same with other words with tradename backgrounds: hoover (vacuum cleaner), nugget (shoe polish), Kodak (camera or film for it). Most are so common many people are not aware that they ever were trade names. Advertising has made them household words. That is no excuse for using them unless every household knows exactly what they mean.

The best rule for trade names is don't use them. Their use can be dangerous. If a report says a hoover blew up and it wasn't a Hoover, the manufacturers may be annoyed enough to sue for defamation. Below are some avoidable trade names and their generic and safe alternatives.

Aerogard	insect repellent
Aspro	aspirin
Bandaid	adhesive dressing
Biro	ball point pen, or pen
Cellophane	transparent wrapping
Coke (Coca-cola)	cola or soft drink
Elastoplast	sticking plaster
Esky	cooler
Gladbag (or wrap)	plastic bag (or wrap)
Jumbo Jet	wide-bodied jet
Photostat	photo-copy
Pressure Pak	aerosol can
Primus stove (lamp)	portable gas stove (lamp)
Singer	sewing machine
Technicolor	colour
Texta	felt tipped pen
Thermos	vacuum flask
Vaseline	petroleum jelly
Xerox	photo-copy

It is the same with Americanisms — very colourful, very "with it", very vague. Americans are the masters of inventing jargon, though Australians are good at it, too. Remember when writing Americanisms, or words imported from anywhere, that many of them are jargon words.

Although you think you understand them, how many of the people you are speaking to have the same meaning. What, for instance, is a "platter"? It depends on whether you are speaking to a disc-jockey (but what then is a "disc", or is it "disk"?) or a chef. The dictionary only lists one meaning.

Consider recent impositions from overseas like "de-escalation", "Reaganomics", "detente", "hospitalized". Just what do they mean and what can we use instead? And before you get the idea that we import all our vague new words, think about "industrial disputation", or even worse "wage fixation". Look up fixation in the dictionary.

Trying to be "with it" with words can lead to more problems. There are some words which have a dictionary meaning and a different one colloquially. What do the words "grass", "gay", "birds", or "chicken" really mean? Take "grass", for instance. Advertisers say you can turn grass into lawn with a particular mower. To other people grass means marijuana, to others a police informer. In Northern Ireland an even newer version of the word, "supergrass", has come into being to refer to someone who informs on leaders of the Irish Republican Army. "Grass" and the others mentioned are colloquialisms with double or triple meanings. Avoid them.

Politicians and public servants all too often try to impress by using not so much big words as too many words, especially ones with vague meanings. Don't quote them: translate them, even if it means decoding them first. "It is anticipated by the administration that. . ." really means "the council (or government) expects. . ." "Of the order of" has no other meaning than "about". Trying to impress has no place in broadcast writing. Being understood has.

Using cliches is more a sign of laziness or lack of a good vocabulary than it is of trying to impress. Avoid cliches "like the plague". They are words or phrases that have been over-used, or they wouldn't be cliches. When they came into use they were colourful, even accurate and certainly catchy, which is why they became too popular. There is almost always another, better way of saying the same thing.

Be careful with superlatives in broadcast writing, even about sporting events, where they are usually used to excess. Naturally a reporter wants to make a story sound as interesting as possible, but it is easy to overdo it. Leads like "Australia made a disastrous start in the first test against the West Indies" makes it difficult to use the word "disaster" when a truly disastrous situation arises, such as an earthquake. "Disaster", like many other strong words, is already debased by mis-use. Keep the big guns of the adjective range for the really worthy stories. Don't waste them trying to increase the impact of a lesser item.

13 Use the present tense, active voice.

Only verbose politicians and pompous civil servants speak in passive voice. This inverts a sentence so that object comes first and uses complex verbs and "by" — The mat was sat on by the cat. Be alert to the "by". It is often the indicator of a needless passive.

Present tense and active voice reflect natural speech patterns and fluency. There is no need to descend to the "so he says to me and I says to him" level of back fence or bar gossip. It is easy enough to maintain a clear speech pattern style with a natural flow of everyday, normal words. The clearest and most immediately understandable way of saying something is always the best.

Ignore the criticisms of angry grammarians. What makes them angry is the mixing of tenses which often follows from deliberate use of the present tense. In speech all but the most pedantic mix their tenses every day. They use a past tense verb when something was said, because the saying actually took place in the past, but a present tense verb to re-tell what was said, because that was the tense used by the speaker.

For example — using the same hypothetical example as before — "Prime Minister Hawke TOLD Parliament this morning Australia IS at war with New Zealand." TOLD because it actually happened this morning, which is already in the past, but IS because that is what he said and it remains the tense the speaker used, even when it is reported.

Conciliatory grammarians call it historic(al) present tense. Others say it is wrong but probably speak that way themselves.

Of course the reporter must be careful that the "is" is still valid. If the fictitious war was all over in half an hour because the dispute was settled and no one was hurt, the tenses would have to be changed. The sentence might then read: "Australia was at war with New Zealand this morning, but only for half an hour." Then the report would go into the details.

Journalists have to be similarly careful when using continuing verbs like "believes", "understands" and "agrees". They must be sure that the person being reported still believes, understands or agrees at the time of broadcast as they did when they spoke earlier in the day.

Present tense is the best in broadcasting, but it must be right in meaning, even if it is sometimes debatable in grammar.

Passive voice is another matter. Avoid it. It wastes words and is often imprecise. Perhaps the most frequently used example in officialdom's speech which appears in lazy reporting is "is expected to be". Who expects what to be what? Find the answers to those questions and a better way of writing the story in the active voice becomes obvious.

14 Write out all words, figures and initials as you want them read

Again, normal speech pattern is the guide. If the story is about the RSL and the newsreader is to read the letters (because it is an organisation better recognised by its initials than by its full name) then write R-S-L. If the full name is to be read, spell it out in full. There are dozens of examples of this, and while the initials do not make a word in their own right they cause little problem: B-H-P, A-C-T-U, I-X-L, C-R-A. But don't expect the newsreader to say "United Nations" when the copy reads "UN". Write "U-N" if the initials are to be read and "United Nations" for the full name.

Be specially careful with initials like UN and US, because they also run the risk of being read as "un-" or "us". It is probably better to write "American", if that is what you mean (remembering that there is more to America than just the United States), or spell out the words "United States". Be precise in descriptions and there will be little problem.

The same applies to SA and WA. Within South Australia and Western Australia newsreaders are so used to these contractions that mistakes are unlikely. But do the letters mean the noun or the adjective—South Australia or South Australian? Make sure by spelling them out. It takes a little more time, but it saves a possible error. Outside those states the letters cause even more problems. SA can also mean

South Africa and there are probably other interpretations for the letters WA. If you want the reader to say "South Africa", run no risks. Spell it out.

It is the same problem with acronyms — initials which make words if not meanings. If the newsreader is to refer to NATO, UNICEF or CHOGM, write them that way, in CAPITALS and without full stops or spaces. To make sure listeners know what the names stand for by spelling the names out in full at the first mention.

15 Write numbers so they are easy to read and understand

Radio and television news organisations differ in the way they present figures in stories. Some spell out figures (one, two, three etc) up to nine, others up to ten. All use figures up to 99, but some use figures to 999; i.e. five people, 15 cars, and in some newsrooms 350 trains.

Most write out "hundred", "thousand", and "million", so the "350 trains" above may appear as "three-hundred-and-50 trains".

It is easier for a newsreader to say 12-hundred-and-50 than to risk a mistake in reading 1,250. What if the copy read 12,50? The newsreader would have trouble deciding whether it was 12-hundred or 12-thousand with a zero left off. Also, 12-hundred is almost always preferred to one-thousand-two-hundred.

Use precise figures only when they are important to the story — the exact amount of a cost-of-living rise, for instance — otherwise all large figures should be rounded off. For instance 4,998,321 will be expressed as "about five-million". If it is a little less it may become "almost five-million". Write out "dollars". Don't use a $ sign in front of figures.

The word "percentage" is always spelled out, as is "per cent".

When recording voting figures say "75 to 69", inserting the word "to" to avoid any problem posed by a hyphen being misunderstood or mistyped.

Never say "over 30". The correct style is "more than 30". Over means above.

In summary: spell out numbers to nine (or ten), then use figures from 10 or 11 to 99 or 999 (according to house style), and a combination of words and figures to express figures from 100 or one thousand up.

Usually you end up with one, nine, 10, 99, two-hundred, one-thousand, five-thousand-and-50, 11-thousand.

These are guidelines which can be upset by reader preference. If the newsreader asks for figures to be presented in a different way, write them that way. The newsreader is the one who runs the risk of making a mistake on air.

In spite of decimalisation, many people still say "3½- million" rather than "3.5-million" (in written style 3-point-5 million). The second is correct but either is acceptable. Use whatever sounds right.

Statistical stories with their strings of figures, percentages and comparisons are difficult to handle in broadcasting. Television has the advantage of being able to provide visual aids, but radio must rely on words, trying not to be boring by repeating them too often. Radio is not a good medium for such stories and their writing requires special attention. Often they are so important they cannot be ignored. Look for different ways to compare, using different words, and don't hesitate to round out figures to make their understanding that much easier. If the council's budget is $34,653,471.33, in broadcast news it will be "more than 34-point-6-million dollars" or "nearly 35-million dollars".

Note the hyphens between figures and words used together. This is to make sure the reader clearly associates the two.

16 Punctuate to help the newsreader; the listener can't see it.

There is no need for a listener to hear the punctuation, nor even to imagine it. It should be evident from the way the story is read. Broadcast news writers use all sorts of punctuations in their copy. Dots and dashes appear all over the page and it doesn't seem to matter as long as the newsreader knows what is wanted. To make sure of this, some newsrooms impose a punctuation style. It is wisely based on normal punctuation since, like normal spelling, this is what intelligent readers find easiest to read. It is amended to meet the special needs of broadcasting.

Commas (,) should be used only where they are needed for a genuine but brief pause in the reading. Reading aloud shows where. This means many commas which appear in normal positions for print may be left out in broadcasting, and sometimes vice versa (like the one before "and" in this sentence). But never leave out a comma if it may affect the precise meaning. Clarity justifies an extra comma.

Full stops (.) should be used as normal. If it is the end of a sentence, mark it as such with a full stop.

Dots (. . .) are used to mark extended pauses (not in place of commas), or where a sentence is genuinely unfinished, as with a partial quote.

Dashes (—) indicate the sort of abrupt pause that comes with a change of intonation, as when inserting a clause or phrase which need not be there for the rest of the sentence to make sense; e.g. "The Premier says the bill will be introduced on the 17th — that's next Tuesday — as long as drafting can be completed by then." Make sure not to confuse dashes and hyphens in your copy. A dash is written as three hyphens close up with a space before the first and after the last (---). A hyphen (-) is a single stroke with no space before or after.

Quotes ("like this") must not only be made abundantly clear to the reader but also to the listener. It is not good enough simply to put in the quotation marks and leave it to the newsreader to make clear by intonation what words are being quoted. It is best to avoid direct quotes altogether in written scripts — radio and television have the advantage of recorded inserts to allow people to speak for themselves. Where no insert in available and the quote is essential to the story, word the sentence so that the quotation is absolutely clear without using quotation marks. But put them in to make doubly sure. It is difficult for even the best of newsreaders to get some quotes across clearly. It is not acceptable to use the Americanism "quote-unquote". Australians don't speak that way.

17 Listen to what you write; don't just read it.

For beginners this means talking to the typewriter — literally. Sound the words to yourself as you write them, loud enough to actually hear them and not just imagine you can hear them. Even among practised professionals, perhaps especially among such people, no one will laugh. The experts know that it is the quickest and most certain way of recognising word sequences which don't sound right, even though they are grammatically acceptable.

Talking to your typewriter means there will be no mistakes with what are known as dangling modifiers. Take this example: "A 25-year-old labourer was sentenced to ten years in prison for rape in Central Criminal Court today." It sounds ridiculous because there are two modifiers which are wrong. In print, punctuation may make it acceptable, but never correct. The rape did not take place in Central Criminal Court and nor was it committed today. A broadcast journalist should write: "A 25-year-old labourer was sentenced in Central Criminal Court today to ten years' jail for rape." It is a frequent error. Talking to the typewriter and listening to what is written is a good safeguard. It will also show up other clumsy or ugly word patterns and tongue-twisters before they reach the newsreader — as long as you are talking to your typewriter in a voice you can hear.

Even after virtually writing the copy aloud, there is no excuse for not checking it aloud when the story is complete. It will have to be checked for timing anyway.

Talking to the typewriter may not be necessary once broadcast style comes naturally, though there are many experienced broadcast journalists who still do it. They make very few silly mistakes.

18 Make corrections clearly.

In an ideal newsroom there are no corrections on the copy which goes to the newsreader for on-air presentation. In these days of word-processors or computers and screens in front of the reader visible corrections in the copy are unthinkable. But in copy to be read from a typed script on paper, when a correction is needed there is a right way to make it. Don't use newspaper sub-editing symbols. They require interpretation. Score out in full the word or words in which the mistake has been made. Black them out so that the reader is not tempted, even unconsciously, to try to read through the black to see what the error was. Natural curiosity tempts everyone to try it. Print the correct form of the word or words immediately above the correction — no hurried scrawl, please. Typing it in is even better but not always practical. Make sure the correction goes through to all copies of the script if carbons are being used.

If there are more than three corrections on any page of copy, type it out again. Corrected copy makes for risky newsreading.

19 Keep copy neat and tidy.

Proper layout for broadcast copy differs in radio and television. The generally accepted script page layout in a radio newsroom is to use A4 paper of a type and weight which will not "rattle" on air when pages are turned or moved. Set a wide left margin — 30mm is a minimum — so there is ample room for the reader to hold the page. Start the story well down from the top of the page, at least 50mm, and use double spacing. Use double-double spacing between paragraphs.

Never continue a sentence over a page. If the page end occurs before the sentence is complete, don't cram the last words onto the bottom. Write the sentence again on the top of the next page and score it off the bottom of the previous page. Make sure that the first page of everything you write carries, usually in the top right corner, an identifying catch-line for the story, the writer's name, the total duration of the news item and the time and date of writing. If there is more than one page of copy, put "MORE" at the bottom of the first page and write the catch-line and the figure "2" at the head of the second page. No matter how many pages there are, the end of the item is always marked "END", or with some accepted mark that indicates that there is no more.

Keep typewriters and word-processor printers clean — they are the tools of your trade — and make sure the ribbon is delivering easily readable copy.

When writing is complete make sure the copy is delivered in good condition. Mutilated copy is difficult to read, so don't drop it on the floor and tread on it. Don't eat lunch over it or put coffee mugs on it. Never use paper which is crumpled. It rattles when being read on air.

20 Write the way you speak.

This can't be stressed too often — but remember to speak well.

Radio, which has only words to rely on, has been called the medium of the imagination. What is said — what the journalists write to be told — should create images in the listeners' minds. The writer's task is to create verbal pictures. This can't be done by tired words. "Colourful", "interesting", "dramatic", "traumatic" and "tragic" are examples of words which have been used so often, usually loosely and inaccurately, that they cease to mean anything and thus add nothing to your story. There are more precise words that can better describe the colour, interest, drama or tragedy of a news event.

Then there are redundant words and tautologies like "a little bit pregnant" and "completely destroyed". Check the dictionary. If something is destroyed it's destroyed. There is no need for qualification. It applies in phrases, too. "Appointed to the position of" or "have been engaged in producing" are two examples, and there are dozens more. They produce hackneyed, unimaginative mental pictures, if any at all.

Once you understand all the guidelines and the reasons for them, all that remains is to do it. To make the process easier there are three "C"s to add to journalism's normal five "W"s — Clarity, Conciseness and Colour. Broadcasting needs all three, but the most important is clarity.

Broadcast news writing should sound to the listeners as if the newsreader is telling them what happened and in a way that is entertaining, authoritative and absolutely clear. That's not easy. It doesn't mean keeping the audience amused or clowning up the script like an advertising jingle. It means writing it in such a way that the listener's attention is won and held by the naturalness of the words, no matter what the content.

It is the factual reliability of the content which lends the authority, every bit as much as a sombre "dark brown" voice. Yet no newsreader — even the best of them — can sound as though he knows what he is talking about if the facts are not written reliably into the script. "Let the facts speak for themselves" is an old saying that is almost the whole truth about good broadcast writing.

To get it across properly even the facts need a little professional help from good writing and clear voices. Never sneer at the "entertainment" tag with which some people try to denigrate broadcast news. The broadcast media are entertainment media. Everything they do to stay in business is aimed at catching audience attention and holding it, so that the same people will tune in again tomorrow and next week. Broadcast news can be no different.

It has been mentioned before, but it is worth repeating: listen to the way people speak. Listen in buses, bars, classrooms and canteens, even at council meetings. People speak in a subject-verb-object pattern (who did what to whom; who said what about whom). They speak in idioms, sometimes in incomplete sentences, but it is usually easily understood. They speak that way because they have a rapport with their audience which is usually one other person.

This is why broadcast news in one city varies in language from that in another. The language of New Orleans is not that of Adelaide or Townsville. Nor are the idioms or colloquialisms. A radio station which sets out to attract the teenage audience may use jargon words from areas of interest keenly followed by those in their teens. A station catering for a mature audience will not. It will be much more accurate and reserved — conservative, perhaps — in its choice of words. The key thing is clarity. Does the audience know and understand the words being used? If not, the words are wrong, not the audience.

Within Australia there are differences between one city and the next which go beyond local pronunciations. There are words which mean one thing in Sydney and something else in Melbourne.

It would be easy to distinguish the differences between the language of news in New York and old York, Capetown or Canberra, even though the audiences and the newsreaders in all four profess to speak the same language. It is less easy for a writer in Australia to sense the smaller language differences between the cities and regions here, yet this is what must be done.

Broadcast writing, especially for local radio and television stations, is writing for a particular audience and should follow the language and idiom of that specific audience — follow local language fashion, not keep abreast of it and certainly never try to lead it. Because of this, writing for a national news service means what you have to say must be understandable immediately to a much wider audience. The wider the audience, geographically and in age, the more careful the writer must be with colloquialisms or "local" words. Being too obviously colloquial debases authority, which damns a news service even more than too much stiff formality.

No matter where the writer works, the language used must sound natural to the audience being catered for by the news service. Those in broadcasting speak as people do in everyday life, except they eliminate trivia, profanity, most of the slang, vogue words and all the faulty grammar. Reaching an end result that still sounds natural is the art of writing for broadcast. With about two million words to choose from it is demonstrably possible.

In spite of this, clarity is more than just words. Choice of words is important, once the writer clearly understands the story to be written. It is axiomatic that he who does not understand cannot make other people understand. Thus, any reporter's first task is to understand the story and to ask questions until he or she does. Only then is it possible to write it for others.

Reporters are translaters for the audience. They must take the copy or the spoken words of people who write or speak less well, or perhaps those who deliberately use ornate or complex language, and make sense of it for the public. This is one of the most difficult aspects of broadcast writing.

Many public relations officers — there are exceptions — write as if they want to shine. Most politicians and senior public servants delight in pompous language, even when they are not trying to obscure the real meaning of what they are saying. All journalists, print or broadcast, have to find out what the welter of words really means and then use words which convey that meaning.

"At this point in time", a phrase beloved of politicians, really means "now". They say it either because they think it sounds better or because they need thinking time before saying something else. There are dozens of examples, probably hundreds, and they change with the times. If the phrase means "now" then that is what a journalist writes. "Currently" is another useless word. What does it mean? It might mean "now" or "for the time being", but usually it means nothing. If the meaning does not change when "currently" is left out, leave it out.

Look at this example of obscure and wasteful words: "At this point in time it is anticipated that the construction of approximately 41 floors being erected on behalf of the Ministry of Works at the intersection of Smith Street and Jones Street should occasion an expenditure of the order of, in round terms, slightly in excess of 33-million 300-thousand dollars." What the speaker really means, though he could not bring himself to use such blunt language, is "The Ministry of Works now expects its new 41-storey building on the corner of Smith and Jones streets to cost 33-point-3-million dollars." About 23 words instead of 53 and if local knowledge and language style permit it could probably be trimmed even further without loss of meaning or accuracy.

It is obvious that an essential tool of trade for a journalist is a dictionary. Never use a word unless you, as the writer, are absolutely sure of its meaning. If you don't know, look it up, and make sure of the spelling while you're at it. Spelling is important. It is a lame excuse to claim that the audience can't see the spelling so what does it matter. It does matter, because newsreaders see the spelling and a mis-spelled word can cause a hesitation or even a mistake. Most newsreaders — and journalists often enough have to read someone else's copy — are accustomed to seeing words spelled correctly. If they see "bare" when it should be "bear" the meaning is changed, so there is a brief pause while the reader's mind works out the sense of the story before reading on. Even silly errors like "there" for "their", which is surprisingly common, can upset a reader's concentration and spoil what otherwise is a well-written story. If a word is wrong, the mind automatically tries to correct it before reading on.

The following rules for broadcast writing apply to everyone, though not necessarily with the same weighting or in the same order.

1   Understand what you are writing, even if it means asking a lot of questions or doing a lot of research.

2   Listen to experienced journalists speaking and read what they write. Learn from their compression and skill with words.

3. Be precise. Know the meaning of every word you write. If you don't know it, check it in a dictionary.

4. Be original. Use your own words rather than parroting those of others.

5. Hear what you write. Read it back at speaking speed and loudly enough to hear it, so you can change difficult or long words and phrases which don't sound right.

6. Learn from changes made by the editor or sub-editor. There is a reason for every change made and if you can't see it, ask.
7. Talk to your typewriter until a verbal style of writing is automatic.

When you are eventually at the typewriter ready to tell the story, bear in mind the following advice from three experts with words.

George Borrow in *Lavengro* wrote, in the 1850s, "It is no easy thing, plainly and directly by word of mouth, to tell a story, but to tell it on paper is difficult indeed, so many snares lie in the way. People are afraid to put down on paper what is common. They are anxious to shine, and people who are anxious to shine can never tell a plain story."

A century later, Ivor Brown, in his useful little book *A Word in Your Ear* added another relevant observation: "The cardinal sin in the use of words is obscurity. It is a more common and more afflicting nuisance than is pomposity."

And Somerset Maugham so succinctly said: "To write simply is as difficult as to be good."

Radio is the only medium in which a journalist is also his or her own technician. This means technique goes beyond words and includes how to record them and edit them, as this journalism student is doing.

(Picture: Charles Sturt University)

Techniques 1
Mainly how to do it in radio

Technique is using the tools of the broadcast journalist together with the best words in the best style to achieve the best result.

The first two basic techniques—proper use of words and proper use of a microphone—have to be practised together if the end result is to be good broadcasting. The most effective way to demonstrate this, though not by any means the easiest, is to re-write newspaper copy into broadcast style and then record both, the original newspaper story and the broadcast rewrite. The difference becomes obvious.

But even to do this means first mastering a microphone. Use a plug-in microphone of reasonable quality. Never use the built-in microphone with which many portable recorders are equipped. They may be acceptable for recording group conversations in family or classroom situations, but they are not good enough for broadcast work. Nor should you use a remote-control microphone, with a switch that starts and stops the recorder unit. They are seldom of appropriate quality and the start-stop system is not fast enough for journalism.

Before starting, go through the preparations outlined in the chapter on equipment: check batteries or power supply, make sure the recorder is clean, is properly loaded with the right (preferably erased) tape or cassette and that the spools are turning freely. Do a quick voice check to see that the unit is recording effectively.

Read again the paragraphs on how to hold a microphone, then try this simple exercise. Choose two or three sentences or lines of poetry which you can confidently repeat several times in exactly the same manner — as though you are speaking to a slightly deaf person who is about two metres away. (There is no need to shout, but neither should you whisper or mumble.) Then choose three locations which will yield quite different recording results. There are three suitable locations in most homes. The first is the lounge, or a bedroom, both of which usually have carpet, curtained or draped windows (certainly not exposed, reflective glass) and usually upholstered furniture. Such surroundings reflect little sound. The second is the kitchen or bathroom where the walls are usually smooth and reflective, as are the furniture and the floor. The third is outdoors, usually in the backyard since it is furthest from traffic noise. Once away from the back wall of the building there is nothing to reflect sound, but plenty of unexpected noises may intrude.

In each of these three locations try speaking your chosen sentences, first holding the microphone at the recommended distance of 20–25cm from your mouth, then at arm's length which is usually almost a metre, then at about three metres. In each case make sure your voice is entering the mike effectively, which means it should be slightly below mouth level and held upright or angled towards the mouth. For the three-metre example set the microphone down at an appropriate angle on something not too hard, switch on the recorder and move back three metres before speaking.

Remember to present the lines in exactly the same way on each occasion — same volume, same intonation, and of course the same words.

The playback will show why reporters, or anyone using microphones, choose locations carefully, handle the microphone with care and hold it at the best distance. The lounge/bedroom recordings will almost certainly be best, because sound reflections have been controlled and outside noises fairly well shut out. The kitchen/bathroom experiments will probably sound as if they were made in an oil drum and the outdoor ones, except that at short range, will have included all sorts of other noises — wind, trees rustling, dogs barking or birds chirping, even a neighbour's lawnmower, and traffic.

In all locations, with the microphone at arm's length the voice begins to sound distant. It is called "off-mike", as though the speaker has turned aside or is not quite where he or she should be. At three metres the voice is definitely distant. Depending on other noises it may be almost inaudible.

The test may also show that even in supposedly controlled conditions other noises can intrude. Was the refrigerator running? Did it account for a whine on the recording? Unless you check carefully for sounds not normally noticeable the microphone will hear them — the television in the next room, dripping taps, air conditioners; almost any sound to which humans have become so accustomed that they don't realise its there. Microphones don't discriminate.

With the best locations and the best microphone distance established, try the comparative readings of newspaper copy and copy written in broadcast style. Don't choose newspaper feature material or that written by a columnist. These are often written in styles which approach that used in broadcasting. Choose extracts in conventional news style, which probably means reading material from the news columns. Do the re-writing first, so that at one sitting you can read, perhaps three newspaper excerpts, each followed immediately by its broadcast re-write.

If the difference is not apparent immediately it is most likely the re-write has not been well done. Until your broadcast style presentations sound like someone telling a story rather than reading it, the re-writing needs improvement. Check again with the chapter on words. Only after broadcast style is mastered on the typewriter or computer terminal and in static presentation can the business of making voice reports begin.

Voice Reports

There are several types of reports for radio, often worked into a "package", but each component of that package has to be perfected separately if the sections are to fit together. There is usually an introduction (intro) to the item, read by the newsreader in the studio and ending with a "throw" to the prepared report. The preparation usually means the report is edited and dubbed to a cartridge, so that it is complete in itself. However, within that recording may be a voice piece from the reporter on location, perhaps some natural sound from the scene such as chanting demonstrators, often a short segment from an interview or a news conference and as often as not a round-up and sign-off from the reporter.

All this, from intro to sign-off, is the responsibility of the reporter, even that section which he or she will not present in person.

When the report comprises only an intro, throw and journalist's report, this is the simplest form of **voice report** and the whole item will seldom last more than 50 seconds. It may be longer in ABC newscasts and it will certainly be longer in a current affairs program. Each additional insert which adds to the content and variety of the package will make it longer, but it is a major item which exceeds a minute on most commercial radio newscasts.

Most stories on commercial and ABC radio news take the form of voice reports, so it is necessary to master the basic techniques of voice reporting.

Voice reporting technique involves both a choice of words and the delivery of those words. Too often reporters sound as if they are reading something they have written rather than telling a story. They may well be reading it, but it is poor reporting if it sounds like it. Unskilled reading lacks life. The whole idea of using a voice report is that the reporter, who has experienced the event at the scene, tells the audience what a trained observer saw and heard. If there is no advantage in having the reporter present it, then write a report for the newsreader to read. The end result will be better.

A reporter at the scene should sound as though he or she wants to tell people what happened. The voice should sound as if the reporter is genuinely interested in the story. If you are not interested, how can you expect listeners to be interested?

Voice reports from the scene, or prepared in the studio after returning from the news event, are still not the whole report. Even if there are no further components to be edited in, there is still the **introduction** to write, with its throw.

This isn't always an easy task, since the intro has to attract listener attention—it is, after all, the lead. It must say in general what the story is about, often giving several of the facts, without giving any information which is in the voice report itself. This is worth remembering when preparing on-location voice reports. Try to prepare an intro, even if only mentally, before recording the voice report, so that the completed item will flow from beginning to end without repetition.

If a voice report is being prepared in the studio, it is easiest to start with the introduction and its throw, then prepare the voice segment.

Introductions can be as short as one sentence, with the throw built in, or they can be two or three sentences. They are seldom longer unless the report is only one segment of a large, composite story, such as the annual Federal Budget, a major disaster like the 1989 Newcastle earthquake, a major bushfire or a round-up of widespread industrial action. Whatever it is, the voice report should expand and elaborate what has been said already, illuminating the initial facts contained in the lead to the voice report by adding the colour, emotion or atmosphere which can only be gathered at the scene.

Additional segments within the voice report itself are invariably short — only a few seconds. If those inserts require more time, treat the story differently. It is no longer a voice report.

The **throw** can be written in several ways. The simplest is to say after the intro, "John Smith reports", thus telling the listeners that the next voice they will hear will be that of reporter John Smith. Or it may be "John Smith reports from Mount Panorama" if that's where the story is. It is simple and effective, but sounds repetitive if used more than once in a short news bulletin.

A better way is to say, "As John Smith reports, the race had a dramatic start." In this way John Smith's report is firmly linked to the event. The throw tells the listeners that John Smith was there — maybe still is there — saw and experienced what happened and is about to tell them about it.

Those who listen to radio news will recognise the throw, "As John Smith reports from State Parliament, the government's decision has been attacked on the floor of the House." In this case, as in the previous example, the throw gives facts on which John Smith is about to elaborate, so the report must follow smoothly from that point.

Remember it is the reporter's responsibility to provide the sub-editor or bulletin editor with the intro, throw and completed voice report "package". The smoothness of the final composite package depends on the original reporter and on no one else.

The news-writing rules which say fact must be clearly distinguishable from comment and which prohibit bias apply equally to reports on tape. Voice reports are not a licence to speculate. They give a specialist reporter the opportunity to put a story into perspective. In broadcasting, as in print, experienced rounds reporters are expected to background the events they report — background based on experience, not bias. Personal comments are for colleagues, not for listeners.

Voice reports add life to a story because they are usually less formal in language and construction than material presented by the newsreader. Overdoing the informality can destroy the credibility of the report.

To make reports properly requires a **good voice**. Most newcomers to broadcasting have to work on their voices, not because they were born with deficient speaking equipment, but because over the years people, not deliberately conscious of the way they speak, fall into bad speech habits. The most common faults in novices (more apparent on radio than in television where vision helps) are:

- laying stress in the wrong places.
- speaking too fast.
- slurring words and talking in a monotone.

News presenters, including reporters who have learned their job, speak at between three and four words a second. This 180–240 words-a-minute speed is comfortable for most newsreaders, reporters and members of the audience. Any faster becomes difficult to understand, any slower sounds dull and pedantic.

A speaker who lets his or her voice drop too much at the end of a sentence risks not transmitting some major point of the story. The two most important parts of a sentence, as far as delivery is concerned, are the beginning and the end. Many reporters tailor their writing so that the key words or facts are positioned to receive that emphasis.

One voice coach — also an experienced announcer and newsreader — tells novice newsreaders that the best voice is the one they would use when talking to a slightly deaf aunt sitting about two metres away, as if on the far side of a wide desk. He chooses an aunt as an example because such a person normally likes the reader but is not of the same generation, so is tolerant but slightly aloof.

This ideal voice will change from station to station, according to its style of presentation, but it is a good starting point. It means the reader must speak clearly to be heard, must lay the stress in the right places to be understood effectively and must avoid foolish mispronunciations.

The same applies to voice-reporting journalists. Their particular type of delivery will be affected by the story itself and the conditions in which the report is being delivered, as well as by any stylistic demands imposed by the station or the news editor. Reports must be in conversational language, with what actors call "light and shade" in the voice, yet sound as though the story is being told to a friend, not to the boss.

Every report must add to the facts given in the intro. Voice reports are used to highlight the top stories and to add interest to others. If they don't do this, there is no need for a voice report. Having a voice report in a newscast just to give the newsreader's voice a rest is poor journalism.

The best voice reports make it clear that the reporter has experienced the event being reported. The content will be better or worse according to the reporter's individual descriptive skills and the time and effort put into it. If the "I was there" feeling does not come through, it is a poor report. Experienced radio and television reporters can ad-lib accurate and absorbing reports from their notes, but usually they do so of necessity, not from choice. Most prefer to take the little extra time to do a better job. Ad-libbing from notes is only for those who have the experience at both note-taking and delivery to do it properly. It is not for beginners.

Every word of a voice report should be thought out carefully for maximum impact, accuracy and brevity, just as in written reports, and then enunciated with equal care. Once such a report has been recorded there is little, often nothing, a sub-editor or editor can do to improve or amend it. Unless there is time for a complete rewrite and re-recording, it is a fait accompli. A sub-editor who has the time may drop or rearrange a sentence, but it is more likely a deficient report will just be dropped.

Reports from the scene permit a first-person style of reporting not usually accepted in other circumstances. Reporters on tape can say "I saw" or "He told me" when appropriate, as long as it adds to the story. It is natural, since the report is a personal account, and such first-person remarks often explain why the reporter is at the scene. But use first-person reporting with care. Some news organisations ban first-person reports completely. Others tolerate them. Few encourage them. In many cases first-person reporting is lazy reporting. The need for it has to be obvious in the report itself for its use to be justified.

Voice reports for radio are simpler than those for television. The reporter can make notes and read from them. Because of this the requirement that good broadcasting style be maintained in voice reports on radio is even stricter than it is on television, where the picture can help tell the story.

In the field or at a studio desk, write voice reports to suit your way of speaking. In the field you may have to do this in a notebook, since typewriters or laptop computers are impractical to carry around. If you take notes in such situations, take time to make the notes readable; it saves time in presenting them. If you have difficulty getting your tongue around something you have written, stop and re-write it. Rewrite it again, and again if necessary, until it is easy to deliver. The end result will be the better for it.

As in studio-written copy, avoid pompous language, vogue colloquialisms and jargon. There are plenty of other words in the language which will tell the story.

Remember that in presenting a voice report many listeners will identify more with the reporter than with the newsreader. The listeners know the newsreader is reading from prepared copy, even though in most commercial stations the newsreader may have written some of it. A voice report transports listeners in their imagination to the scene. The reporter is their eyes and ears at the event, there to relate accurately what happened to whom, where, when, why and how.

Interviews

Interview segments, whether they stand alone or are part of a voice report package, are a major part of radio reporting. How to prepare for an interview, how to conduct it, what questions to ask and why, are discussed in a separate chapter. Here we consider technical and ethical aspects of interview technique. Why do we insert interview segments in news bulletins? How do they affect editing and how are they affected by editing?

Not many years ago it was considered exciting and different to hear someone other than the newsreader speaking in a radio newscast. Now it is expected.

Radio news requires brief interview segments. What is needed is called "clean audio" — a segment in which the newsmaker gives a crisp critical, explanatory, or forecast comment on the story being reported. The important thing is that it stand alone without requiring the reporter's question to explain its content, context or importance. It also has to be "clean" technically.

The ways of asking questions to yield such responses are explained later. Too often the reporter records several minutes of interview from which one brief segment must be chosen for use. If that segment is to stand alone it will probably be of no more than 10 or 20 seconds. If it is part of a voice report it will be even shorter.

How do you choose which answer, or segment of an answer, to use?

The comment from the newsmaker — the person being interviewed — must go to the heart of the story. It must refer to the main facts given in the introduction. A comment on any other aspect of the story, though perhaps relevant in a longer report, is difficult to fit into the duration of a news item.

Take a simple example: a politician denying allegations of corruption. Even though the reporter writes a story which leads with the denial, the audience expects to hear the accused politician deny it personally. They also expect to hear how the politician feels about the allegations.

Many politicians are experts in what is termed "news speak" — the quick 10 to 20 second "grab" that explains their position in simple English, with the right inflections and emphasis; ideal for radio. They have learned to express their views in a couple of sentences, since they know that is all the radio reporter can use. Many politicians and other regular newsmakers pay tutors to coach them in interview techniques.

Sometimes reporters are not so favoured. An angry or distraught politician who gives an involved answer explaining his or her position at length, is not suitable for easy editing. The reporter still has to find a brief segment which "says it all", or at least as much of it as possible.

There are two alternatives. The reporter can put the question again and hope the politician can summarise more effectively; or try to find a suitable segment within the first answer.

Faced with the second alternative, the reporter may need to listen to the interview several times to find the appropriate segment. Listening to the interview carefully as it is recorded can save a lot of time.

It should be fundamental that the reporter listens to what he or she is being told, but some seem more intent on ensuring the recorder is working or re-reading their list of prepared questions than actually listening to the person they are interviewing.

Ethical considerations also arise. Finding a suitable segment may seem simple enough, but does it honestly represent what the speaker said? Nothing should be done in selecting or editing to change or distort the meaning of what the interviewee said in the whole response. The meaning of what is said is always more important than the actual words. It is too easy to use a brief segment out of context, and how many politicians, or other people interviewed, complain they have been quoted out of context? Sometimes it is an excuse on their part, trying to back down on what they said. All too often it is not; it is a case of poor or unethical reporting.

Any significant qualifications made by the person interviewed must be included, if not in the edited interview itself then somewhere in the report. Editing which results in distortion by omission is another cause for complaint.

Sometimes the broadcast journalist is required to ask the same question or questions of a number of people. This is the "vox pop" straw poll (from the latin "vox poluli" meaning voice of the people) — an attempt to report random opinion about a particular news subject. The answers are edited together, but the report is honest only if precisely the same question, in precisely the same words, is put to every one of the respondents.

A reporter may have to record several interviews with different people on the same subject. These people have different views and are usually answering different questions, or the same question put in a variety of ways. It is dishonest and unethical to edit them in such a manner as to suggest that one is responding to another's comments, or arguing in person with the holder of the other opinion. The only occasion on which this is acceptable is when two or more people are present and each has the opportunity to present a case.

Any editing which suggests that people are arguing points when they are not actually in each other's company is ethically wrong.

Even in simple interviews care must be taken in choosing segments for inclusion in the news or any other program. It is the reporter's responsibility to see that the interviewee is not misrepresented. It is no excuse to say you had to choose a brief segment "and that's the way it came out". Professional integrity demands that reports be fair, whether the reporter agrees with what the interviewee has said or not.

It is all part of being honest with your audience and yourself in telling the essential facts of the story. In editing a segment from an interview the first consideration is that it truly represents what the person had to say. Include the segment most pertinent to the main facts. Then, if time permits, consider other segments which may be more colourful.

There may also be the opportunity to use another segment of the interview in rewriting or updating the story for later bulletins.

When a broadcast reporter covers a speech, finding segments truly representative of the whole can be much more difficult, but the ethics of the situation are the same.

Those who are conversant with such situations know not to plan recording from a printed hand-out or copy of the speech. Few speechmakers follow their written material that closely. It is much better to start the recorder at the beginning, ignoring the "thank yous" and "I-am-glad-to-be-here" niceties, and then pay attention to what is being said.

To do this means arriving sufficiently early to set the microphone in a position to record, or to arrange a "split" from the public address system. Either way, the recorder should be at hand, so those sections of the speech which may later make up an honest and balanced report can be noted as they occur. Note the tape counter numbers for the approximate start and finish of those segments, as well as an indication of their content.

Listening is important, but so is making notes while listening, because much of what is said may have to be reported, not replayed from tape. Those who don't listen effectively, as any worthwhile print reporter would, will have to listen through the whole lot again before beginning to prepare a story—an inexcusable waste of time. A reporter who has not listened carefully can't pass on what is truly representative of what a speaker says.

Even in broadcast reporting, listening is more important than recording. If no segment is suitable the reporter can still write from notes, if the speech is worth reporting.

Voice inserts from a speech or other reported events must add something to the report to be worth using at all.

A note of caution: make sure the segment is of sufficient technical quality. It is pointless to use a tape where background sound competes with or distracts from what is being said. Audience attention will never be won or held by reports that are hard to hear, let alone understand.

Natural Sound

The use of natural sound improves the interest and quality of a news item. The sound of chanting demonstrators outside Parliament House can lift interest in a news report. It creates sound pictures which the printed word can't, and usually before the report can be seen on television.

In reports from the Mount Panorama motor racing circuit at Bathurst, the audience will expect to hear the sound of cars in the background of the report. The editor certainly will.

Recording and using natural sound can cause new problems. Trying to record a report in the atmosphere of a rowdy demonstration usually results in too much uncontrolled sound and an inaudible report. An extreme case, maybe, but the same is true of most natural sound. A reporter has no control over it. The mix is rarely right.

The simpler way is to record a "grab" of the natural sound, or whatever is required, for several minutes. Then write the voice report well away from the noise. When phoning the end result to the newsroom, as reporters on the scene invariably do, the recorded sound plays down the line with your voice in a controlled mix.

The same method can be used to insert a segment of interview into a voice report. Cue up the recorder/player to start playing back at the start of the chosen segment, set the unit on PAUSE and start sending the report. At the cue for the insert release the PAUSE button and a voice report plus interview is the result.

The quality of the recorded sound in such circumstances is not good, but experienced newsroom staff can demonstrate how to get the best quality from a telephone line.

The ideal, if time permits, is to make the mix at the studio.

Appropriate sound boosts any story: the sound of an ambulance or police car arriving at or leaving an accident scene; a brief segment of a fire chief directing operations; the sound of stock being auctioned in a story about cattle prices; or the sound of children playing in a story about child care. They all add realism to a reporter's words, but only when the background sound is controlled.

Composite reports

All the elements discussed—voice reports from journalists, segments of interviews or speeches and background sound—come together in many of the news reports heard daily on radio. If more than one element is present, plus the introduction and throw, it is called a composite report.

In such reports the introduction—that piece of written copy which permits one report or portion of a report to follow naturally—usually contains the principal facts, or the most important aspect of the story. It is the lead.

To move from the introduction to the voice report, interview segment or entire packaged report which follows requires a throw, and there are many variations which can add something to a report. A sub-editor may suggest changes to a reporter's intro or throw to make it follow from the previous story, especially if the two stories have something in common. Or it may be that the previous story used the same phrasing and a good sub hates to hear words or phrases repeated.

Throwing to a voice report from a staff reporter soon becomes routine, which is a danger, since the throws can become repetitive. Throwing to an interview is never routine. Not that it's difficult; it's not, but the throw is so varied that no two are the same. Yet there is still a how-to-do-it guide which is so straight-forward it is almost a formula.

Most interviews in radio or television news are short clips of one answer, or part of an answer, and television uses even shorter clips than radio — as short as 10 seconds, often only a few words. Radio news sometimes uses two brief answers. If the answers are both short and well edited together there is no need to include the reporter's question in the broadcast insert.

Compare the following two ways of presenting a key question and answer and the better one is immediately obvious. The facts of the story on which Mr Brown is commenting are given clearly in the introduction, after which the newsreader says:

"John Smith spoke with Mr Brown this afternoon" and in comes John Smith's voice from tape asking a question which Mr Brown answers. Acceptable, but barely. The question would have to be spectacular to warrant inclusion and if the throw was repeated even once in a bulletin it would already seem stale. That is a lame effort compared with a throw which says:

"Mr Brown is angry at losing the election by such a large margin."

Then Mr Brown comes in, the anger in his voice evident, with an attention-grabbing answer.

The difference is that the question has been written into the introduction so that no time is wasted hearing it asked in the insert. Nor is there the confusion of hearing the reporter intrude with a question between the announcer's voice and that of Mr Brown, who was the person introduced and expected. Writing the question, usually in indirect speech, into the end of the introduction, is the best throw of all for an interview segment.

In the second throw the name of the interviewer is not given since his or her voice is not heard. Staff members need be identified only when their voices are heard. Otherwise the audience doesn't care who asked the questions. It is the answers which matter. Offering two names in quick succession, the interviewer and interviewee, is cluttering the throw needlessly.

Sometimes it is necessary to introduce both the interviewer and the interviewee, usually when the question is a strong one or the manner in which it was asked has an effect on the answer. If this must happen the last name read by the newsreader should be that of the first voice to be heard. That means that if the first voice on the tape insert is that of the reporter, the throw might read "Mr Brown talked this afternoon to John Smith", and in comes the voice of John Smith with the question. If John Smith's question is included after the first response, so that he must still be identified but his isn't the first voice heard, the throw might read, "Reporter John Smith this afternoon asked Mr Brown why he lost the election so heavily." Up comes the angry voice of Mr Brown and later, with a second question, comes John Smith's voice.

Reporters who ask good brief questions don't say much in an interview so there is seldom any need to identify them. Sometimes the radio station which employs them insists that they be identified to help build their image in the community. Even then it is often best done with a simple back-announcement — like the statement which comes after the playing of a record: "That was Mayor Smith speaking to 1PQ's John Brown." No more.

The best throw is almost always the question, in some form. It saves time and it brings the key person into the story immediately.

But be careful not to use the question as a throw, with or without the interviewer's name, and then leave the question on the head of the tape insert. Nothing sounds worse than having a question repeated. It makes John Smith and his newsroom colleagues sound foolish.

Remember that it is essential to identify the person being interviewed; it is not important to identify the reporter, though sometimes it is advisable. It is done not as an ego trip for the reporter but to let the audience know who asked the questions. Those who care probably already recognise the reporter's voice.

A successful radio reporter must master all elements of the composite report, including the introduction and throw. It calls for perseverence and practice, but the more often it is done the quicker and easier it becomes. Even the most versatile reporters have their favourite package formats. Some like to end their report with an interview clip, others to sandwich the same material half-way through, leaving themselves the last word and sign-off.

Each station or network also has its chosen or preferred format, especially for sign-offs. You have heard them: "John Smith, ABC News, Brisbane", or "John Smith, National Network News, Canberra", or "John Smith at State Parliament". They are house styles with which all staff or casual correspondents must comply. It is also the aim of all aspiring broadcast reporters to deliver such respected sign-offs.

Dub-editing

Once a report has been recorded it has to be edited before it can be used on air.

Ideally a reporter is able to record a voice report without making a mistake and record an interview from which one clip can be excised cleanly. This is the aim, especially in straight voice reports or simple voicer/interview wraps. It saves valuable time in the field and at the editing desk.

The ability to tell a story clearly first time, without ums, errs and hesitations, is becoming even more important as radio reporters are increasingly expected to report live during news bulletins. Senior reporters are getting used to delivering their reports "in one take". But in most radio reports it is still necessary to edit.

Electronic (dub) editing is universal in news work. It involves transferring segments of recorded material from the original tape to another tape, and in the required order.

Imagine there is a recorded interview from which a small segment is to be used as part of a composite voice report. It may be something recorded on the recorder phone that needs further editing before it is suitable for on-air use—the interview may be too long, or the voice report may have a false start or a stumble part-way through.

Before explaining the recording of cartridges, it is necessary to explain the principles of dub-editing. Sometimes it is better to edit the required segment from the master to another machine, either reel-to-reel or cassette, before the edited insert is transferred to cartridge.

It is possible to edit segments directly from cassette to cartridge, but it does create problems. On most cart. machines, every time the RECORD button is pressed to make an edit, it places an electronic stop pulse on the tape. This is so the cartridge will run through after use and re-cue at that point. If more edits are made more pulses are put onto the tape and they have to be removed or the cartridge will stop on air every time it comes to a pulse. Newer cart. machines edit segments together without the annoying pulses, but not all machines have this facility. So the choice of editing procedure will depend on which machine is available in the newsroom. If the pulses can be "wiped" without risk to the edited program, or the machine is a recent model, edit directly to cartridge. If there is any risk, edit first to something else, then make the cartridge.

Two tape recorders are needed to dub-edit — one to replay the original material, the other to record the edited material. They must be connected from the output of the replay machine to the input of the record machine. This is usually done through a mixer, but for simple voice editing two recorder/players can be linked by simple patch cords.

The first step is to find the start of the first segment of what will be the final edited version. How this is best done depends on the type of replay unit being used. If it is a reel-to-reel unit, set it on cue and manually turn the tape spools until the precise spot — the exact point at which the segment begins — crosses the replay head. Then take the tape back about 6cm from the head to allow the machine to reach proper play speed and avoid any "wow" on the new recording. If it is a cassette unit of good quality, play through the lead-up to the opening segment and listen carefully. Spool back and play it again and when the last sound before the section to be dubbed is heard, press PAUSE.

Find a suitable starting point on the recording machine and zero the counter so the start can be found again quickly once the recording is completed. If the recording machine is a cassette unit make sure the start of the recording is well clear of the blank leader on the cassette. A cassette machine starts more promptly from PAUSE than from RECORD, so take advantage of this. Set the machine to RECORD while in PAUSE. When PAUSE is released, it will start to record instantly.

Now both machines are cued to dub. Set the original (master) to play and the receiving machine (slave) to record by releasing both PAUSE buttons simultaneously. The required segment will be transferred from one machine to the other.

A second or two after the end of the required segment stop both machines. Check the recording by replaying it. Check that the recording level is what it should be and that there are no extraneous noises on the tape. If the dubbed segment sounds as it should, continue the editing.

Find the start of the next section on the master tape and cue as before. On the recording machine, find the last word of the first segment and PAUSE the machine at that spot and press RECORD ready to receive the next segment. With both machines re-cued, make the edit by dubbing the second segment in exactly the same manner as the first. Check the recording again.

If the second segment dubbed follows the first with no click, no dead spot, no excessive pause and no change in sound level, the edit is a good one. If you have miscalculated you may have cut a word from the end of the first segment or the head of the second, in which case make the edit or edits again.

Repeat the operation for as many segments as are needed, but remember to check each edit before continuing to the next. Once all the segments have been dub-edited in the required order they can be dubbed again, as a complete unit, onto a cartridge for on-air use. Now the edited tape becomes the master.

Bulk erase a cartridge and place it in the cart. recording unit, making sure that the two machines are properly connected—the output from what is now the master to the input of the cart. unit.

When all is ready to record press RECORD on the cart. machine, which puts the stop pulse on the cartridge tape. Then, while holding the RECORD button down, press PLAY on both cart. and replay machine. Start the cart. unit a fraction of a second ahead of the replay. When the last words have been transferred, hit STOP on the cartridge machine, though if the editing has been tidy there will be no further sound after the intended last word. Then set the cart. player to FAST FORWARD and the cartridge will re-cue. Check the cartridge to make sure it holds what is wanted, no more, no less.

If the end result is satisfactory, label the cartridge clearly and accurately with the story name, date, last words (out cue) and running time. Then it is ready for use.

More experienced radio journalists make "running" edits, but this is not recommended for novices. This system, used in most newsrooms, requires that the editor listen carefully to the start of each segment so the precise start is remembered. Then the master machine is re-spooled a few seconds and played again. At the precise edit point, the record unit is set in motion. It saves time for the experienced but it can ruin a lot of edits for those gaining the experience. Ability to run-edit comes with a "feel" for editing and that comes with practise.

Cut-editing

Dub-editing is quick and relatively easy to master, but it can rarely produce the quality of editing demanded for current affairs and documentary programs.

The quality of cut-editing is better for two reasons. The master is always on reel-to-reel tape — which offers a wider recording surface and moves more quickly than a cassette, and all work is done on the master — which means there is no loss of quality from successive dubbings. Cutting, or physical editing, is impossible — certainly highly impractical — on narrow and confined cassettes.

Before cut-editing, make sure which is the PLAY head of the reel-to-reel unit to be used. This is critical. It is on this head that the precise editing points are found.

Segments can be cut-edited with greater precision than they can be linked by dub-editing. As an example, assume that a very small portion is to be edited out of an interview — a cough, an "um" or an excessively long pause. The editing steps are the same whether the section to be cut out is short or long.

- Using the cue control, find the end of the portion which is to be retained (the start of the piece which is to be cut out). It may take several "rocks" back and forward to get it exactly right.

- Mark the tape lightly at this point with a chinagraph pencil, setting the mark across the tape where it passes the head. For extra safety draw a line on the tape in the direction (left) of the material which will be discarded (mark the "waste" tape). Play the tape forward to the start of the next section to be retained (the end of the section

to be edited out). The cough or um or pause will be entirely within this section of tape.
- Mark across the tape as before, only this time put the chinagraph waste tape mark towards the right, back into the tape to be cut out.

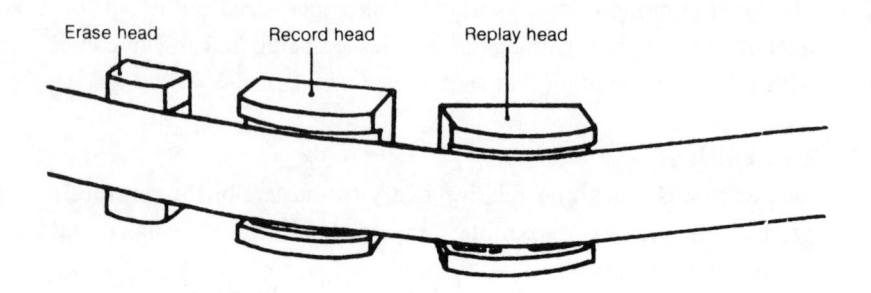

The erase, record and replay heads

- Loosen the tape from the recorder so it can be placed in an editing block and cut the tape with a razor blade or scissors at an oblique angle at the two edit points which have been marked. The angled cut is used because it allows for a quick cross-fade of any sound which is on the tape and also because there is a larger area of contact between the two sections of tape about to be joined. Check that the piece of tape cut out carries the "waste" mark drawn along it when the edit points were marked.

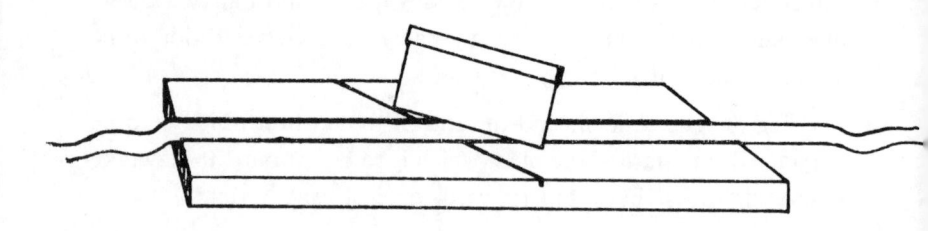

Cut editing using razor blade

- Place the cut ends of the tape together in the editing block, taking care that they butt neatly without overlap, that they are not twisted and that the backing side of the tape (the shinier side) is up.

- Lay a piece of adhesive splicing tape about 3 to 4cm long, across the backing side of the tape, press and rub firmly.
- Slide the tape out of the block to trim the splicing tape back to the exact width of the recording tape, again using a razor blade or scissors.
- Play the edited segment to make sure the desired result has been achieved, then move on to the next edit.
- Some advice to be remembered whenever cut-editing.
- Never, repeat never, cut tape with a blade, scissors or anything else, against the heads of the tape recorder. It risks damaging expensive equipment.
- Always slide the tape out of the edit block rather than pull it out. Pulling risks breaking the splice or stretching the tape.
- Don't discard any edited-out tape until all editing is complete and you are satisfied with the result. If any re-edit is likely later, keep the off-cuts even longer by taping them together for possible re-use.

Most current affairs reporters and documentary producers prefer to record at 7½ ips because it allows for more precise and tighter editing. Anything recorded at that speed uses twice as much tape as the same material recorded at 3¾ ips. With twice as much tape there is twice as much space between words, making cut-editing easier.

The risk in trying to clean up interviews by taking out coughs and other unwanted sounds is that the first sound of the following word may be clipped off, or perhaps the final sound of the previous word. Sometimes, if there is not adequate space on both sides of the offending sound it is best to leave it rather than take any risks, especially since it is the master tape.

It is unwise to try to cut out short pauses just for the sake of tightening up an interview. The end result will sound unnatural, since everyone pauses from time to time when speaking. If the interviewed speaker doesn't, it will sound strange, as if the thoughts are just tumbling out. There is a fine line, no matter what type of editing is used, between having the interviewed person express thoughts succinctly and having them sound as though they never draw breath or stop to think, but just fire out their thoughts and opinions in a continuous stream. Another tight editing problem evident in today's radio news bulletins is the brief comment from a news-maker that ends on a wrong inflection. It is obvious that the person had more to say and the listeners are left wondering what it was. The impression is that the interviewee was cut off in mid-sentence and that is usually exactly what happened.

Dub-editing and cut-editing each have advantages and disadvantages. There are editors who discourage cut-editing because they claim it wastes tape. Once the required segments have been cut out of an interview the rest is usually thrown out. Over a period this amounts to a lot of tape, but there is no alternative. Tape which has been cut and spliced can't be used again, at least not safely. A splice may break or jam in the machine, since splices deteriorate over time. Also, there will always be a sound drop-out at each splice point when the tape is re-used.

There are still many applications for cut-editing. Current affairs and documentary producers still prefer this system because it edits the original tape — the best quality available. It needs only one machine, so it does not tie up studio facilities or an editing suite. If only a few cuts are needed it is faster than dubbing and it is the only effective editing method if extraneous and unwanted sounds, such as coughing or interjections, have to be cut out.

The advantages of dub-editing are that the tape can be recycled and the uncut original can be re-used for subsequent programs. Dubbing is quicker when there are a number of edits to make; other sounds can be mixed in and levels adjusted as editing progresses. Another advantage is that edits can be rehearsed to see how they sound before the actual edit is made, though this takes time. A poor edit can be remade, given time, so that the end product can be near-perfect from an editing point of view, if not in sound quality.

But dub-editing is time-consuming for small editing jobs such as taking a small segment from a long interview. There can be loss of continuity in background sound. It requires two tape recorders and a busy studio can't always afford the time or the equipment. Perhaps most serious of all, it is not as precise as cut-editing. It is difficult to take out a cough or a single unwanted word. On top of all this there is the risk of an electronic "click" at every point where an edit is made, especially if the editing recorders are not in perfect condition.

News items are usually brief and news editors are prepared to accept less than perfect quality in recording and editing to get the story to air quickly. Quality is improving as "in-the-field" recorders, recorder phones and car-to-base radio systems perform better.

Journalists generally do their own editing in radio. If they are detained in the field for another story and have to send their tapes back, they should suggest to the alternative editor what segment or segments they think best for on-air use. In both cases the judgment for news purposes is made on content rather than on sound quality. With good equipment there is little excuse for a journalist returning with anything less than good quality material.

The best television journalists understand camera techniques, even if they never handle equipment themselves. It helps them record better reports from the field.

(Picture: Channel 7)

Techniques 2

Extending the how to do it to television

Many of the techniques used in radio reporting carry over into television, but in television the picture is the master. The picture is both television's greatest advantage over other news media and an ever-present problem for television journalists who want the words they write and the news items for which they are written to be accurate and without distortion.

Anyone working in the medium soon realises, whether they like it or not, that the picture is paramount. What people see overrides, or at least conditions, what they hear.

This does not mean words have no value in television, nor even that they have less value than in other news media. Words are essential if television's picture is to reflect reality, but the words must be written to fit the picture. If there is any clash, the picture will win. Television reporters must write so that their words complement the pictures, not vice versa.

People have two major senses by which they absorb information: sight and sound. Of the two, sight is by far the more efficient. People can read much faster than they can listen to spoken words. They can absorb the content of a television picture in a flash, quite literally in a split second. How accurately they absorb it is another matter.

Contradictory though it may seem, most people who are paying attention hear more accurately than they read or see, unless they have the opportunity to study a picture for a long time. Once again, it depends on how accurately and clearly the audio information is presented.

When words genuinely reinforce pictures on television, providing information the pictures lack and explaining or qualifying those parts of the pictures which need support, the information delivery system is at its most efficient. This requires that both camera operators and journalists do their job properly.

Viewers are quite capable of taking in both sight and sound simultaneously when they are complementary. If they clash, the picture overrides the sound, even when the picture is less precise or less informative.

Television is considered a powerful and effective medium, yet most people remember little of the material they see. Most recall less of what they see on television than what they read in a newspaper or hear on radio. It need not be so. American studies show that when television news is prepared and presented in the best way, with words truly complementing pictures, retention rates (the amount of information remembered) are substantially increased.

So writing style for television journalists, if there is such a style, is the writing style for radio adapted so that the writing fits the pictures so well that they become one message. The picture thus becomes part of television style.

The first technique to be learned in television reporting is how to properly lay out a news script. In radio, as long as the copy is clean and the writing clear and in good style, there are few problems. Line length on the typewriter does not matter much in radio but it does in television. There is a universally accepted way to set out a television script, universal because it is so practical and effective.

Television deals with both pictures and sound, so part of the script page is allocated to each. Normally a script page is divided vertically by a line, real or imaginary, about a third of the way across the page. The left third carries information about the pictures (video) and the right two-thirds the information relating to the sound (audio). In the production of commercials, or in programs where there are many picture changes demanded and not much in the way of sound instructions, the page division is different, but for news it is constant through most Australian television stations: the left third for pictures regardless of their source and the right two-thirds for sound, which means words to be read as well as any other sound regardless of its source.

Precise chronology is essential in television presentation, so it must be preserved clearly in the layout of the script. For instance, if it is required that the picture appear exactly as a reader begins a script, or a prepared cartridge begins to play, then the picture instruction and the sound instruction must appear on the same line across the page. If the picture is to show a split second before sound begins, then the picture instruction must appear above the sound one, so that they will occur in that order. Preparation depends on the journalist's ideas and planning, or sometimes those of a news producer. Execution depends on a director, not the journalist, so the instructions to the director must be precise.

One of the problems in television production, including news programs, is that there are so many people involved. Compare it with the simplicity of radio. In radio the journalist prepares the package on a cartridge and writes into the introduction where the cartridge is to be played, how long it runs and what its end cue is. Anyone can present it because it is straightforward and there are only two sources of sound, the mike and the cart. player.

Compared with the logistics of television even the production of a newspaper seems simple. A newspaper's production, at least from a news point of view, is linear. The reporter writes, the sub-editor corrects, checks and lays out the pages, it passes to the platemakers and then to the printers. It all happens more or less one step at a time.

In television it is not so. A reporter writes a story, usually incorporating pictures in one form or another. The reporter does not take the pictures—someone else does—though the reporter may have a hand in their editing. The reporter will also have a hand in preparing the final sound track which will usually be played from a cartridge as in radio, except that this cartridge carries both the edited picture and the sound—a composite videotape. The report may also be played from an edited videotape and a separate audio cartridge. But the reporter plays no part in the final presentation, when information converges from many different sources at the director's command.

In television, different people in different locations contribute to the precisely-timed presentation on air. The newsreader has to ensure that the words on the script (or the autocue) are presented at the right time.

The operator in the videotape room makes sure that tapes are in the right order and ready to play. This is sometimes still called the telecine room, dating from the day when cine film was played from there into television cameras. If camera graphics are to be used the floor manager in the studio makes sure the right graphic is in the right place (this can be done elsewhere in the station building) and that the reader is looking at the right camera when he or she starts to read. In the control room the switcher looks after the pictures to make sure the right camera is on the right person and the right tape player is called into operation. The audio operator makes sure the right sound source is used, whether it is a studio microphone, a cartridge or tape, or sound is played from a videotape player.

Fortunately most television news operations cut a few production corners by standardizing their presentation methods, but it still means that the journalist's script is the guide for all others involved as to what should happen to produce the right end product. It is the news director's task to make sure it will all happen smoothly. He or she takes the scripts in the order in which the editor (or line-up sub-editor) has prepared them, and makes sure that everything required will happen. The director integrates pictures from the studio cameras, from videotapes or film projectors (rare these days), from slide projectors and caption scanners (or any of the many versions of them), from character generators (which put writing onto the screen), and often from two or more of these at once.

Ideally, information relevant to all pictures and sound should be on the script. As the script originates with the journalist, this means that a good television journalist should know all about production in the field and have a working knowledge of production in the studio as well.

A sloppy script can lead to sloppy production, unless someone else is doubly alert. Proper layout helps. Once the page is divided vertically, there are some general rules.

The top right corner of the page should carry the following information:

Catchline — as in print or radio, a one-word (sometimes two-word) tag based on content, by which the story can be identified. The catchline goes onto everything associated with the story, the videotape, cartridge, prepared artwork.

Duration — this refers to the total duration of the item, including intro and any videotape inclusions and should be written in minutes and seconds.

Date — the date of telecast, not the date on which it is written or photographed. Insert the telecast time, too, if there are several newscasts in the day. This is to make clear for which bulletin the material is intended.

Name — The reporter's name or identifying initials come next, so others who must handle the copy can tell who wrote or re-wrote the item. Both are important so both should be included. If there is a separate tape editor, his or her initials are added as well.

That means that the top right corner of the page should look like this, even though the information may not be available until the the script is complete.

> Buaffaloes
> 0:57
> Jan 4, '91
> MM/RP/BN (author, sub, editor)

Also — some television stations insist that the script list the picture and sound sources included in the story, in the order in which they occur; e.g. Live/VTR with cart/VO graphics.

Because of the use of ENG equipment has become almost universal throughout Australia, most television stations present their news from videotape "packages" edited ready-for-air before news time. This means that most scripts will carry only an introduction to be read from the studio and the instruction to "take VTR". In and out cues must still be provided, as in radio, and the total running time. This is necessary so the editor and producer can work out accurate timings for the bulletin.

Now to the layout of the script itself. Because there are so many short-cuts used in different newsrooms, the layout described is the basic lay-out, with everything included, since this is the starting point from which the others have been developed.

Leave space at the top. Some television stations print special script paper, often with multiple carbons. Others expect journalists to prepare only the original and have a typist prepare the final error-free copy from which the presentation will be made. Still others use a word-processing computer system which automatically lays out scripts according to a prepared formula.

The space at the top is for the director's instructions. On un-printed copy paper leave a consistent amount blank at the head of the page; 5cm is a minimum. All the top-of-the-page information explained above will soon fill part of this, but there should be a very clear gap between the bottom of that data and the beginning of the script proper.

Make your page divisions clear. Whether the page has an actual line to separate audio and video portions does not matter as long as the script writer adheres rigidly to the divisions. Never allow type to overrun this dividing line.

This page division is in use wherever people read from left to right and top to bottom of a page.

Double space everything to be read on air at any stage of the production. This means even if the script is to be used in the making of a package for on-air presentation from video tape, it should be double spaced. This spacing is easier to read. Only the data lines at the top of the page or instructional data within the script which is not be read on air, should be single spaced. Instructions should also be clearly ringed in bold pen or felt-tipped pen to make doubly sure it is read as an instruction.

Make sure the typewriter is delivering a clean, black, easily-read image. Faint images are difficult to read in the bright lights of a studio, even in the lighting of a production booth which may be used to create the packaged video story.

Keep paragraphs short, as in radio, with double-double spacing between them. This is in the interests of easy reading. Wide spacing makes it easier for the newsreader to keep the place on the script, which he or she has to do even when reading from autocue.

"End" or "More" should appear at the foot of each page, so it is clear to the reader, director and everyone else involved in the production that the story is either ended or there is more. The word "END" or "MORE" should be typed or written boldly under the last line of copy and then circled equally boldly. Encircled material is never to be read on air. When a report continues onto a second script page, many directors like to see the foot of each column marked to indicate what happens over the page; e.g. "VTR continues", "Cart. plays on".

Number the pages after page one. If there is a second page it is only necessary to put the catchline and the page number on the top right corner. No other information is needed. But it also pays to mark the head of the video column to show which video source is continuing, and the same for the audio column; e.g. "VTR playing", "Cart. playing".

Make all instructions clear, concise and accurate and make sure they are in the right place. This is best understood by looking at an example or two. Every television news story begins with an introduction, normally read from the studio by the newsreader. The script page will thus read, in the video and audio columns:

Cam	In Canberra today...
(For camera. May have a camera number added)	(These are the words the reader actually reads. It is unnecessary to use the instruction MIKE.)

If, when the introduction ends the picture is to come from a prepared videotape package (or videocartridge package) which carries both picture and sound, the instructions are simple and clear.

VTR (or VCR)   VTR (or VCR)

But perhaps all the sound is not on the prepared tape. It may well be that the edited videotape carries the picture and only the background sound recorded together with the picture. The written words of the script are on a prepared audio cartridge. Then the instructions, still on the same line in each column, will read:

VTR   Cart./VTR for b/g

And so on throughout that item and every item. Both the director (or switcher) and the audio operator know from the script in front of them exactly where their material will come from.

Still or moving pictures may come from T/C (telecine), SOF (sound-on-film, also from the telecine room but not used much in news these days), or camera graphics (pictures, diagrams or maps in one of many forms set up before a camera of some type). Other forms of visual information may come from one of the many types of character generators in use in television stations. This is the source of the lettered information telling the viewer where the news item is from or who is speaking. The more complex these electronic gadgets, the more facilities they can offer ---varieties in face and size of type, colours, split screens, even amimations.

Audio can come from an equally diverse range of sources, though news producers try to keep the number in regular use as small as possible. Audio can be V/O (voice over, which means someone is actually reading the words into a microphone while the picture is from some other source), cassette, cart., or VTR (which means the videotape carries the sound as well as the picture—the normal situation).

End cues must be accurate. An end cue, usually the last three or four words of the script, is an absolute necessity to warn those presenting the item on air that it is coming to an end. Even though videotapes are electronically cued so that a buzzer or beeper sounds when there is 10 seconds of tape to play, it is normal to write on the script both audio and video end cues and the exact duration of the video or cartridge. Even if both picture and sound are from the same videotape the end cue is essential for the director and audio operator to be able to cut cleanly to the next item.

If the news item being played has a normal reporter sign-off then "sign off" may be all that is needed as an end cue. If it does not have a sign-off, then the last words of the script being read or played MUST be inserted as a cue.

The duration of the tape, cartridge or other source must also be included to tell the on-air operators whether the material runs 10 seconds (0:10) or one minute 14 seconds (1:14).

The duration and end cue should be written together with the audio or video instruction and circled to indicate clearly that they are instructions, not script to be read on air.

Reporting for television

Reporting for television has much in common with both radio reporting and newspaper reporting and yet has a manner of its own. It shares radio's basic conversational style, whether the words are from a reader in the studio or from a reporter and recorded to be presented with pictures. It shares with newspapers the necessity for concentration and the physical presence of the viewer if it is to be both seen and heard.

Television is neither radio with pictures nor a development of the movie industry, though it has wrongly been described as both. It is television, and television journalism is as separate and distinctive a form of journalism as television is a separate and distinctive form of entertainment.

Television journalism is logistically complex and full of apparent conflicts compared with other types of journalism. It is rigidly constricted by its own techniques and technical requirements yet totally unrelenting in deadlines. This means television journalism needs the best journalists available if it is to be done well.

Television journalists must understand and accept that television news is part of a medium which is not primarily a news medium. Television journalism, properly done, may be the most effective means ever invented of telling people what is happening in their world, but it is part of a medium primarily concerned with entertainment.

So television news, even on the ABC, must reconcile itself to the fact that it is the informational arm of a medium which survives on its entertainment value. News must therefore be entertaining as well as informative or it will lose ratings — for commercial television this means losing income. Television news editors know this. Their continuing dilemma is how to inform those who watch to be informed without losing those who view essentially for entertainment.

It is not a problem peculiar to television. In every medium the way in which journalists would like to present the news has to be tempered by what the audience wants.

Television journalism is a team effort. It involves camera crews as well as journalists in gathering and editing the stories, technicians and engineers to help prepare those stories for air, production staff to put the news to air, and most of the staff of the television station for the complex organisation which makes regular television broadcasting possible. For practical purposes, however, before a television journalist can become competent, he or she must know about pictures. This means co-operation with and understanding those who operate cameras in the field.

Journalists involved in television reporting, whether in a stand-up, voice-over report, scripted pictures taped on location, interview, or any combination of them, must realise that the picture provides a substantial part of the story. So it is necessary for journalists to know how that part of the story is gathered. The picture is a part, often the major part, of a story for which the television journalist is responsible.

In the real world journalists are not permitted to handle cameras as part of their work. There may well be valid industrial reasons for this but in the training of journalists for television it is unfortunate. The best way to understand how anything is done is to try doing it yourself. No amount of telling and explaining can achieve what can be done by some hands-on experience. Problems become evident in the shooting and more in the editing. By doing both for himself or herself the journalist learns what those problems are and how they can be overcome.

In a working newsroom a journalist may be expected to take part in the editing without having had any part in the initial shooting. For this reason the more a reporter can learn about the work of the others he or she works with, the better.

Television reporting techniques explained in this book are taken in order of pictorial complexity rather than scripting complexity, simply because the reporter has to understand what is required of the camera operator to do the job properly. They are covered in the progressively complex order of stand-up, voice report on location, voice-over scripting, interviewing and then the compilation of a package which combines two or more of these elements.

As in radio, all these require an introduction and throw as part of the total report and these must be included in the final script. Every report presented for television must be a complete script, from intro to sign-off.

The Stand-up

In the simple form outlined here, a stand-up is a form of television reporting which passes in and out of fashion in television newsrooms. Whether in or out of fashion, it is a basic technique which all who intend to become television reporters must understand. A stand-up is a report in which a reporter on the news scene reports directly to the camera. He or she may appear in only some or most of the "takes" or "grabs", but always in such a way that reporter and picture tell a story without the end result appearing disjointed.

Anyone who watches television recognises the throw to a voice report. It is just as in radio, with the simplest form being: "with a report from the scene, John Smith".

Stand-ups should be done with scenes of the location in the background so the picture provides part of the story, whether the picture is of a courthouse, construction site, accident scene or sportsground. Stand-ups are usually, though not always, eye-witness accounts of what happened, and the idea is to give "I was there" credibility to the story.

If such a report is to be made entirely on location it will need planning by both journalist and camera operator and co-operation between them.

When a journalist reports directly to a camera on location it is much the same as doing a live report, which means several things:

- there is no time to stop and think once the report has started.
- there is no opportunity to make use of extensive, or any, notes (there are exceptions to this).
- the reporter must be fluent.
- the reporter must speak clearly, precisely and in good English.
- the reporter must know (because it was arranged beforehand) how the end result will be edited.

This requires planning, no matter how the stand-up is to be done, and stand-ups can be done in one of many ways:

- The reporter can make a simple statement to camera (which must be short if it is to be covered in one take).
- The reporter can make several short statements to camera for later editing together, but they must be shot from different positions or angles to be editable, whether or not they all include the reporter in the picture.
- The reporter can so organise the stand-up that it includes an interview segment, or more than one, which requires even more careful planning.
- The reporter can plan for an overlay type of editing, which means that relevant pictures are shot to be edited over the tape of the reporter telling the story.
- The reporter can combine any of the above to produce a television news "package".

Often the simplest approach is the best, both verbally and visually. Complexity creates editing difficulties which cost time or may cause problems in production or presentation.

There is no sense in recording a report on location or locations if the same report can be presented just as well from the studio by the newsreader, helped by still or taped pictures from the scene. Recording stand-ups consumes time and materials and creates delays in editing, all of which cost money, so there ought to be good reasons for doing them. The reasons are:

- There is increased credibility in a report which shows pictures and sounds from the news scene.
- Such a report offers viewers a change of voice and face.
- A location report can (and should) take the viewer to the scene as if he or she was there, thus giving atmosphere studio delivery can never provide.

If the stand-up can't do any one of these well, the report might as well be presented from the studio, and probably should be.

Stand-up reports are usually shot in short grabs (or takes) for two main reasons. The first and most important is to change the picture information the viewers see. Every change of shot should be motivated by the desire to offer a new scene or a new angle to a previous shot, so that as much information as possible about the event being reported is included.

The second reason is that most reporters, especially those without long experience, can handle their material best in short grabs. Planning all grabs carefully means they will edit together coherently.

The reporter has many things to consider before making even a simple stand-up, no matter in how many of the shots the speaker will appear. It is unusual to see the reporter in all takes of a stand-up. In reality there is no need to see the reporter after the first take has established that he or she is at the scene.

However, setting out to make a stand-up in which the reporter appears in every shot is a good exercise to show how ridiculous jump cuts look. A jump cut results from editing together two segments of tape in which the same person appears in two different positions. It looks as if the reporter, or whoever that person is, has been instantly spirited from one position to another. It might not sound too serious, but it is. Anything that makes some viewers titter, and jump cuts do, is distracting, which is a cardinal sin in television journalism.

In a stand-up the reporter has to plan the verbal content of each shot so that what is said can be edited together smoothly. He or she also has to work out with the camera operator what will be in each shot so that the words and pictures reinforce each other. If they don't, the picture will demand the viewers' attention and the words will be ignored, and with them a significant part of the story.

The best way to do this is for the reporter to jot down the information which must be included in the stand-up, remembering that there is an introduction still to be written and that this will usually carry a major part of the story. The planned pictures will carry more of it. Many television reporters use a clip-board to carry their written notes. It is hard to conceal on camera, but it usually looks acceptable on air and is the easiest way to make notes immediately available when recording.

Having worked out what must be said, discuss the situation with the camera operator. Look around the scene and work out what will appear in each shot.

Rely on the camera operator's judgment on how to frame the sequence of shots and on what should be included in them. Few people can tell a story better on television than a good camera operator, so it is a careless or very hard-pressed news editor who sends out an inexperienced reporter without an experienced cameraman or camerawoman.

Camera operators know how to avoid jump cuts. They can easily be avoided by leaving the speaker out of adjoining takes, but this is not always possible. In an exercise in which the reporter must appear in each shot it defeats the whole purpose.

Jump cuts can be avoided. The simplest and most immediately obvious of such cuts is where the reporter (or anyone else) is distant in one shot with a whole scene between him or her and the camera, yet in the next is close to the camera, with the whole scene behind. How did he or she move so magically from one place to the next?

Another example: the reporter is shown in the first shot standing on the courthouse steps, leaning against the handrail; in the next the reporter is facing a different way, even though standing in the same place, and is not leaning on the handrail. Such apparent trifles are important. One reason why the directors of feature films use "continuity" people is to make sure such silly, jump-cut errors don't happen.

There are journalists who think jump cuts don't matter. Camera operators know better. Jump cuts detract from the smoothness and authenticity of what is presented. The viewers who see them and whose attention may be distracted are the intelligent and observant — the very people most critical of television journalism's shortcomings.

Strangely, the human mind which is jolted by the magical transportation of a person a few feet, accepts without problems the transport of the same person across the street or across the world in a fraction of a second if the pictorial sequence is right. Thus, if the reporter is on the courthouse steps in the first shot but "walks in" to the second shot, in front of the gates of a prison most viewers know is miles away, it is acceptable. But it is acceptable only if the reporter enters after the shot begins.

The distance between locations in adjacent shots doesn't matter. A first shot may show a person getting into a car and the car driving out-of-shot around a corner. It must travel out of sight of the viewer. The very next shot can show the door opening on a plane which has just landed in London and the same person emerge. Because the person concerned has been lost to sight, even for a split second, it is not a jump cut. Yet cutting between shots of the same person at Tullamarine and at Heathrow in London, would cause half the audience to laugh, it would seem so ridiculous. You want the audience to laugh at the humorous stories, not at your mistakes.

In sequence, the reporter works out what will be said in the introduction, then what will be shown in each shot and thus what must be said in each "grab". Then it is the time to dispense with the clipboard and reduce what is to be said to "key words". These key words can be written on a slip of paper small enough to be concealed from the camera while the report is being taped. It takes practice to conceal notes in the same hand which holds the microphone, but that is the ideal place for them. No viewer is disturbed if a reporter sneaks a glance at his or her microphone.

Better still, memorise the sentence, or even two sentences, which will be presented in each take, so that the whole report can be made without reference to any notes. Experienced reporters can report to camera without memorising more than the key words and without notes. Key words, noted and held in the palm of the microphone hand, are there as an insurance policy should the delivery go wrong.

The important thing is to make sure that the two, three, four or more takes which are made will fit together as a continuous, fluent report with the words accurately complementing the pictures. The reporter need not appear in all takes and in most stand-up reports which appear on television does not. In those takes in which the reporter doesn't appear, the script can be read, as long as it is done in exactly the same voice as that used in reporting to camera in the other takes. Keeping the same voice in such different circumstances is not easy and is another of the problems which the would-be television reporter must learn to handle. If the voice production is different viewers will realise that part of the report was recorded differently, probably later. Maybe it doesn't matter to many, but it matters to some and that affects credibility.

There are circumstances when reading from notes during a stand-up is advisable, and in some newsrooms obligatory. Consider the case of a report from the courthouse steps telling what has just happened inside. It is stupid to take risks with the accuracy of names, charges, quotes and the final verdict, so the audience almost expects the reporter to refer to notes. As with justice, reporters should not only be accurate, but be seen to be accurate.

No matter what the circumstances, all stand-ups must be planned. Work out how many takes are needed to cover adequately what must be reported and then work out what must be said in each of those takes. Look for suitable locations for each and work out where and how to stand or walk in (or out), so that the end result will have no jump cuts. Make sure by asking just what the camera can or should see, so that there is no duplication in the words used.

Always remember what the picture shows, even if it is only background. It looks silly if the reporter has a tree sprouting out of an ear, or anywhere else. On the other hand, if the story is about a tree, don't obscure it just to get a better picture of the reporter.

If the reporter elects to remain out of shot for parts of the report, it should not be in the first or last grabs. The reporter should be there to open the report, if only to show the viewers that a reporter was on the scene. It is also best to be in the last shot, unless the report ends with another animate subject, such as an interviewee. It is a reinforcement of the fact that the reporter not only was there, but stayed there to do the job properly. Reports often end with a sign-off, as in radio, and when they do the reporter should be seen.

It is essential to include the camera crew in all planning. Unless the person behind the camera knows what is going to be said and in what sequence, there can be no effective zooming in or out, no panning to include something which is being mentioned in the script. The camera operator must know what is happening if the end result is to be effectively edited. The same applies for an audio operator, if there is one on the assignment.

In most stand-ups the picture should change every 15 or so seconds. It may happen in less than 15 seconds, according to what is being said, but takes seldom exceed 20 seconds. A take of 25 seconds is an absolute maximum. Viewer boredom sets in unless what is being said is so important it needs no picture. When that is so, why have a picture?

The reporter also has to plan ahead if an interview segment is to be included. It is necessary to include in the location report who is to be interviewed and why. It can't be inserted later. How to plan and conduct those interviews will be discussed later.

For practical purposes this means that the interview has to be made first, so that information included in the interview is not included in the stand-up takes or written into the introduction. If the interviewee says something there is no need for the reporter to repeat it.

In a reporting team that works smoothly, the reporter and camera crew plan their attack on the way to their assignment, as long as one of them knows the location well enough. If this can't happen they stop on arrival, gather the principal facts and survey the scene for picture locations and then do their planning. They work out together where they might conduct an interview, if there is to be one, and from where the most informative shots can be taken. Then, while the camera crew sets up, the reporter can work out the overall content and the content of each grab, or at least the first two or three, so that the job can be done quickly and efficiently.

Speed in carrying out assignments, as well as accuracy in reporting, makes news editors and station managers happy. It means quality reporting is being carried out for as little expense as possible—very important in television.

So there is a sequence in the planning of a stand-up, whether the reporter is in all of the shots or in none of them.

- What will be said and how will it be said?
- What will be shown and how will it be shown?
- How will the two fit together?
- What are the best angles and lighting positions?
- In what sequence will it be shot?
- What will the intro be?
- How long will it take to shoot?
- How long will it take to edit?

Some tips for beginners:

- Avoid reading notes except in those situations where they are necessary for accuracy or credibility.
- Let the camera run a second or two before starting to speak in each take. It helps in editing and makes certain the first word is effectively recorded.
- Shoot in sequence wherever possible. It is easier for inexperienced reporters and for the editors.
- Look at the camera when opening and signing off. It looks as though the reporter is speaking to the audience. (This is not always so in interviews, which will be explained later.)
- Don't be afraid to move. It is better for the reporter to move than the camera. Competent but steady shots are better than imaginative but unsteady ones. This does not mean reporters should get into movement habits, such as the popular but overdone action of walking towards the camera while recording a "grab".

- Speak up. Most stand-ups are done outside and will need good speech volume to record adequately. Also, since most television sound recording units operate on automatic gain control (AGC), speaking up helps cut out extraneous noises. At the receiving end it also helps to project across the living room from the television set to the viewers.
- If you need notes for names, key words or figures, make them small, so they can be concealed in the reporter's palm, or so plan the takes that you can look at something bigger without being seen to do so.

All sorts of note-reading tricks have been tried. Huge key-word notes have been scratched in sand almost under the camera operator's feet so that the reporter could read them without appearing to take his eyes from the camera. Words have been written in mud on a powerboat's deck, on clipboards hung on convenient trees, on papers wedged into rubber seals on car windows — anything which makes the notes readable without the reading being obvious.

The whole process aims at an end result in which the maximum amount of information about an event can be passed to the viewers in a minimum of time, without the words and pictures conflicting. Both must form a fluent sequence if maximum audience understanding of the information is to be achieved.

To do this, it is much better to make the words fit the pictures than the other way round, even when reporter and camera operator are co-operating closely, as they should in a stand-up.

Voice-over scripting causes new problems. This is the writing of a script to complement pictures which have already been shot and edited to tell as much of the story as possible. The aim is to produce a fusion of pictures and words which will impart the most information with the utmost clarity in the shortest time. In many ways voice-over scripting is the most difficult aspect of writing for television, but it can also be the most satisfying.

Since television began the preparation of scripts has undergone many changes. When Australian television began, all scripts were written voice-over because there was then no practical means of recording picture and sound simultaneously. There was a complex double-system method by which separate systems recorded picture and sound, one on film and one on audio tape. These were later edited together in a studio editing suite. The apparatus was so cumbersome it was seldom used in day to day news reporting.

In those days it was customary for a film camera operator to go to the news scene and shoot the pictures considered necessary to report the event. A journalist on the same assignment would gather facts to provide information for the script. If there was no journalist on hand the camera operator gathered as many facts as possible and provided what was known as a "dope sheet" to help the editing.

After processing, the mute film (film without sound) was edited. If the journalist assigned to script it could be present at the editing, so much the better. Suggestions from the journalist were usually welcomed. If no journalist could attend, the script had to be written from the edited film.

In an ideal situation the film editor prepared a complete shot list which gave a short description to identify each shot and listed its accurate duration. The scripting journalist viewed the film to see what was in it and to understand the shot list, then wrote the script.

In some ways this system is still the ideal when voice-over scripting is required, as it often is. But time requirements and times themselves have changed. First came sound-on-film, which meant that sound could be gathered from the scene on the film itself as it was being shot. This changed reporting and editing styles, and established the pattern of operation which is now in use with portable videotape recording. And then came electronic news gathering, with even more portable cameras and recorders, with helicopters and field-to-studio live links.

Time pressures have also increased, so although the camera crews and editors can work faster with more versatile equipment, they cover more than they used to, over a wider area. Reporting and editing time gets shorter and shorter.

Most newsrooms have come to terms with time pressure by reducing field reporting to a formula in which the reporter puts as much of the material as possible on tape in the field, as the pictures are shot. This reduces editing time later and may do away with the need for anything but the intro (and the needed cues) to be written back at the studio.

In spite of the ease with which voice can be added to tape in the field, it often happens that script must be written for a succession of shots taken on location with only natural sound. Shortage of time means shot-listing has been by-passed in favour of a quick look at the shots by both editor and writer. Then the pictures are edited to match the script written by the journalist.

Even if the voice-over segment is only a small part of a package report, it is still a second-best way to do the job and those who have been long enough in the business to have experienced shot-list scripting know it. Editing pictures to words saves time but costs quality.

Editing pictures to script often results in "wallpapering", which means showing pictures which do not relate directly to the story being told. The most recognisable examples are lines of unidentified people walking in or out of what is presumably a meeting room while the words explain what happened inside, or of participants in a court case filing or out of court while the words give details of the evidence. There are dozens of examples on television every night.

They are there because television video editors believe viewers must have something to look at, relevant to the story or not. It is almost as if any picture is better than looking at the newsreader. In reality this is not so. When the words and the pictures fail to connect directly, to complement each other, the pictures dominate, which means the viewers' attention is on what they see, not what they hear. The whole story is often wasted.

Video editors used to be able to edit so the pictures told the story in the best visual manner. Any film or tape editor knows that pictures have a natural length — cut shorter and they become meaningless, even indecipherable as images on the screen; cut longer and they may become boring. This edit-before-scripting system is today restricted to quality-conscious productions. In the news field this means documentaries and current affairs programs with lengthy filmed or taped segments.

In the business of learning how to script voice-over material, whether it is a whole news item on edited tape, something much longer for current affairs, or only a segment of a packaged item, novice scripters will improve the quality of their work by writing from a shot-list rather than insisting that the pictures be edited to a prepared script.

For news scripting purposes shot-lists are easy and quick to make. If the reporter whose task it is to do the scripting can see the edited tape it takes no time to jot down the significant points in its content, especially those to which script reference will be made. Most editors are only too happy to supply shot durations, or durations from one point of direct reference to another, if they think it will end up a better script. There are proper formats for shot-lists. They are used in the making of documentaries and feature films, but such fine detail is seldom necessary in news work.

With shot-list in hand and the content of the viewed tape freshly in mind, the scripter must consider even more before starting to write. What is in the introduction, or what will be in it when the reporter has written it? What is in that portion of the report on tape recorded in the field? What is on that portion which will follow the voice-over section? Repetition in a script is poor reporting.

There are some guidelines to bear in mind.

- Voice-over scripts allow for three words a second, counting full stops as words and commas as half-words. Reading on camera may move at up to four words a second, but in voice-over the picture demands much of the attention of the viewer. In any case, slight pauses in the script make for better comprehension of the whole message, especially when the picture is a dramatic or demanding one.

- Don't even try to say what is clearly visible in the picture. Why say "this is. . ." when every viewer can see what it is? If the picture tells the story there is no need to tell it again in words. Use words to say what the pictures can't, to explain, qualify and detail.

- It is unwise to write a script shot by shot, even if the shot-list is accurate enough to enable it to be done. It sounds jerky, even when the timing is precise.

- Try to make the words match the key references in the picture, but not by making them appear at precisely the same time. It seems staged to do so. Words either lead viewers to look for something in the picture or add explanation to what has just been seen, leading or trailing by half a second or so. Common sense is the best guide.

- Thus it is best to time from reference point to reference point in what is to be shown, counting the seconds to find out the number of words required to do the job. If the script overruns the first reference point by ten words (3.3 seconds) and it is seven seconds between reference points, there is room for only ten words and the full stop (3.7 seconds) in the lead up to the next reference point.
- No matter how few seconds are available, there is no excuse for any lack of accuracy or balanced reporting. This is why it can help if
- the reporter who will write the script can see the raw material from the camera before it is edited.

It sounds mathematical and compared with other types of news writing it is, but the aim is the same — total comprehension. It happens only when there is total fluency of pictures and words.

Scripters accept from the start that they must work with pictures which are not natural. It is an edited newsfilm/tape, not an actuality account of what happened. It can only show a tiny portion of the whole event, even if that tiny portion contains the most important aspects. It is up to the script to provide the facts that the visuals can't, facts such as when the events happened, especially why it happened, and if the pictures don't make it clear, how it happened.

Good scripters take care to have the words move at a constant pace. It is no use having the reader race through one portion to keep "on cue" and then dawdle through the next. It can happen, even when a reporter is recording his own scripting. Such speed variation sounds wrong, therefore it is wrong.

And it is disastrous to write a script which overruns the end of the edited tape. This means the words have not ended when the picture has, so the words either go on "in black", run into the next portion of the package for which there are already words on tape, or over the newsreader waiting to read the next item.

When a script has been completed, even if only a short portion of a news package, rehearse it and time it, to make sure it fits. If it doesn't, fix it before handing it in to the sub-editor or producer.

Journalists are directly concerned with the writing of scripts rather than the taking of pictures, but they must remember that the picture is part of the total message. It is often the most important part of it. This means that although the scripter must choose carefully what few words are used, those words do not always have to make sense in themselves—sentences do not have to be grammatically complete. Usually they are and should be, but when the picture carries the story and expresses it eloquently, there is no need for the words to do so. There are all sorts of examples of this. A script for a demolition project ends "And then, promptly at 10:30 . . . (and the viewers see the old building or crumbling chimney come tumbling down).

Television reports are prepared in packages, just as in radio, and the packages include much the same segments: intro, stand-up, voice-over picture, interview segments, natural sound, sign-off. Apart from the intro and sign-off these segments can occur in any order, according to what is most appropriate for the story being told.

No matter what the story, the pictures and words must never conflict. In the viewers' living rooms there must be the most complete union possible between picture and sound.

This book will not try to explain how the important business of video editing is done, because techniques vary according to the equipment used. In colleges or universities students may work with U-matic, VHS or Beta equipment which is effective but slow. If they are fortunate, they will use Super-VHS or more professional VBU units.

Television station newsrooms use VBU editing units in one form or another, or developments of them, but the input can come from a variety of sources. Some still use quad. (2-inch wide) tapes on much bigger machines to do their editing instead of the newer, more compact cassettes. Some edit their segments onto AVR (automatic video recorder) cartridges, or dub onto them after editing, for versatility in the control room.

The range is too wide to attempt to cover, but there are some hints about editing which make it easier for all involved to achieve a smoother, more professional end product, no matter what equipment is used.

Get to know as quickly as possible what is on the tape. Many portable camera-recorder units permit playback on location, even if it is only through an eye-piece viewer and low-quality headphone. If it will play back on the scene for the camera operator it will play back in the car on the way to the studio for the journalist, as long as the camera operator is co-operative. If notes made on the scene are not as adequate as the reporter would like, check with the tape.

This means that by the time the crew gets back to the editing facilities in the studio building the reporter may not know the lengths of all the shots but will know what has to be included. Also, he or she will know what part or parts of any interview should be included in the story and if there has been time enough will have made a note of the cues and where they fall on the recorded tape. This saves a lot of time. Journalists are seldom permitted to do their own editing — the equipment is too complex and expensive — but looking over the editor's shoulder is allowed and has advantages. If the journalist who is to write the intro and the script can see the editing being done, some sort of shot-list forms automatically in the journalist's mind, if not in a notebook. A script also forms in the mind as the editing progresses, which means sensible suggestions can be made to the editor.

Too many editing suggestions, specially ill-considered ones, are not welcomed. They distract and slow up the editor, who in most cases can be relied on to produce a better picture sequence than any but the most experienced reporters can manage. The idea of looking in on the editing is to allow the journalist to write to the picture — still the best way of doing it — rather than providing a recorded script and expecting the editor to cut to that.

In editing speech, with or without a picture, remember to allow the person speaking to breathe. Don't cut so hard at the end of one sentence and the beginning of another, even with a suitable cut-away picture, that when they are dubbed together they sound like one.

If a journalist watching a video editor edit sees a cut made for which there is no obvious reason, he or she should ask about it, but only after the editing is done for the day. It is a short cut to unpopularity to stop the system when there are deadlines to meet. Most experts are willing enough to talk about their work and how they do it, especially to people who show an intelligent interest and want to learn, but only after the pressure is off.

Editing, more than any other part of the television journalist's job, comes from learning on the job. Those who have an opportunity to try editing for themselves should do so. It is the quickest way to understand the problems of video production. It also speeds the gathering of material in the field if the reporter, as well as the person behind the camera, knows how to avoid editing problems.

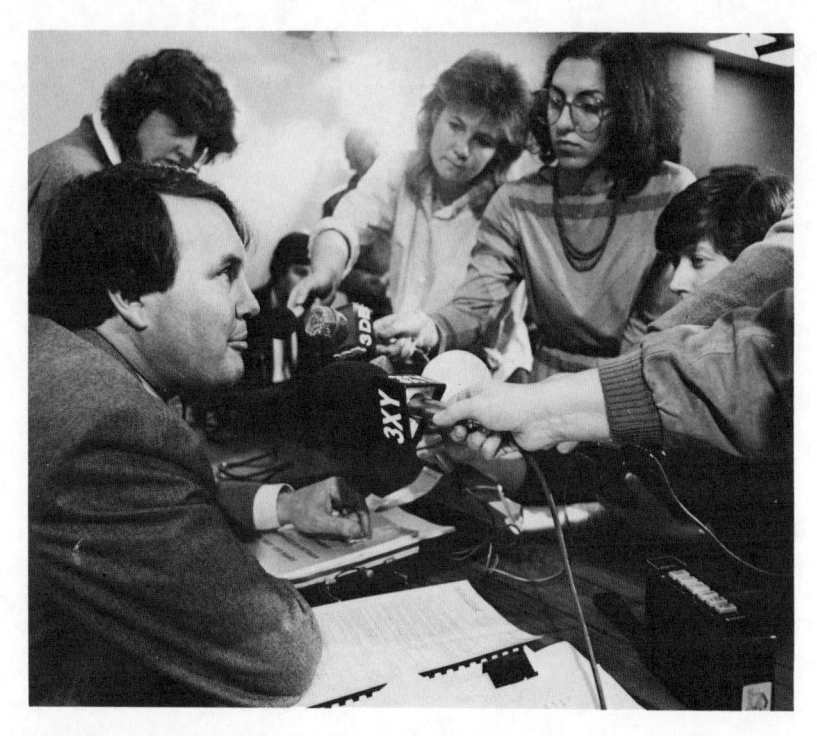

Interview or news conference, it's the best question that gets the most informative answer.

(Picture: Geelong Advertiser)

The art of it

About interviewing, which is an art.

Knowing how to do all this—the reporting, the gathering and presentation of voice reports and pictures, the formation of a competent and interesting news bulletin—is one thing; doing it effectively is another. It requires training and skill.

"Any fool can write," say those who have never tried.

"Any idiot can ask questions," say those who see an interviewer at work and think they could do as well.

Try it. It is not as easy as it seems. Asking questions is one thing. Asking the right questions so that the answers say something is quite another. Asking the right questions in the right way so that the answers are concise and self-contained is another thing again.

This chapter is given its name because it is mainly about interviewing, and good broadcast interviewing is an art. Some journalists who are brilliant in other aspects of their work can never be more than competent in interviewing for radio or television. Even for those who know precisely how it should be done, good interviewing for broadcast still requires a knack which some people don't have and don't seem to be able to acquire.

No matter who is to be interviewed the interviewer should never forget that the purpose of an interview is to elicit information. That may mean seeking facts, opinions, explanations or impressions on the subject matter in question, all in the interviewee's own words. The listeners and viewers can then form their own opinions on what is said and how it is said. If the interview does not yield such information it is a failure.

In broadcasting, especially on television, many interviews generate more heat than light, with interviewees occupying uncomfortably hot seats. In such a position they are not likely to answer spontaneously. They may not answer at all if the questioning is too tough. Sometimes such encounters are entertaining; more often they are not. They are seldom good news interviews.

An interview is not a discussion. The interviewer's opinions are not relevant, so they should not be expressed. There are very few exceptions to this. The audience wants to hear what the person being interviewed has to say. That is why the interview is taking place. The interviewer is there on behalf of the audience, to ask the questions the audience members have no chance to ask for themselves.

The interviewer must appear to be impartial and as objective as his or her knowledge of the subject matter allows. Sometimes it is necessary for the interviewer to play devil's advocate to introduce opinions, even to take a position contrary to that of the person being interviewed, to win a more spontaneous or enthusiastic response. But such an approach should still leave no doubt that the stance being taken is not the personal one of the interviewer.

Don't confuse the position of a news interviewer with that of the "talk show" host or interviewer. Hosts conduct discussion programs and those who are invited to take part in those shows, or who choose to phone in, are encouraged to express opinions so that highly paid broadcasters can express theirs in reply. It makes for lively broadcasting, though it is not necessarily news. It is a show, not a newscast. The interview techniques used are the same as in news, but their intent is different.

The news interviewing process proper begins long before the first question is asked. It begins when an interview is assigned, and for a wise reporter even earlier still. News staff should always read their own publication, and others, to maintain their background understanding of who is making news and why.

Many interviews are undertaken without being specifically assigned. In the gathering of many stories interviews are necessary. Some are thrust onto the reporter at short notice in the process of gathering information. More often there is time to choose who is the best person to interview. It is not always the one who is most obvious or most readily available. Choose the person best qualified to speak on the subject or in the particular situation, and if possible choose someone who speaks well.

Remember that in broadcasting the audience has only one chance to hear and understand what is being said. It is possible to edit out a question which is not clearly expressed, though it is an error if it occurs that way. It is impossible to edit out the answer. It must be clear first time. The best way to achieve that is to ask clear questions.

Almost every phone call a journalist makes seeking even the most basic information is in reality a simple interview. The aim is to elicit information and it is best done by asking straightforward questions.

When an interview is assigned, the backgrounding should begin in more detail. According to the person or persons involved, the interviewer may choose to consult Who's Who?, library indexes, newspaper files, or a variety of other references to gain more information. If the subject matter is a specialised one, the interviewer should consult specialists. Most will usually help willingly enough once they realise that they are being asked so that an interview on their subject will be a useful and intelligent one. The request must be for the benefit of the interview, not of the reporter's ego.

This is an instance where a reporter's "Jack of all trades" level of knowledge is simply not good enough and should be admitted. Not so many years ago a journalist with a few years experience built up a genuine "Jack of all trades" general knowledge which sufficed for most interviews. In today's more specialised world this general knowledge is too often not specialised enough. So don't worry if there is something you don't know, as long as you know where to find out. The important thing is not to display your ignorance by asking stupid questions.

Journalists working for radio or television stations seldom have as many resources immediately available as those working for a newspaper, but they still have to prepare as much as possible for interviews. Current affairs reporters need even more preparation, but most of their programs have research staff to lighten the load.

Take the example of preparing for a relatively simple interview about a new service to be offered by a community organisation. What can be done to prepare for it?

Have any stories been written about the service, the need for it or how it is to operate? Has the organisation sponsoring it sent the newsroom any background information or handouts? Refer to these first.

Then try any contacts who might be able to provide more background on the service or the need for it. For instance, are there any government reports on the subject? Find out.

At a pinch, try phoning a local university or tertiary college to speak briefly with a lecturer who has knowledge in the area of the new service.

All this takes time and too often there is no time to spare. Typically everything is rushed in both radio and television newsrooms, so there will be precious little time for research. In spite of this, the more time spent in preparation the better the interview will be. The "talent" — the term used to refer to those who are interviewed — will expect the interviewer to have at least a basic grasp of what is to be talked about. The more the reporter is prepared, the more the interviewee is complimented and likely to open up.

To go into an interview knowing nothing is an insult to the interviewee and reflects on the professional ability of a reporter and the credibility of the news operation. The best way to see that this never happens is to read newspapers regularly, take in as much as possible of radio and television news and current affairs shows and read as much as possible in areas of personal news interest. Reporters who "keep up to date" diligently can usually handle short-notice interviews with a minimum of preparation, and can manage some "off the cuff".

Three types of interview

Basically, news interviews are of three types: informational, interpretive and emotional. Some involve two, or even all three categories.

An **informational** interview is, as the name implies, about getting information. It is the type in which most young reporters will be most involved when embarking on their careers. At its simplest it involves asking a person who has experienced an event, or has information to impart about it, what happened, so as to gather the information to write a story. Part of the total interview may end up as a segment within the finished story. Depending on the questions, the descriptive abilities of the person being interviewed and the packaging ability of the journalist, the members of the audience may feel they have shared the experience of the event.

An example might be a person who witnessed a robbery telling what happened, or a state premier announcing a major building project.

In this type of interview the interviewer is seeking only information—the facts. A good interviewer will already know most of the facts, and hence the expected answers, because of research already done (or because the facts have already been made available in a handout or speech). The audience wants to hear the key facts from the lips of the authority, the one who really knows. The interviewer's task is to extract the information so that the audience clearly understands both what is being said and the story as a whole. In most of these interviews the reporter is not an expert or authority, but the interviewee is.

Many such interviews arise when a reporter arrives at a news scene with little or no knowledge about what has happened, rushes around gathering facts because the deadline is approaching, then finds someone who can explain what happened because he or she saw it, or was part of it. A quick and informative interview serves two purposes: it informs the reporter and in turn informs the audience at first hand.

But there is a trap in this type of interview, especially in the example just cited. Eye-witness accounts are notoriously unreliable, even inaccurate, even when the witness genuinely tries to tell the truth. People like policemen and journalists are trained to observe accurately but they soon realise how fallible their observation can be. Ordinary members of the public have no such training, nor any obligation to try to see things objectively and in perspective.

Every eye-witness account needs checking, usually with other accounts. The penalty for not checking can be expensive in credibility, if not in court costs.

There are exceptions to this and they are usually the very best of informational interviews, the person who has a dramatic story to tell and is the only one who can tell it; the swimmer who has just beaten off a shark attack, the sailor who has survived a week or a month on a life raft, the family who has just won the lottery. There are many other examples but what they have in common is that only those who have experienced it can tell about it.

In an **interpretive** interview the facts of the story are usually delivered before the interview which interprets them is played. Sometimes the facts are already known to the listeners, as in a "serial" or continuing story which develops over a few days. In such cases the interviewee is usually an acknowledged expert whose opinion, explanation or forecast is sought. This type of interview is also known as a "reaction" interview.

Such interviews require more preparation on the part of the journalist. It is obligatory to know as much as possible about the subject matter of the story before asking the first question. It also helps to know something about the interviewee, at least why his or her opinion is being sought. Only if the interviewer is well backgrounded can he or she hope to pick up the significance of anything new or different which the "expert" has to say, and follow it up.

This type of interview plays an important role in broadcast work. It occurs more frequently than a straight fact-seeking interview, though it may not usually be as memorable as an end product. It is also the bread and butter interview for broadcast current affairs reporters.

A simple example of this type of interview is that which takes place with a cabinet minister after the announcement of a government decision. The prepared story gives the details of the announced change in policy (or whatever the announcement was) and the cabinet minister is interviewed because he or she can explain why it happened, what caused it and what will happen as a result of it. The answers to the questions may well contain information unknown before, but only an interviewer who really knows the background will recognise it for what it is—new and therefore news. Or it may differ from the publicly-known background so the interviewer, provided he or she knows the background, can challenge the validity of what is being said.

When seeking facts, it may be advisable to discuss the nature of the interview with the person to be interviewed before beginning the questioning, to make sure the facts are delivered as concisely and sequentially as possible. In an interpretive interview this is seldom necessary. Usually it is best to get to the questions as quickly as possible so the answers emerge spontaneously and unrehearsed. All that is needed by way of preliminary chat is to remind the interviewee that there is no need to give the facts because they are already a matter of record and already reported. If the interviewer expects answers virtually off the cuff, then the interviewer had better know the facts just as well as the interviewee, or risk being bluffed.

The third type of interview, the **emotional** one, is the one most open to public criticism, usually because the media seem to intrude on private grief in trying to get the interview.

"How can they ask that poor woman how she felt about losing her son down a stormwater drain?" The protest is as recognisable as the sloppy question "How do you feel..?" which all too often destroys what might otherwise be a satisfying interview—satisfying for all concerned, including the audience.

A journalist should always remember that audiences are made up of people, and that people are interested in people and in their reactions and feelings in times of stress. It could be a personal tragedy—difficult for any journalist to handle comfortably—but it is often a case of supreme achievement like winning an Olympic gold medal.

Emotional interviews are not uncommon, so by comparison protests are rare. The audience learns through such interviews the feelings of unionists involved in a long-running strike, or of mothers so incensed at government inaction over road safety precautions that they form a human chain across the road in front of the local school.

It is the strength of the feelings and emotions—anger, joy, fear, delight, anguish, laughter—that the interviewer has to capture. It calls for tact and sensitivity, especially in cases where the emotion is grief. It also demands impartiality to the point of detachment, which is not always easy.

The news conference

There is another type of interview most journalists encounter sooner or later; the **news conference**. It used to be called a press conference before the broadcast media arrived and sometimes still is. It is not a fourth type, since it invariably becomes one or more of the first three, yet it presents problems found nowhere else. For a news conference journalists from different media gather—too often compete—for a common interview. The requirements are no different from those explained above, but the techniques may be vastly different.

In some ways news conferences are the least productive type of interview, simply because too many journalists are there trying to extract some response from the interviewee. It need not be that way and often is not. Media practitioners have become astute enough to realise that in unthinking competition they are cutting each others' throats.

News conference organisers have also become more astute and realise that a mass gathering of reporters is the best way to get information across unchallenged. Usually the news conference is called by the interviewee to get the reporters together for a hand-out.

At most news conferences there is little chance to conduct a fair and balanced interview. The person who called the conference arrives, usually makes an initial statement which everyone records or notes and often opens the conference to questions, knowing that the handout information has already been effectively passed. It is a type of media manipulation which can get out of hand unless reporters are alert.

The first problem for the broadcast journalist is that if anyone in an audience is to hear anything, all the microphones have to be at the front, on the podium with the major speaker. Often there is a battery of microphones attached to the front of the podium or lectern, or whatever the speaker is using. So rule one is to take a long microphone lead, so that no matter where the recorder has to be, the microphone can be within listening range. Rule two, closely associated with rule one, is to take some masking or insulation tape, so that the microphone can be taped in position and not knocked down, inadvertently or deliberately, by someone else.

The second problem arises when it is time to ask questions. With so many journalists clamouring to have questions answered, few stand any chance of having those questions "heard" by the microphones in front of the speaker. They are too far away and facing the wrong way. So note the questions, even if there is no record of who asked them. Questions asked in such situations are in public domain. Anyone can use them, together with their answers.

In the past, when radio and television reporters were so shortsightedly competitive that each insisted on asking his or her own questions, the same questions were asked over and over at news conferences. Even live coverage of some major conferences didn't put an end to such a ridiculous practice. The use of more sophisticated editing equipment and the ease of editing videotape has changed all that.

The conference caller can still manipulate the news media by managing the question time. When everyone asks questions at once, the respondent can choose which question to answer, or even who to answer. Thus the person calling the conference is clearly in charge of proceedings. This still happens and will continue until reporters learn to make use of each others' questions.

There is no reason why everyone present should not record the answer to a good question, no matter who asked it. The print reporters present will certainly note it for their use. Neither is there any good reason why either the same reporter, or another who wants to follow the same line of questioning, should not ask a follow-up question to make the situation even more clear. Exclusive stories don't come from news conferences. But if reporters want to act intelligently instead of aggressively, news conferences should yield news and not just selected information chosen for release by the person who called the conference.

For radio and television purposes, a news conference is a story which has to be told either from the studio or by voice report on location, with interview segment or segments inserted, regardless of whose questions are used. They can be written in. The important part is to record the responses "loud and clear". If each reporter has a chance to ask a question, well and good, though there are seldom that many intelligent questions worth asking.

Regrettably it is radio and television reporting that has made news conferences less productive than they were when only print reporters attended. It is the broadcasters also who have given the "doorstop" interview such a bad reputation. Politicians know that broadcast journalists, television journalists in particular, want a short statement which gets to the nub of what the person has to say. So they prepare just such a short statement to make on the doorstep of parliament, or wherever else they are interrupted by journalists seeking short, sharp interviews. The result is that the short statement is precisely what the politician wants reported and not what the journalist really wants to hear. It is almost certainly not what the public, whom the reporter allegedly represents, would have asked if they were given the opportunity.

No matter what type of interview it is and regardless of who is the interviewee, the interviewer should treat the interviewee with courtesy at all times. It doesn't matter whether the person interviewed is a fool, a shyster or a convicted criminal, the journalist is only an interviewer, not a moraliser, inquisitor or attorney. Be respectful but not subservient in all interviews of all types. There is no need to be servile to anyone, regardless of their age or rank. Neither is there any place for arrogance or superciliousness. Interviewers are there to get information, not to make fools of their interviewees or of themselves. If either is a fool it will show in the end product without further effort on the reporter's part.

Interview locations

There are three basic locations for interviews: in the studio, at the news scene and on the telephone. There are advantages and disadvantages in each.

The advantage for the broadcast journalist in a **studio interview** is that he or she is working on home ground. There is technical assistance on hand to make the recording, which means the journalist has to think only of the questions and to follow the answers carefully. There is no need even to operate a tape recorder. In a studio the journalist may not even have to hold a microphone.

The disadvantage of studio interviews is that many interviewees are intimidated by the studio surroundings, especially in a television studio. A radio studio, with its switches, dials, recorders and headphones can be bad enough. A television studio with lights, peering cameras and floor crew is far more disrupting. For many people, especially those who are not accustomed to being interviewed, the studio situation is too strange and unnatural for them to relax and do the job well.

If the reporter knows his chosen interviewee has never been interviewed before, it is best to opt for an **on-location** setting, even if the chosen location is right outside the studio door. At least both interviewer and interviewee are on neutral ground.

Sometimes the on-location location is, either by necessity or choice, a place where the interviewee is most comfortable, such as a home or work place. In gathering interviews for use in newscasts, which means they will be used as short inserts, it is usually a case of the interviewer going to the interviewee. It saves time. It is the current affairs interviewer, with quality in mind and with a little more time to do the job, who has a choice of location.

There are problems in being on-location, but they are technical ones rather than matters of content or the comfort of the interviewee.

From a purely news point of view **the phone** has a disadvantage which exceeds all others. It is impersonal. Too often reporters meet people on the phone whom they have never met, nor are likely to meet in person. They don't know them, yet they expect them to divulge accurate information. Over the phone it is hard to tell whether a person is telling the truth or lying, saying it with a sneer or a smile. There is hardly a single reporter, working in radio or anywhere else, who doesn't admit to relying on the phone as a most convenient last resort but who would prefer to interview face-to-face. Broadcasters can seldom afford such time-consuming luxury.

In face-to-face situations the reporter can see how the person questioned responds—non-verbal communication, as it is called, can transmit a lot of information. So, at the scene, the reporter can ask that extra question that puts all previous answers in a new light, or at least makes clear the interviewee's attitude to the subject in question. This the telephone interview can't do.

The telephone interview can't capture the intangible, the look in response to a question, the shrug of the shoulders which says something words can't. Over the phone there is only what people say and how they say it—often that is a lot, and very revealing—but all too often it is not the whole story, or even the whole reaction to the story which the reporter wants. So telephones are fine for hard facts, but it takes a very experienced telephone reporter to winkle out an in-depth interview, with all its nuances, over a length of wire. It is too easy for the person on the other end to give superficial answers and get away with it.

Telephones are used almost without exception to gather information on the "disaster" round; the police, ambulance, hospital, fire station calls checking on accidents and mishaps. True, most of this reporting is informational—seeking facts rather than explanations—but not all of it. In many cases it is the only way such a round can be achieved. There is no time for the much preferred personal visits every day.

With this in mind here are some tips on using a telephone for gathering news:

Don't ask "anything doing?" It happens most often during phone checks on police or industrial rounds and it almost always invites a comfortable and work-avoiding "no". Why should the person on the other end of the phone bother to tell you anything, unless that person is a valued and cultivated contact of years' standing? Look up your "Where is it?" contacts book and it is quickly evident how many people you call every day, or at least regularly enough to maintain the sort of contact which will prompt them to tell you anything which might make work for them. Most often they will fob you off.

Do your homework before getting on the phone. Know what's going on. True, it will often be necessary to phone a contact without a specific inquiry, but still avoid the "What's doing?" approach. Make up a question, especially if it can be one which shows genuine interest in the contact you have been cultivating. Never make it sound as if you don't care whether there is anything to report or not. It leaves the impression that you, and by association your reporting colleagues, are lazy.

Be clear in your own mind what it is you want to know before you get on the phone. Have some questions thought out in advance, even if not on paper. Then ask them, so it appears there is good reason for the call.

Be authoritative when you ask questions. Make clear that you have the authority of your employer behind you in every inquiry. To do this you will have to identify yourself and your employer on almost every occasion. But then there is no reason why the person on the other end should not know who he or she is speaking to and who they represent. After all, it is where the eventual news report will appear.

No matter who you talk to, be courteous. It is the same with face-to-face interviews, though possibly more difficult to achieve on the telephone.

Be alert to any reference to something you don't already know about. If you have backgrounded yourself properly for the telephone interview and the person still manages to mention something you don't know, perhaps you have a whole new story. Keep up to date with all the latest happenings on anything you are asked to report, especially if you are expected to report it by telephone interview.

Always be ready to conduct an in-depth interview — presuming, of course, that you have done enough homework to be able to conduct one. As the name suggests, interviewing "in depth" means inquiring more deeply than what appears on the surface of any event or situation. It is a good rule to ask at least one more questions than you need for the day's immediate news story. The answer may indicate that there is more to the story than you think. If there is, don't be content with the half of the story which is readily available. Exhaust all avenues of questioning in one area before you move on to another. Make the most of the limited time you have on the phone, but don't ever assume anything. Ask that extra question to make the respondent's inference or suggestion absolutely clear.

Don't hang up too quickly. Once you have the information for which you first made the call, ask if there is anything else your respondent might like to say. Is there anything else happening in that person's area? Sometimes — admittedly only sometimes — the reply results in a better story than the one chased originally. It is always worth the try.

In all this, remember you are representing a company, perhaps a whole organisation, and certainly a newsroom with other journalists. Never do anything which will prejudice their work in news gathering. Perhaps the most obvious aspect of this is to remember to say "thank you". Courtesy costs nothing, but its rewards are immense. Next time you call, that same person will remember the polite "thank you", or any other courtesy you have offered, far beyond the subject of the interview itself. This may sound trite: it's not. There is no excuse for discourtesy by any journalist, even to those few interviewees who choose to be rude. Politeness is a professional necessity.

Interviewing by telephone has only one advantage — time. It is also an essential tool for gathering background information and arranging a time and place for a proper interview.

Planning the questions

Having done as much research as possible and thought out carefully who is to be interviewed, plan the actual questioning carefully. This does not mean that every step from start to finish should be worked out in advance. It is better if it is not.

Planning means working out what ground is to be covered — far more important in broadcasting than in print, where a selection of the material can be made by the reporter after the interview is completed. In broadcasting, especially gathering information for a news item, planning helps cut the interview down before it starts to that which is important enough to have a chance of being used.

A good broadcast interviewer tries to record no more than is needed to capture the information sought. In some news interviews this may be as little as one well-planned question. In other interviews the total recording time cannot be estimated in advance because there is no way of knowing what the interviewee is going to say. He or she may say something quite unexpected, which means the interviewer should follow it up. It could lead anywhere.

Current affairs reporters usually plan their interviews in greater detail. They forecast the way the interview will progress, setting out the areas to be covered in the most likely progression, but always allowing for surprise digressions.

Few good broadcast interviewers write out their questions. This does not mean they don't write out anything. In the process of planning they **make key-word references** to the areas they intend to cover (in news seldom more than one or two, unless it is an unusual interview) and beside these, more key-word clues to the actual questions they want to ask. Each one of these questions is mentally rehearsed, to make sure it can be expressed succinctly and clearly. In the interviewee is an expert in the subject he or she understand a vague or loosely worded question; the audience may not.

There are two very good reasons for not writing down the questions, or at least for not taking them into an interview in written form. An interviewer using written questions tends to read them, so that in the middle of what should be natural conversation the question suddenly sounds stilted and artificial. Worse, artificially-delivered questions all too often invoke equally artificially-delivered answers.

The other reason is that an interviewer with written-out questions is so busy checking the wording of the next one there is no time to listen. The next question may or may not be delivered well, but is it the right question? Was there something said that should have been followed up? No one can read and listen attentively at the same time.

Listening is the key to good interviewing. It is far **more important to listen** than to have all the questions ready. In some ways it is better to listen than to have any prepared questions at all, even as key words. No one advocates going into any interview without some idea of what should be asked but a good listener who is adequately prepared finds that questions flow naturally from what is being said.

Just as important as not writing down your questions is not giving the interviewee a list of the questions. This can ruin the interview. Those who want to know ahead of time what is to be asked usually try to cram all the information into the answer to the first question. There is no intention to spoil the interview, after all the interviewee is part of it. It is a natural reaction for a person who knows he or she is going to be asked about certain things, to jump the gun and come up with answers, but not necessarily the ones the interviewer is seeking.

Occasionally reporters seeking interviews with top-level businessmen, or even some public officials, are told by the "great man's" public relations assistant that an interview will be possible only if a list of the questions is provided. There are ways around providing what is asked for and still safeguarding the wording of the questions.

Usually it is the public relations person, not the "great man" in person, who wants the list of questions, so that guides to the answers, or even precise answers, can be prepared in advance. People don't get to be "great men" of industry or government without knowing their jobs well enough to answer most reporters' questions without the aid of a public relations assistant.

There is no reason to be coy about what areas the interview is to cover, in fact there is good reason to be open about it. If the intention is to ask the head of BHP about the price of steel or co-operation with the Chinese in a joint venture, he has a chance to check some necessary figures in case he needs them in the interview. He certainly doesn't need to know what the question will be.

If, however, the intention is to ask about BHP's plans to build an office in a regional town, the chief executive may well have to look up quite a deal of detail if he is to answer the question adequately. It is fair to give him that opportunity by telling him in advance that there will be a question about the office. But he still doesn't need the wording of the question. That would certainly ruin the spontaneity of the answer.

So don't tell anyone what the questions will be, only what they will be about, and even then it pays to ask the questions in an order other than that in which they appeared in the advance notice. This means the answers are not rehearsed but are delivered genuinely and naturally.

Location reporting has special requirements

When you arrive at an interview location, no matter where it is, take a look around. Forget about the questions—by now already reduced to a cue card of key words—for long enough to select the best possible spot. In a studio the chairs will probably have been set up in advance. In the field it is another question. It is useless to stand on a wharf in a screaming gale to interview a waterside worker or anyone else. It is a natural position for him, perhaps, but useless for an interview.

Look for the **natural situation**. If the interview is with a ship's captain, try the ship's bridge, the captain's cabin (if invited in) or the saloon. They are places where a captain would naturally be found. For a manager, an office is a natural setting, for a traveller the airport, for a doctor a hospital or consulting room. It would be totally out of place to interview a ballerina about dancing while she was milking a cow, unless the interview established that there was very good reason for such a situation.

There are other things to watch before any questions are asked. The weather — where is **the wind** coming from and can the interview take place in shelter? Inside is comfortably safe for television interviewing, but may not be natural for the interviewee. In any case even though the camera crew has lights, it takes time to set them up and artificial lighting is seldom as good as natural light.

And what about **the light**? It is the camera operator's task to attend to getting the best possible picture but a bit of understanding from the journalist can speed things up. Open shade usually offers the best lighting conditions because it softens the hard shadows of sunlight and means the interviewee doesn't squint when looking towards the camera or interviewer.

Should the interview be conducted **standing up or sitting down**? For hurried jobs standing is easier and quicker, but will it look and sound natural? It need not sound relaxed; many interview situations are not relaxed ones. It is easier to get someone standing to face the right way, to position him or her so that the interviewer can stand close enough to ensure good quality sound. This is not always easy in a sit-down interview.

In an office, where there is little choice but to interview across an office desk, try organising a position across the corner so that both interviewee and interviewer can be heard well. If it is impossible to get good sound from both and there is no chance of using two microphones, favour the person interviewed. Questions can be handled again later or written into the final script.

Framing questions

Now to the questions themselves. Whether it is a good question or a poor one depends not so much on what it asks, but on how it is asked. It's not too difficult to work out, mentally or in writing, what should be asked, but it is another thing to ask the questions well.

In simple terms **the best questions are blunt** ones. Use as few words as possible without being rude. In broadcast interviews the journalist must come to the point quickly. If there is any chat to take place before the interview, that is when it happens—before the tape recorder or camera is turned on. Get the pleasantries out of the way, then get down to work.

This means that in broadcasting the major question can come first, a thing few interviewers in print choose to do unless their interviewee is very experienced. If the major question will be difficult or embarrassing for the interviewee to answer, it is usually best not to put it first. The interviewer should have made a list of the areas to be covered, so there should be no difficulty in starting with some other question, one that will be answered fluently and comfortably. Once the interview is moving easily, that's the time for the hard question or questions. The other material can always be edited out later.

How to frame the questions is one of the real skills of interviewing. Anyone who has watched interviews on television or listened to them carefully on radio recognises that some journalists are much better interviewers than others. It's not that they get more, or even better information, but that they seem to do it so easily. A good interviewer doesn't intrude too much, so that it is the interviewee who is doing most of the talking. The good news interviewer is almost not there; only a voice asking brief questions to keep the interviewee talking interestingly.

This is done by asking **true questions** which demand true answers, not by asking apparent questions which may not need answers at all. Ask questions, **don't make statements** which vaguely seek agreement or otherwise from the interviewee. It also means you ask questions one at a time, preferably in a natural and logical sequence, and **never string two questions together**.

Short questions which are to the point and incapable of more than one meaning usually result in short, to-the-point answers which are easy for any listener to understand. Of course there are exceptions, since interviewees vary in their ability to express themselves.

Take those points one at a time.

- An **apparent question** is one which sounds like a question but really isn't. It does not specify what information is sought. All too often a less than efficient interviewer asks a question like "And what about the budget?" Well, what about the budget? What is the question? What is the interviewee expected to answer? There will be an answer, i but it may not be what the interviewer expects and it may allow the interview to get out of hand. There are dozens more examples which should spring to mind. The question does not do the job for which it is intended: to get an answer to something specific. Had the interviewer asked "Why did you support $30,000 for drainage works?" the answer would have been equally precise.

- **Making statements** is another sign of sloppy interviewing. Too many interviewers, even those who have done some homework beforehand, come up with statements like "Councillor Smith says your drainage plan is wasteful," and leave it there. It is not a question. It is a statement that leaves it up to the interviewee to frame the question. He or she may reply: "I don't agree with that." More likely it will be "So what?" in which case the interviewer has to re-put the question or move on to a new one without getting an answer.

  Making statements also means that the interviewer's voice is heard at least as much, perhaps more than that of the interviewee, which is poor interviewing. It is also very difficult to edit, because the answers don't make sense on their own.

- Another type of **statement question** — it is a question, but a poor one — goes this way: "Do you agree with Councillor Smith, who says that your drainage plan will waste council money?" The likely answer is "No," which means that the interviewer has had to use 16 words to elicit one. Many statement-questions are much longer than that. Sometimes the interviewer embarks on a lengthy exposition of background before getting to a question that can be answered with a "yes" or "no". Any question that can be answered with one simple word is a poor one unless such an answer is wanted.

- There are often occasions on which the answer sought is a blunt **"yes" or "no"**. On those occasions be careful not to ask a question that rules out both of them: "Is it a waste of money or not?" What can the respondent say? What would "yes" mean? It is also important to make sure the context of your question is absolutely clear, both to the interviewee and the audience, or the response might be a confounding "it all depends what you mean by waste". If you have done this you can afford to keep it simple and straightforward: "Is it a waste?" The answer must surely be "yes" or "no".

- The perfect follow up question in almost any situation is **"Why?"** – the best word in the interviewer's verbal repertoire.

  Asking questions in their natural and logical sequence is not as difficult as asking them well. Those who listen to what the interviewee is saying find it a lot easier to do both than do those who spend time worrying about the next question. It is not only polite to give the interviewee full attention, it is good interviewing technique. It is not difficult for those who have done sufficient preparation. They can listen in confidence because they know questions will come naturally.

- **Listening** is far more important than making notes, even for print journalists conducting an interview. By listening and paying full attention the interviewer truly hears what is being said, not just the words used. The true meaning is sometimes apparent only to those who see the raised eyebrow or hear the subtle change of emphasis. Mere words can't pass on such subtleties. Radio can catch most, television even more.

  For all that, it often pays a broadcast interviewer to make notes. It is not necessary to note anything that is already on tape, but there is much more to an interview. What of the background information divulged either before or after the taping; other observations to be jotted down in case they slip the interviewer's memory; and perhaps most importantly names and pronunciations to be checked. It is stressed elsewhere in this book but it is worth stressing again; wrong pronunciations, of names or anything else, brand an interviewer as either ignorant or uncaring. Either results in a loss of audience involvement or credibility or both.

  When making a radio interview, being **observant** means noting how the interviewee behaves and dresses: does he or she smoke and how much, does he stroke his beard or does she constantly fiddle with her handbag. All sorts of human mannerisms help make the interviewed person more real to those who listen but can't see. There are dozens of possibilities which may be mentioned briefly to add life to a brief insert.

  In television such mannerisms reveal themselves, sometimes when they should not. Having a nervous interviewer swing from side to side in a swivel chair can ruin the recording.

Who wants to be interviewed?

It quickly becomes apparent to those who do a lot of interviewing that there are different types of people on the other side of the microphone.

There are those who want to be interviewed; politicians, sporting personalities, celebrities or would-be celebrities. They usually have something they want to say and it is in their best interests to be interviewed, even though not all of them are good interviewees. Their jobs, and in many cases their egos, make them keen subjects, even when they have nothing new to say. With most of them the problem is to keep them from "waffling" or straying from the point of the question.

Then there are people who don't want to be interviewed, for any one of many possible reasons; they are in some sort of trouble, they are upset about something, have something to hide, or perhaps it is just shyness. This is where tact and careful handling of the pre-interview "chat" can work wonders. The reporter has to persuade such people that it is in their interest to be interviewed. Again there are several reasons why this should be so. Once the interview is started, it needs more tact and unruffled questioning to keep it going smoothly.

There are also those who are antagonistic. These people think all journalists are like some of the interviewers on television who throw questions like a heavyweight boxer throws rights to the jaw. The antagonism is often a false front, even when it is openly expressed. Such people are usually unaccustomed to the media and are afraid the journalist will make a fool of them. Tact of a different kind is needed to calm such people down and relax them even before starting what would be a normal pre-interview explanation or "chat". It might take two or three "throwaway questions" — ones which can later be edited out — before such people talk freely and confidently enough for the interview to be successful.

Another group, fortunately a small one, will not be interviewed unless it is done anonymously. They don't want to be named or identified in any way. Sometimes there is good reason and the interviewer should be certain to ask what it is. If the reason does not seem genuine, press for a normal interview, with proper identification. It is always more credible that way.

And there are some who don't want to be interviewed at all. When this happens the interviewer has to remember that people have a right not to be interviewed but that need not prevent the journalist from trying persuasion. Ask the reason for the refusal. It may be a business deal which may be prejudiced — a good reason perhaps — it may be something else. If the reason does not seem adequate, keep persuading, politely.

If the reason does seem reasonable, accept the situation. If a new story has emerged, an alert reporter wants to be the first to get it, so make arrangements for a later interview, just as soon as it is possible.

Controlling the interview

In all these interviews, the interviewer must remain in control of the interview process, especially with the first type of person who is enthusiastic to be interviewed. Make sure your question is answered. If it is not, ask it again. The original question can and should be repeated, if the respondent appears to wander deliberately to avoid an obvious answer. Sometimes it is a case of the original question not being understood, in which case it should be put again in different words, but it should still be put again. The repetitious portions can always be edited out if the end result sounds ungainly.

Never be afraid of repeating a question, or an answer for that matter. If an interviewer stumbles over a question, start it again. The stumble can be cut out later. If the interviewee stumbles in an answer, or stammers or stutters or simply stops, take the time to explain that it doesn't matter. It can be edited out so he or she will not be embarrassed. Just ask the question again and get the answer again.

The first time a question is put and answered is usually the most natural, however, so always try to get the interview to run smoothly first time and never discard the first take until satisfied that the second one is better.

Interviews themselves fall into two broad categories according to circumstances — the expected interview and the unexpected one.

In an **expected interview**, the reporter knows of the assignment sufficiently far in advance to make specific arrangements to speak to the interviewee in a set place at a set time. It is arranged, usually by phone, so that both parties arrive knowing what will happen. It is often in this arranging process that any necessary persuasion is done to get the reluctant person to the microphone. All the necessary introductions are made in advance and much of the background information is gathered well before the interview takes place.

The un-arranged, **unexpected interview** is the type which occurs with little or no notice. In such an interview the reporter finds a witness to an event and begins an interview on the spot. Or perhaps he or she just arrives at the office or home of someone suddenly thrust into the news—usually a person who is accustomed to the media, fortunately—uses as few words as possible on an introduction and explanation about why an interview is needed and gets on with the job.

Basic interview procedures

The aims of the interviews are the same, even if the level of preparation is different. The techniques are the same, even if in the unplanned interview the preliminaries are rushed.

What are these techniques, other than the planning and asking of questions which have already been considered?

The first is always to **make sure the needed equipment is ready**—as ready, or even more ready than the reporter. Recording gear should always be ready to go without notice. It is embarrassing to arrive for an interview only to find that there is no tape, or that the reel-to-reel recorder has no take-up spool. It is even worse to find after an interview, especially if it has been a good one, that the batteries were flat and the end result is useless or non-existent. Check first.

Always check the equipment before leaving to make an interview. In television, the camera operator is responsible for this, though it doesn't hurt the journalist to help. In radio, the journalist is also the recorder, so whether the equipment is all there and works or not is the reporter's responsibility.

Check again at the last minute before beginning the interview, no matter where it is. It is better to check outside the door than inside in the presence of the person to be interviewed. Taking time to check in those circumstances can disrupt what could otherwise be a fluent start to an interview.

It is also important to **get there on time**. If an arrangement is made for 10 o'clock, be there by 9:55. It allows time to check gear, to take a last look at the question cues or the background notes, to straighten a tie or tidy up after a journey.

Appearance is important. Reporters on the job represent more than themselves. They represent the news organisation they work for in the community it serves, so they should always be dressed appropriately.

Once on location, whether it is an office, a waterfront or an airport lounge, take a quick look and listen. To get the best sound, **find a location** which cuts out as much extraneous noise as possible. Make sure the recording takes place well away from air conditioning, refigerators or anything else which makes a noise. If the location is an office, see if incoming phone calls can be stopped by the switchboard until the interview is completed. The test recording, if done on location, can check for these noises as well as voice levels.

Television also has to consider the light and to set up the camera accordingly. Back-lighting an interview always causes problems. It may mean blinds have to be closed or extra lights set up to balance the light flooding through a window. While the camera operator is attending to all this, the reporter can get some of the preliminaries out of the way. It is also the time to set the microphone in its best position and to check sound levels. This can be done without annoying the interviewee by explaining, honestly, that the aim is to get the best possible picture and sound.

Outside, bright sunshine causes hard shadows. It also causes either the interviewer or interviewee to squint. Aim for open shade where the shadows are softer. Before recording a word, **check that all names are right,** not just spelling but pronunciation as well. Check how he or she likes to be introduced—given name, nickname, initials only—so that it can be properly written into the introduction. It may affect the way he or she is referred to in the interview. Check also that his or her title is accurately understood. It is poor journalism to introduce a secretary as a treasurer, or a general manager as a director.

Placing the microphone in the best position is not often difficult in radio, but in television it is considered best to keep it out of the picture. There is no reason for this other than aesthetics. Everyone watching knows there is a microphone, so it seldom matters if it shows. For all that, there is no need to make it more obvious than necessary. A microphone has a magnetic appeal to some who are not used to being interviewed. They talk directly to it, even lean towards it, so putting it in the right place can be important for more than just sound.

If the microphone has to go on a desk between interviewer and interviewee, make sure it is well cushioned and will not pick up reverberations from the desk surface. In such circumstances anything touching the desk — a foot inadvertently touching a desk leg or a hand drumming on the desk surface or moving across the desk — can cause disastrous and unexplained sounds on the tape. Set the mike on some papers or on a note pad.

In television, the best interview position is to have the person being interviewed looking towards the camera and the interviewer away from it. The angles involved will change according to the interview location, but side-by-side positioning always looks clumsy and unnatural. The right position is usually helped by holding the microphone in the hand away from the camera. It opens the angle between the interviewer and interviewee, rather than closing it, and this makes it easier for the camera operator.

Whether interviewing for radio or television, the reporter must always keep firm control of the microphone. It may make a nice human touch for an infant in the arms of a mother being interviewed to reach out for a visible microphone (it is disastrous on radio where the listeners can't see what is happening) but in any other situation it spells trouble. There are interviewees, usually enthusiastic politicians or zealots for a cause, who would like nothing more than to take the microphone into their own hands. Some try it.

The reporter is in charge and will remain in charge as long as the microphone is under control. Resist any attempt by anyone else to touch it or interfere with the mike by drawing it away, even if it means starting the interview again. If the interviewee goes on interminably and the interview is hard to finish, just say thank you and take the microphone away. The interview stops there.

How to deliver the questions

Even after the questions and their sequence have been worked out, there is still the problem of delivery. In radio, understanding relies on both interviewee and audience hearing clearly the questions and the way they are asked. Television often enables an audience to see the questions being asked and answered. The problems of delivery are the same for the journalists in each medium.

The first essential is to **speak clearly** in short questions. Some of the audience may not be paying full attention, especially on radio, so what is said must be unmistakably clear. Short, clear questions encourage short, clear answers, and it pays to explain to the interviewee beforehand that this is what makes the best interview. Long, rambling answers tend to be boring and usually won't be used. If they are used because the content is important, the attention of the audience will tend to drift. If the interviewee strays from the point or becomes long-winded, interrupt. Ask the question again or stop the interview completely and explain that it has been stopped because the answer was getting out of hand.

Be interested in the topic of the interview and in the questions. Animate your voice. If it sounds as if the questions are being read from a sheet of paper, especially if they are read without interest, there can be no quibble if the answers sound equally uninteresting and flat. Too many young interviewers have monotonous voices. They sound as if they are going through the motions of the interview, but aren't really interested in what they are doing.

The more interested the interviewer sounds the more likely the person interviewed is to give his or her best to the interview. It is a compliment to have an interested listener, and that is what an interviewer is. **Look interested** too, not only on television but on radio as well. Let the interviewer see that you really want to hear what is being said.

In asking the questions **be forceful in delivery**. There is no need to shout, but never sound apologetic.

When the interviewee is talking, **keep quiet** and let that talk continue unless or until it strays from the point or gets too long. Never inject "yes", or "right, right", or anything else which indicates agreement with what is being said — or disagreement for that matter. Remain the obviously impartial interviewer. If it seems the speaker needs some encouragement to continue, an interested look or a nod of the head will do the job without impairing the content of the interview or its editing.

For the same reason interviewer mutterings like "I see" and "um" can be annoying for the audience and frustrating for the editor. They also suggest the interviewer doesn't know what he or she is doing.

Question starters

In almost all news interviews, and perhaps most current affairs ones as well, the best questions seem to begin with one of six words. Each of them guarantees an answer of more than "yes" or "no". They call for an elaboration, justification, explanation or comment — just the type of answers which are most keenly sought in news, on radio or television. Those words are:

Who. . .? which asks a fact and gains a name in reply.
When. . .? which also asks a fact and gets a time or date in reply.
Where. . .? asks another fact and gets a location as reply.
What. . .? elicits an explanation or description of what happened.
Why. . .? asks for an opinion or an explanation and gets it.
How. . .? asks for, and usually gets, an effective description or interpretation of what happened.

All these questions have their place in almost every interview, but the least used and possibly the most informative of all is "why?" It is the "why" that gets to the nub of most things.

Reporters who start their questions with these words will get proper answers and not be flustered by a brief "yes" or "no". These words almost oblige the person being interviewed to make his or her position clear.

No matter how much there is on tape by way of interview, most of the facts will be written into the introduction and presented on air before the interview begins, except in the case of interviews which are outright narrative. This is fair enough, since journalists can usually recount what happened more clearly and in fewer words than most other people, even witnesses to the event. Thus the story will give the facts and the interview will give the reasons, excuses, explanations, reactions or forecasts about what will happen next as a result of the event reported.

This is the most convenient and most effective way to use interview material in both radio and television news. It is another story in a direct narrative interview where the person being interviewed is the only one, or one of very few, who can actually tell what happened. In such interviews, usually dramatic and absorbing for interviewer and audience alike, the explanations, excuses and all the rest are usually included in the answers. Such interviews almost conduct themselves.

One question which has been overworked and consequently irritates many of the audience is "How do you feel...?" The idea is acceptable; after all the aim is to make known how the interviewee reacts to an event, even an intensely personal event. The problem is usually the tactless, even unfeeling way in which the question is asked. Often such a question is entirely unnecessary. It is apparent, even on radio, how a person feels. Everything a person says and the way it is said tells the audience how that person feels, so why ask the question at all? This sort of insensitivity, particularly if the person is distraught, labels the interviewer as either callous or stupid and loses audience sympathy.

In some cases a "How do you feel" question is asking the impossible, not because the person asked does not feel, but because the question calls for an expression of inner emotions from a person who does not normally express such feelings freely. It should be no surprise when they express themselves in cliches or don't express themselves in words at all.

If it is reasonable to ask about people's reactions, the art is to ask briefly and tastefully. No one questions the interviewer's right to ask "What is your reaction to the opposition's statement that...?" or "How do you respond to...?" or even "But the mayor says that...?" The interviewer's problem is how to reduce this type of reaction-seeking question to a simple, straightforward one. Too often the interviewer becomes so entangled in explaining the background or the reason for the question, that the question itself becomes vague and unclear.

When the interview is over, check names, initials, pronunciations, anything that will help in the story itself which is not covered in the interview. For a radio journalist the job is just about finished, but not so for the television reporter.

The television interviewer on location has to **think forward to the editing** to make sure that the end product will fit together. When the main part of the interview is over it is time to consider **reverse, or cutaway questions**. This inter-cutting is a technique in which the camera position is changed so the interviewer is seen asking the questions but the interviewee is not seen answering them. It is not necessary to record a reverse for every question, but it is up to the journalist to know which ones will, or may, be needed.

In news work many interviews are reduced to one or two questions, even though five, six or more may have been asked during the recording. The selected answers have to fit together when edited without the picture of the interviewee appearing to "jump". Maybe the interviewed person was smiling in answering the first question but scowling for the second, or leaning forward in the first and back in the second. In either case editing the two together will look clumsy. This is where reverse questions come in.

Reverse questions, or a brief shot of the interviewer listening and reacting to what is being said, can also be used to edit down excessively long answers to something more manageable. But they have to be well done or they look as clumsy as the jump cut they are intended to replace.

Shooting reverse questions

The best and simplest way to shoot reverse questions or reaction shots is to do it immediately after the interview in the same location. It automatically has the same lighting and sound characteristics. On such occasions it pays the journalist to explain to the interviewee what is happening, otherwise it is strange to hear the same questions put again without any answers expected.

And it must be exactly the same question or questions. Any change in the wording can make the original answer meaningless or misleading. For this reason is pays to note questions as they are asked, or if this is not possible, to play back the interview to listen to the precise questions, so that they can be repeated. Some television interviewers use a small audio recorder as well as the television equipment just for this purpose, and for planning the editing later.

Consider the difference in meaning which would result from asking, during an interview with the organiser of a charity jumble sale, "What sort of things will you sell?" and then in the reverse question wording it, "What sort of things won't you sell?" It is an easy error to make, especially after hearing the initial answer, yet it makes that initial answer mean just the opposite.

Often it is not possible to make the reverse question on the spot. The interviewee may not have time. The office may be needed for something else. Perhaps there is no room for the camera to move to the right position to shoot the reverses. In such cases both journalist and camera operator have the responsibility of finding a second location which looks and sounds the same and setting up the camera so that the journalist appears to be in the same location as he was at the actual interview. Getting the camera position wrong makes the end result seem artificial and the edits obvious. Being too high or too low, on the wrong side of the interviewer's face, or even too far to the side, can ruin the best-asked question.

If the camera looked over the interviewer's left shoulder for the main part of the interview so as to get the subject of the interview almost full-face and only slightly to the right, then the reverse should see the questioner from the reverse angle — as if looking over the interviewee's right shoulder so as to see the interviewer almost full-face and only slightly to the left. The two will then intercut cleanly. Having to do this away from the original interview scene makes it doubly difficult.

If the person who has just been interviewed can be persuaded to stay to see the reverse questions made he or she will realise that every attempt is being made to present the interview honestly, with no wrong emphases being injected during the editing process. It will also be obvious it is not just an ego trip for the reporter.

Then pack up and leave quickly. In radio this is easy. Television has more gear to move, but the journalist can help the camera operator to get the place cleared away, making sure no mess remains.

Outside the door, stop and check again. Is there anything that has been forgotten? Look at the notes made beforehand and make sure all areas have been covered. If there is a gap in reporting, it pays to find out before the crew leaves the premises. Check also that the interview is safely recorded, by replaying a few words. If it is not, there is still a chance it can be repeated, after checking the equipment.

In all interviews time spent in planning is always repaid in the recording and editing. The smoothness in editing the end product also endears the reporter to the editor, colleagues and to the employer.

One of the key points to remember is not to record more than is necessary. There is no need to have the recorder running during any warm-up period. It may not matter much in radio, except that it adds to editing time. It adds much more in television. By recording only useful material, editing time in either medium is cut to a minimum.

The reporter is not obliged to ask the interviewee whether recording may start or not. In an interview situation it is obvious that there will be a recording made. It is usually best to make it obvious that recording is starting, either by visibly turning on the recorder or making some comment which lets the interviewee know that his or her voice is now being recorded.

This can present a different problem in telephone interviews. It is neither ethical nor legal to record a telephone conversation without the consent of the second person. For all this, it is not necessary to ask for permission to record. If you have telephoned for an interview the person phoned knows that at some stage there will be a recording.

It is best to tell the person that the recorder is being started. If the reporter asks "May I record?" the answer could well be "no", even though the person to be interviewed never thought about it before. Asking provides the opportunity for this obstruction. Telling the person that recording is beginning still allows the interviewee to object if he or she really wants to, but it seldom happens. The person being recorded can tell that the recorder is still operating, by the "beep" sound which is fed back down the phone line by the recorder unit.

Planning the end product can continue on the journey back to the studio, provided the reporter has some means of playing back what has been recorded. While the camera operator drives, the reporter can work out what portion or portions of the recorded interview will be used and what the "in" and "out" cues are for those sections. By the time the crew has returned to the studio, the reporter should be able to tell the line-up person precisely how long the interview segment will run (to the second) and how long the whole item will run, including the intro.

Whether the reporter does the editing, as is customary in radio, or someone else does it, as is customary in television, it pays to label the tape clearly. Every tape should carry on its identifying label—usually provided by the newsroom—what is on the tape, if necessary and possible where it is on the tape, and the speed at which it has been recorded. It should also carry the reporter's name and the date of recording. So a typical reel-to-reel tape for editing should be labelled, "Smith interview (and perhaps the subject or Smith's position), by Jones, Feb 21, 3:15, at 7½ ips."

"The voice of the people"

In both radio and television the "vox populi" type of interview requires yet another special technique. "Vox populi", or as it is called in the newsroom "vox pop", means "the voice of the people". Such an interview, or more correctly a series of interviews, conducts a straw poll of the opinions of people in the street.

The idea is to record a number of opinions, responses or reactions to a particular statement, event or occurrence. But in doing so the reporter must remember to ask the same question every time, in precisely the same words, if all the answers are to be relevant. If the same question is put, a string of answers can be edited together one after the other without the question being repeated too often on air.

Normally there is an introduction which gives the facts of the story, so that the audience knows what it is about. Then come the "vox pop" responses, strung together as briefly as possible, to give a quick assessment of how the information was received by the "ordinary people" in the street. Obviously the art is in framing the question in such a manner that each answer will stand alone (It does not need the question in front of it to make each answer intelligible). The answers need take only a few seconds each, preferably less than 10. Long answers destroy the effectiveness of the story.

"Vox pop" interviews lose their interest value quickly if they are used too often. After all, they have nothing but interest value, since no one can contend that such an interview of so few people can be an accurate representation of public opinion. It is snap opinion from a few people, not a public opinion survey. But there is no doubt that when used properly a "vox pop" can add interest to a news or current affairs program.

Don't make promises

Perhaps a final point on interviewing. After any interview at all, whether it be an individual one, a news conference or a "vox pop" involving several different people, never—never—announce to anyone when it will be broadcast. It is seldom the reporter's responsibility to decide what will be put to air in any specific bulletin or current affairs program. There is no way the person conducting an interview can know what other news is or will become available to compete for limited news time.

Telling people that an interview will be used at such and such a time on such and such a station is asking for trouble. It embarrasses the reporter who makes such a silly statement. It embarrasses the person interviewed, who may have advised friends and suggested they watch. It can embarrass the management of the station when an irate interviewee phones in and asks why an interview has not been broadcast.

The easiest way out is never to promise anything. By all means say, if asked, that the interview is being recorded for inclusion in the 11am news if that is the case, but always leave a loophole. There can be no guarantee that any item will be broadcast at any time, so don't give one.

More research, more careful writing and editing and more time for considered presentation are the basic requirements for current affairs broadcasting. It is only one of the many avenues into which broadcast reporters can expand.

(Picture: Channel 10)

Wider aspects

Some comments on current affairs and documentaries.

$\mathbf{A}$ journalist wit is supposed to have said that while the radio news reporter chases fire engines, the public affairs reporter is down at the fire station talking to the fire chief about how to improve the service. There is something in that. It illustrates one way in which the approaches to news and current affairs differ.

A range of program formats come under the umbrella of current affairs radio and television. Some, like the ABC's "Four Corners" cause Royal Commissions and result in public figures being jailed. At the other end of the spectrum and visually much more spectacular is the sight of a camera crew chasing an allegedly shonky business operator over back fences.

In radio, current affairs programming ranges from the prestigious ABC programs "AM" and "PM" to an announcer on a small country radio station, whose task it is to fill the 9am-noon time slot, asking his or her prospective interviewees to bring with them a list of suggested questions. It does happen.

The number of current affairs or public affairs programs on radio and television rose rapidly in the late '70s and '80s with the advent in Australia of popular, as opposed to serious, current affairs. Highly-paid broadcasters, only some of them trained journalists, began interviewing newsmakers on air and expressing their opinions on anything they thought might interest their listeners. Those who were good at it won high ratings and endorsement from the ratings. The era of "infotainment" and the talk show had arrived.

Some AM stations—like 2GB in Sydney and 3AW in Melbourne—went over to a total talk format, mixing talk-back with discussion.

At about the same time, television executives began experimenting with more public affairs television—nightly current affairs programs and breakfast talk shows.

The ABC showed the way years before with programs like "Four Corners" and "This Day Tonight", which enjoyed popularity among the traditional ABC audience, and it was an ABC "ex-patriate" Michael Willesee and others like him who proved that current affairs programs could also rate on commercial television.

By the late '80s the Nine Network's "A Current Affair" had a stranglehold on the 6.30 time slot in most capital cities, and regularly topped the ratings. And the spectacular success of the same network's "Midday" program, conducted by a "hard" journalist turned "soft" host, confirmed that "info-tainment" had also arrived in television.

It all meant more jobs for journalists and camera crews, but the rise in radio and television current affairs output has also seen a change in the way current affairs is covered.

On breakfast television talk shows, for instance, the researchers are directed by an executive producer or chief of staff in lining up those who will be invited to appear on the program. They discuss the main points as the researcher and guests see them, discuss and arrange the preparation of any visual material needed before program time, and organise any props needed during the interview.

The researcher also produces the first version of the on-air introduction to the interview, and suggests possible lines of questioning. A presenter may do half a dozen or more interviews during one day's program, and needs to be "fed" background material on each. While they read widely to keep as up-to-date as they can, the presenters can't be expected to interview a series of people on different topics without a bit of help.

If an interview is about a new book, the interviewer may have had time to scan it, but rarely to read it thoroughly, because of other commitments. So the researchers on these programs are very important—they often decide the way the interview will be conducted.

The changes have been most far-reaching in radio. The size of the station usually determines the size of the staff assigned to help the on-air personalities produce and present their public affairs programs.

A small country radio station may only have the on-air presenter to line up those to be interviewed and he or she may have to rely on the local newsmakers to provide interview suggestions. Many of those to be interviewed during one morning's program may be contacted the day before and allocated a particular time. Or they may be contacted the same morning before the presenter goes to air, especially when their interview is prompted by a news story.

If the station is a bit bigger, there may be an assistant to the on-air presenter. It may be a secretary assigned only to help in the run up to, and during, the program. It may be someone who can offer more help.

In the major capital city stations, particularly the talk stations and the ABC, there is a large group associated with each of the major talk programs — usually a producer, a researcher, and several others to help contact people in the news.

All stations, large or small, rely on co-operation from the newsroom. They need to know what news is breaking, and who is likely to be available to talk on a particular topic. That's why many of the senior researchers and program producers are senior journalists. Most have more background in journalism than their on-air presenter. Sometimes it is the producer or researcher who is the "real" journalist in the team. They are the ones with the contacts and the background knowledge who know where to go to find suitable speakers for an interview segment.

It is one thing to know who you may be able to talk to, it is another to know who is the most appropriate person and also the person who is the best radio or television "talent". And to know where to find that person at a few minutes' notice is another valuable asset.

A current affairs reporter for a program like "PM" or "The 7.30 Report" has more time than a news reporter to devote to the preparation, gathering and presentation of a story. Consequently the report is expected to go into much greater depth.

The main difference between news and current affairs is that a current affairs item looks at as many of the news angles of a story as possible and looks at them in one story. It must present background information to put the event, announcement or decision into perspective. A current affairs reporter seeks out alternative views to those put forward in the initial story. He or she tries to round out the story, to make sure it is complete, so that the end result is a balanced explanation of the event, announcement or decision.

A news reporter will seek out the same background, angles and reactions but will seldom have the chance to use many of them in the same report. Hourly deadlines mean that most major stories have to be written several times. With each rewrite new angles are information are included and material already broadcast eliminated. This way each new angle, even if closely related to the original event, tends to become a separate story.

The news story may last a day or two in its various forms – longer for major serial stories – but because of the nature of news bulletins, no single story will try to cover all the angles at once. Few items try to present the whole picture. There isn't time.

The current affairs reporter should have the time to do a complete job.

Sometimes, for reasons of economy, the reporter who does most of the news reporting and best knows the subject is detailed to write the current affairs report. Sometimes the longer report is done by a completely different team. It depends on staff numbers and station policy. A foreign correspondent, for instance, would cover both news and current affairs stories.

Where a news report may last 50 seconds or a minute, often less, a current affairs report can run anything from two to ten minutes – more if the program's producer considers the story of sufficient merit and interest, like the Middle East crisis of 1990. The story and its many facets were given wide coverage for months – the hostages, the refugees, the economic blockade, the build-up of armed forces in the region, the politics, and the television "war" between the leaders.

Take an item closer to home, like a ministerial statement, as an example of the differences in approach and treatment given the same story by news and current affairs programs.

The first news reports will contain the details of the statement, in which the minister announces a government decision. The story contains the decision itself, the reasons for it and its implications for the future, all in less than a minute—six to eight sentences, between 140 and 180 words. Even at its simplest it can be handled in any of three ways: a straight read, read with voice report, read with interview clip. For succeeding bulletins the reporters seek comments on the decision from the opposition as well as representatives of those groups which will be most affected by it, such an employers, trades unions, farmers, businessmen or mothers at home. Each time the resulting stories are brief. Each time the "bones" of the initial story will be included but the lead will be new information. Each time the style of presentation should change so that even with minor content changes the story will sound different.

Sometimes, usually in the longer bulletins, the lead is a composite of decision and reaction, or opposing reactions. Probably no two bulletins on the same station on the same day will use the same version of the story. The thrust of the story changes with each new injection of fact and opinion. That is the nature of radio news. Where possible the stories, even the shortest of them, will have a voice report of some kind, perhaps from the political reporter, perhaps with brief inserts from the announcement itself and later from those who comment on it. Again, it is unlikely that any single insert will be used very often, or that more than two inserts will be used in the one report.

The current affairs reporter has the task of drawing all the threads of the story into one complete and balanced item. If the decision was announced early in the day and has already been heard on radio news for some time, the current affairs reporter may choose to begin his or her story with a summary of the reaction to it, assuming that the majority of the audience already knows the basic information about the decision.

For all that, the current affairs report still has to carry the essential points of the announcement. It is never safe to assume that anyone has heard anything often enough and completely enough to have a thorough understanding of it.

The item is also likely to include the key part of the minister's actual announcement, certainly at greater length than what was used in the news bulletins. Then, all in the one item so they can be compared and assessed, the current affairs report will carry comments from an appropriate member of the opposition, discussion of the political or economic implications of the decision with an academic or a respected senior political journalist, reactions from community groups which may be affected, and most likely end with a summary which ties all the strands together.

A good news reporter, one who really knows the job, can also prepare reports for current affairs programs. A good current affairs reporter is usually a good news reporter as well. The differences are in approach and productivity. A news reporter is expected to provide new items, or new angles on already broadcast items, for as many of the daily bulletins as possible. A current affairs reporter will usually do only one story a day, sometimes two, so is expected to make a much more comprehensive job of the end result. There is more time to devote to the research, the planning, the gathering of the information and the editing.

There is also much more "lead" time for current affairs; that is the time between editions of the program or the time allowed specifically for the preparation of a report. In news, especially if the story is an important one, there is no lead time at all. The editor is quite prepared to break into a bulletin already on air to insert a "newsflash" if a genuinely important event has just happened. At a maximum, a news reporter's lead time is the next bulletin, usually less than an hour away. In the breakfast or drive-time sessions it may be only half an hour, which means about 20 minutes to get material ready.

A current affairs reporter has more time than that. Depending on the time of the event being covered and how often the program goes to air, there could be a whole day, two or three days, even a week, to get it ready. In some cases television current affairs programs work on a lead time of two, three or four weeks. "Four Corners" reporters may prepare no more than one story every couple of months; longer if the story is a complex one.

In radio, most current affairs programs go to air daily; in television, nightly and weekly. If news breaks late in the day, current affairs staff can still be under intense pressure to get together an in-depth report for inclusion in that evening's program. Sometimes the only way to do it is to interview people "live", in the studio or on location. It makes production more complex, and some of the control over the length of the item is lost, but it gets material to air which would otherwise have to wait until the next day. The ABC's "PM" does it often.

All reporters need the same contacts and sources, but those in news use those which require time-absorbing research much less than reporters in current affairs. Most current affairs programs have researchers on staff, so that the backgrounding takes the reporter no longer than necessary.

Also, there is a greater tendency in current affairs to use reporters with specialised interests or academic backgrounds. A news reporter needs to know something about almost everything, or at least know where to find out in a matter of minutes. Current affairs, because it is expected to go much deeper, can afford to employ expert reporters in economics and politics, and other subjects frequently in the news, like the environment. In current affairs, where the interviews are longer and therefore in more need of direction by the reporter, the research must be complete enough so that the reporter can keep the conversation going in the required direction.

Perhaps the most frequent criticism of radio news is that it is so short and so simplistic. The same critics lavish praise on current affairs programs, all too often simply because they are longer. In reality, they are different versions of the same thing—both impart information to an information-hungry public, one as briefly as possible, the other as completely as practicable. Summarising the essentials of a major story into a few well-chosen sentences while retaining total understanding is often much the more difficult task. Many news reporters would love the time and resources available to reporters on current affairs shows and are jealous of their research facilities. On the other hand, too many news reporters think that preparing material for current affairs must be easier, since for current affairs reporters the clock runs more slowly.

It is not so. A five-minute current affairs report, compared with a one-minute news report, should have five times as much information built into it. It is not a case of "just allowing the interviewee to run on". A good current affairs program should move no more slowly than news; it should only seem to do so. Without a steady flow of new and interesting information the program will pall, and the audience will tune out.

Much the same can be said of a whole range of programs based on news: radio specials, features, talk shows, sports programs, even commentating, and "live crosses", which occur when there is a major event happening. They all involve journalists, working either as news reporters or current affairs reporters.

Consider the highly competent reporting which occurs when there is a major flood or bushfire. Reporters are called in from wherever they are, in news or current affairs, to make sure that all the information possible is passed to the waiting audience. They do the job without any of the audience knowing or caring what the reporter's everyday job is. In news, current affairs or the preparation of so-called special reports, good broadcast journalism is the basic requirement.

At some time in their careers, most reporters will be asked to provide material for a sporting program — perhaps the most frequent of all special programs. This means that all journalists, even those normally on political, council or court duties, must have a working knowledge of the rules of major sports and perhaps some of the minor ones. That means that in Australia a reporter should have some understanding of both forms of horse-racing, greyhound racing, cricket, tennis, all codes of football, motor-bike and car racing, basketball, and now that we are performing well in the international arena, in yachting and hockey. Few do, so the assignment editors have to be careful who they assign to what program or story.

The more a reporter knows about all sorts of things, including an understanding of a variety of sports, the more versatile and more useful that reporter will be. Writing sports stories is perhaps the major specialised area in informational broadcasting, and one of the least well done. For confirmation of this, listen to almost any news service during the "silly season" around Christmas and New Year, when much of the news concerns reports of cricket, tennis and yachting.

True, many such reports are no more than results — who beat whom, by how much and in what conditions — but if it is a major sporting event it is another matter. The story then requires all the attention of any major news item, with voice inserts from the winner, the loser, from the spectators, the umpires, comment from the experts. It is built up, in news or current affairs, just as any other story, because sport is still news. People want to know what happened, when and how.

That means that anyone involved in sports reporting should spend the same time in research and in preparation as for any other story. They should read what is available, or at least as much as possible, on the more popular sports. Most regular sports writers and broadcasters do this anyway, and keep the critical information they come across for later use. It usually comes in handy. They keep up-to-date rankings on the sports they cover and know where to find up-to-date information on sports not regularly covered. Many keep files on individual stars, teams or even grounds, depending on the sport. They maintain the same close contacts as a first-class political reporter, so they always know where to find players, coaches, managers, trainers or other administrators they need to make their stories complete.

It is the responsibility of the sports specialist to keep his or her audience up to date with happenings in that particular area, in just the same way as any other reporter in the news field. That means having an understanding of what is reported. It also means preparing reports in a language which the audience can understand, even those who know little about the sport in question.

The language used is the most frequent criticism levelled at sports reporters. Many seem to think that because they have built up an understanding of the sport and learned its jargon terms, they can use them in their reports and be understood. How many Australians, glued to their radio and television sets during the America's Cup competition, would have stayed there had the reporters, most of whom become fairly knowledgable about yachting, used terms such as "pointing higher", "slots" or "reaching" without adequate explanation? They worked hard to make sure those jargon words they had to use were readily understandable to the audience. They were good journalists.

Yet listen to any weekend's sporting extravaganzas on radio or television and there will be plenty which is not readily understood. Worse still, the same terms will be used over and over, whether they are understandable or not. Why are so many kicks "towering" and why do so many more pass "across the face of goal"? It is verbal laziness, or worse, incompetence. And these days no teams "wins", "loses" or "is beaten". Such words seem too tame for sports reporters. They have to use hyperboles such as "hammered", "decimated", "thrashed", "took out" or perhaps "were taught a lesson". It wouldn't be so bad if they could think up some new exaggerations, but those in use are so hackneyed that "win" and "lose" sound refreshing. Such reporting is not good journalism or good broadcasting.

Sports reporting is far more parochial than most other reporting in Australia. Among journalists in the southern states, who understands the object of a game of Rugby or League? Probably even fewer than those in the northern states who know how to score in Australian Rules, despite the arrival of interstate teams. Anyone who wants to be a journalist, let alone a sporting journalist, should find out.

It can be argued, of course, that sport itself is parochial. What the audience, regardless of medium, wants to know is what happened to "their" team. Did it win or lose and how? Reporters should remember that sports reports are for partisan audiences, but this does not excuse partisan reporting. Reporters, no matter for whom they broadcast in what town or city, are still impartial observers, reporting what happens, even if it is "their" team which is involved.

The same can be said of any kind of special or specialised report, in the arts, in science or medicine, in education or anything else. Such reports are usually the work of people who know their subject matter. They must know it so well that they are immune to the intensely-held opinions of people on either side. It is almost a truism that the more specialised the subject the more intense the opinions held about it. Journalists have opinions, too, but it is poor journalism to allow them to show in reporting.

Time and again reporters are thrust into the position of having to prepare special reports in areas in which they may not be specialists. Think of the regular broadcasts on traffic flows, unusual weather conditions, beach reports, or what's on in town for some festival. The information may well be gathered by people working in the specialised field, but on most occasions the final report is prepared by a journalist.

No matter what the report is about or for what kind of program it is intended, the aims remain the same: what does the audience need to know, what does it want to know, and what will interest its diverse members? With these yardsticks in mind a competent journalist who has a reasonable understanding of what is happening in the world outside the newsroom can prepare an acceptable report in a minimum of words.

Sometimes special programs can be initiated by the journalists themselves. In the process of researching the background to a council decision to build a new swimming pool, the reporter concerned may become so interested in the facts uncovered that it becomes obvious the audience will also be interested. Why not? It may not be a reasonable rule to say that what interests the journalist will also interest the audience — that is too subject to personal whim — but it can be a reasonable indication. Many fascinating radio specials have resulted from an alert reporter, working on one story, finding background facts which build into another. Sometimes they are so absorbing that they are the foundation of what has come to be known as a documentary.

Documentary is a term which applies to film and broadcasting only. It is the broadcast equivalent of a major feature article, or even a series of feature articles in a newspaper or magazine. As with feature articles, most of them arise from the news, but not exclusively so.

Documentaries, whether on radio or television, fall into two basic types, regardless of their style of production: news documentaries which deal with matters of current interest and as such must be prepared in a relatively brief span of time; and cultural/sociological documentaries which deal with lifestyles, customs, institutions and art forms. All documentaries are concerned with people and what affects them, but they still fall into one of these two basic categories. Even the most profound documentary programs about the great events of history are about people, are told by people involved personally or through personal research, and explain what those events mean to people today. In a documentary, the journalist is one of the involved people.

Documentaries must be factual — there is no excuse for getting facts wrong — but they are not always so scrupulously impartial in their presentation. Many successful documentaries are dramatised re-creations of events. Such re-creations by actors playing parts are obvious and popular on television, like the "Dismissal" mini-series which re-created the political events of 1975 which lead to the sacking of the Whitlam Government. But re-creation is not so obvious on radio. It has to be made clear to the audience by the program's producer that the voices being heard are not those of the real people, but those of actors. The event can still be very live and realistic—the program is a poor one if that is not the case—but it can be a misleading, even dangerous fraud if the listeners don't recognise the program for what it is, a re-creation.

The essentials of good documentary making are present in all news and current affairs programs but more than just essentials are needed in a documentary. They also need abundant research plus imaginative production and presentation. All good documentary producers are first and foremost good reporters, but in expanding into documentaries they become interpreters. They have to explain complex issues, sometimes so involved that the meaning of what has to be explained is concealed beneath a mass of much more obvious, but perhaps misleading, facts.

Before anyone can start writing a documentary all relevant material has to be researched so thoroughly that no apparently misleading fact will divert the proper course of the production. Every aspect of the background has to be sought and checked, using press clippings, relevant books, government reports, independent reports, specialised magazines and recognised experts on the subject.

The producer often interviews dozens of people, including some only remotely connected with the documentary's topic, who may play no part in the final product. These are witnesses to events, participants, others who have conducted similar research before. The research people dig, dig and dig some more.

A documentary producer doing the job properly will live, think, breathe and dream the subject matter from the earliest stages of planning until the final mix is made. He or she may be hard to live with for that time, but the documentary will benefit from it. All the information presented will be interesting and relevant, with no avoidable errors of fact or anachronisms which can destroy a program's credibility.

All this scavenging for material and striving for total comprehension usually means that the hardest decisions are those about what must be left out, not what should be put in. This is the same whether the end product is planned to run five minutes or 50. Only those who have done thorough research can make those hard decisions with confidence knowing that the right material has been used.

The five or 50-minute reference is also relevant. If good documentaries are the result of good planning, the duration of the program is part of the planning process. It is no use setting out with the intention of making a program to run five minutes and then making it longer because there is too much material. If it was considered worth five minutes of audience interest at the start, it is probably worth very little more in spite of what material is found. There are exceptions, but few.

Because radio relies entirely on sound, radio documentaries set out to create an atmosphere and to appeal to the listener's imagination. Radio deals in the music of the spoken word. A well-chosen presenter reading a fluent script is an acceptable presentation, but the voices of the actual people, speaking in their own words, are unbeatable.

Music can help build an atmosphere. Use "Roaring '20s" music and the audience automatically shifts itself into that decade, even if not in personal memory. But use recognisable music, or a recognisable type of music, only if you can use it sparingly—unless, of course, the documentary is about music.

Atmosphere, with or without music, is necessary in both major styles of documentary production—narrative and non-narrative. The narrative documentary, in which the carefully assembled segments are linked by an equally well-prepared script which a narrator presents, is usually considered the easier to make; though no documentary is easy to make.

Often the best narration comes from the ad-lib comments of those involved in the topic. They speak with a conviction born of experience and a depth of understanding or emotion which is hard to write into any script. The more the content and continuity emerge from the material itself, the closer the documentary comes to the second type of production. Skilled producers often claim the greatest documentaries are those with little or no formal narration, a "stream of consciousness" technique—the most difficult of all, but also the most satisfying.

Make the beginning and end of any documentary memorable. Obviously, the interest must be sustained for the entire duration of the piece, but the beginning and end should be the high points of that interest. If the first impression on the audience is a good one, preferably a compelling one, they will listen or watch for more. If the end is equally compelling, that is what will be remembered most. Few people remember all of what they see or hear, but if the subject interests them enough they remember the beginning and the end, and more of the middle.

So the beginning is critical. No amount of time and effort in getting it right is ever wasted. It has to be succinct. Documentaries often begin with a series of brief comments from segments of interviews which are repeated later in the program, like headlines before a news bulletin. They must be short—only a few seconds each. Twenty seconds can seem like an eternity on radio. If that seems an exaggeration, count the seconds that elapse in silence next time a voice report doesn't "come up" in a news bulletin, or an expected interview insert doesn't show on television. Three seconds is alarming. Five is a disaster.

The "headlines" technique is widely used to begin a radio documentary because its success is proven, but there are many other ways of starting a program. Sometimes music is used as a "scene-setter", or unusual sights or sounds are used to attract audience attention. Beginnings can charm, shock, tease, intrigue even offend the audience, or parts of it, just as long as it impresses enough people to keep them tuned in.

One of the great documentary writers, Edward R. Murrow of CBS radio and television, firmly believed that nothing caught attention as well as the right words. Since his time many have tried to emulate his use of words but few have succeeded. These days narration is seldom used right from the start. Even in documentaries which use narration for continuity, a more impressive beginning and end are almost mandatory.

The big problem with the "stream of consciousness" technique is that interest and continuity must be maintained throughout without the use of narration, aside from a brief introduction to the program. Everything must unfold from the mouths of the people who are playing the parts, or playing themselves by being included in taped inserts edited together. There will be natural sound, perhaps sound effects and some music, but no written words to be read after the introduction. Those involved must tell their story and in the successful editing together of the individual segments they tell the whole story. No interviewer is ever heard. Of course an interviewer is there.

Making the interviews for such a documentary requires many hours of planning—many more than for a documentary using narration. It also occupies many more hours of interview time. After it has been planned how each segment will follow logically from the one which precedes it, each interviewee has to be virtually "coached" into telling his or her story the right way. The producer can't put words into people's mouths, nor emotions into their actions or voices, so often the planning has to be changed to allow for interviews which did not "come out" as they were planned.

The immutable in all documentary-making is veracity. In a "stream of consciousness" documentary none of the questions will be heard in the final program. Each answer either has to be self-contained or seem to flow naturally from what has been said immediately before. This means that questions which begin "Do you think . . .?"—a poor question in any circumstances—cannot be used at all, even when they would otherwise be suitable. Every question must begin with a who, what, where, when, why or how, so the answers will make sense in themselves, needing no question as a "peg".

It sometimes takes hours to win the confidence of some of the people involved; after all it may well be their past which is being explored. It may take several different askings of the same question to get the answer that fits neatly into the documentary plan.

Once all the interviews have been recorded satisfactorily and the natural sound "grabs" and music all organised, the long process of post-production starts. For most documentary editors this means going through the tediously slow process of transcribing the required interviews onto paper or computer and editing them in that form. Usually there is time in the production of a radio documentary for this to happen. At a minimum, and only if time is short, the producer must make detailed contents lists of all tapes carrying usable material, with times and cues for those planned for inclusion.

Naturally, before anyone enters the studio for final editing, there must be a detailed plan of the program format, where each interview segment begins and ends, which piece of which natural sound will be used, precisely where and for how long, which phrases of which pieces of music will be mixed in and exactly where.

Until such a plan is complete in every detail it is a waste of time going near a mixing console. It is an expensive waste of valuable editing time and equipment to spend minutes finding a brief interview segment which "should be about there" on one of the tapes. It demonstrates poor planning and worse preparation. Producers go to the production studio to produce, not to decide on the rundown of the program.

As the tapes are edited, tighten up each segment. This means "closing up" long pauses in an interviewee's answers—unless the pause itself is eloquent and adds impact to the reply. It means editing out the "ums", "ers" and "ahs" which detract from the flow of the program. It can be argued that a good producer makes an interviewee sound better than he or she really is by such detailed editing. This is true, but the interviewee will certainly not complain about being made to sound better. The program benefits and so do the listeners.

Unless it is deliberately intended for effect, make sure the same comment is not repeated from the mouths of two or more speakers. Time is too precious on radio to be wasted by repetition. It is also wise not to let any one voice continue for too long. This is a particularly difficult problem to overcome in "stream of consciousness" documentaries, but segments can be broken up with natural sound, sound effects, or music. The audience needs a break from time to time to absorb all that has just been said.

Often two or more people in the same radio documentary have voices which sound much the same. They have to be re-introduced from time to time so the audience is in no doubt who it is they are hearing.

The pace of the presentation can also be maintained by varying the length of the interview segments. A minute-long statement from one person should be followed by one which is much shorter, or perhaps longer, and when the initial person speaks again it should be for a noticeably different period.

Most documentaries end with a final statement of some kind. It can be provocative, challenging, decisive—anything but a damp squib. Its function is to summarise the content, to remind the listeners of what has been explored and to set them thinking about the facts presented. It would not be permitted in news, but it is in a documentary if the program is to come to some sort of conclusion. It is more usual, though, since the presented facts speak for themselves, to encapsulate the arguments and let the listeners make up their own minds.

Broadcasters seldom take sides on controversial issues. Those who do jeopardise their responsibility to themselves and to their audience. For all this, producers should not be afraid to say that what they have found out from their research and inquiries is right. If there is any doubt, either say so in the documentary or don't say it at all. The facts must be right, because on virtually every issue there is an opposing point of view and its proponents will be quick to challenge the credibility of the program on any grounds they can find.

Documentaries require long and detailed scripts, whether written as narration, dialogue or the written-down thoughts expressed by those involved. Handling such a script creates problems for the presenter. It is difficult for any presenter to sound natural and interesting for an extended period. In radio, three minutes is an extended period. After a time even the best voices begin to sound boring.

The best way to avoid this is to break up long passages with a mix of natural sound or music, as long as it is appropriate. It helps rebuild the atmosphere and gives the presenter a chance to start again in a fresher, less dull voice.

It is not unusual to use appropriate music under voices to help create or amplify a mood, but the music must be well chosen and must never conflict. This means there should be no narration or interview over a vocal. Proper use of music is a skill on its own. It is good presentation to use music under dialogue or commentary and fade the music up at the end of the spoken segment. It is even better if, when the music fades up, an appropriate vocal begins. It takes careful timing and usually many rehearsals, but the effect is worth the effort.

No matter how effective or clever the production technique, it can be destroyed by over-use. It enhances the production only while it is not repetitious. Following every voice segment with music, no matter how well done, soon loses its effect or becomes annoying.

The secret of good radio production is in the chosen mix of audio resources. It must never be predictable or patterned. The production choices are wide enough to allow every program to have its own individuality, regardless of content.

And in television . . .

Everything said about radio also applies to television documentary production. In spite of the fact that the picture always dominates, sound is still important and television uses the same sound sources as radio. The dominance of the picture in television documentary-making is both an advantage and a disadvantage.

With a picture, atmosphere and mood can be created instantly, with or without appropriate music. The picture can provide much of the information and all of the description which in radio has to be provided by someone's words. This means that in covering many subjects television can say more in less time than radio can hope to achieve. But the medium's very efficiency in imparting information is a trap. Although viewers absorb information more quickly from television than from radio, there is a limit to the amount they can take in and understand. Since a documentary sets out to present a detailed examination of a specific subject, every fact presented is there for a purpose. If any is not understood, the point of the documentary may be lost.

Television's ability to present a torrent of information far outstrips the ability of most viewers to understand what they are seeing and hearing. There is thus a pace beyond which no documentary should progress. Getting that pace right is a problem not encountered in radio.

A television documentary has to maintain continuity in pictures as well as sound. Usually the two progress in tandem through the planning and production stages, but it is possible for them to get out of step. Obviously, in an interview segment where the audience not only hears what the person involved has to say but also sees it being said, there is perfect co-ordination between the two. That's the easy part. It is the pieces between interviews which need double planning. And, of course, the beginning and the end can also cause problems because their importance is no less than in radio.

Pictures have a natural length, according to most video editors. In news reporting, a reporter pressed for time may get away with the editing of pictures to fit a prepared audio track. For documentary work this is not good enough. The words must be written to fit the pictures. Doing it this way genuinely allows the picture to tell its share of the story. The words are both complementary and supplementary, even though what they say makes a vital contribution to the whole. So in the making of any type of documentary the script writer works to the pictures. This does not mean that the writer does not have a hand in the preparation of the edited pictures. Usually their order is well planned, so that they fit together as both picture and script in exactly the way the producer envisaged.

To make this work the planning of both pictures and words must precede any camera work, even purely static or mute pictures such as background shots and scene-setters. If there is any departure from this detailed pre-planning, the picture is amended first and the script re-drawn to fit it. Such departures seldom happen if the planning is done well. When it does happen, it is usually because of something unusual, a cameraman's magnificent picture which shows so much it can't be shortened, the unexpected departure of some key person, or perhaps the destruction of a building by fire.

In television it is rare to see a narrator actually speak his or her lines, though it happens when the documentary makers use a "star" as narrator. There is sometimes a brief explanation by a station presenter, only a few seconds, before the program begins. From then on it is usual to set the narration against a background picture, since television believes people should always have something to look at. Even these background pictures are usually well thought out in advance, since they tell a part of the story, maybe a large part. If the script is well written it refers to the pictures, even if not by direct reference.

Television documentary interview segments can afford to be a little longer than those in radio, since viewers can see as well as hear the speaker. Even so, they should not run too long with only a static shot of one person. Instead of reverse questions or reaction shots, so popular in news and current affairs, documentary producers prefer what is known as the "overlay" technique, or "second reel". This is where a relevant picture of what the speaker is talking about is introduced over the continuing voice. It thus makes what is being said more clear and positive, gives the viewers a change of picture and allows the picture from the interview to be brought back as required to show body language, gestures or mannerisms which will add to the impact of the statement made. Overlay is the frequently used term these days and it is also common in news and current affairs stories, but to a lesser extent.

When edited film was dominant in television—film is still popular in many documentaries because of its versatility—"second reel" was the term, since the overlaid film was played by a second projector from a specially-edited second reel of film.

Success in production depends on the planning. After planning is past the elementary stage this means involving many others. The camera operator (or the senior operator if there is more than one) can offer useful advice on what pictures will best tell the story. The audio operator can warn in advance of difficult sound problems. The lighting specialist may have problems he can forecast. The producer need not follow any of this advice if it does not match his or her concept of the program, but a wise producer will listen carefully.

Thus the planning of a television documentary is little different from the planning of a radio one, except that there must be continuity in both the audio and video strands and between the two. The picture allows television to handle changes of location, people or even time, simply by changing the picture. Most producers choose to fade to black, pause a fraction of a second, then fade up on a new picture with its new associated sound. By television production's standards it is quick, easy and effective. Because the pictures are hardly ever the same on successive occasions—probaby on no two such cuts in the whole program—it is a production technique which does not pall through over-use.

Today helicopters, but then it was cars that moved news crews from location to location. And a car was needed; old sound recording equipment was huge and heavy.

(Picture: ABC)

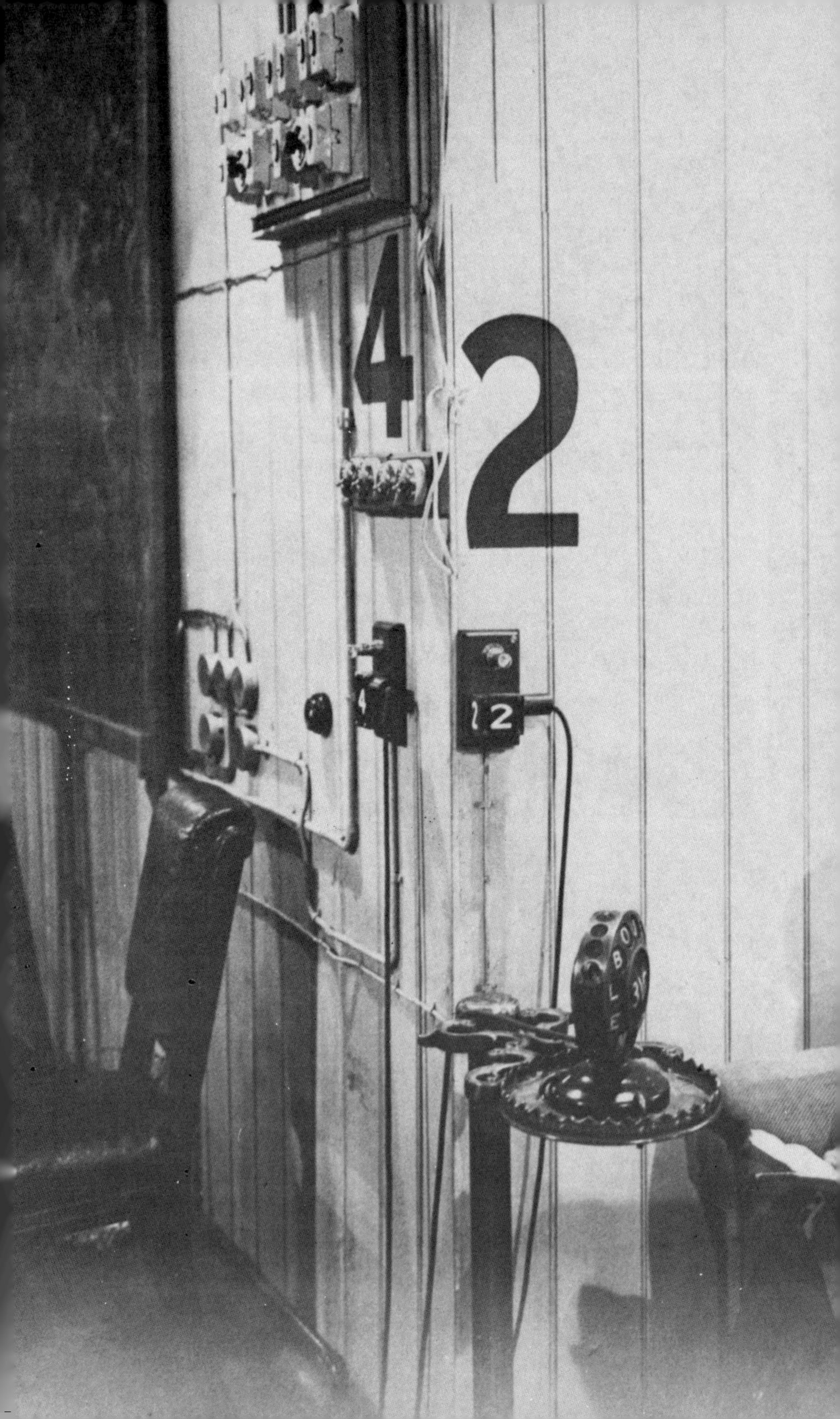
4
2
2

How the ABC announcers presented the news in its first Sydney studio more than half a century ago.

(Picture: ABC)

Times and techniques in radio have changed even more than the dress of broadcast journalism. There was a formality about information radio before the Second World War and the coming of the transistor.

(Picture: ABC)

Studio interviewing in current affairs became less formal in the 1960s but still seems clumsy and encumbered by today's standards.

(Picture: ABC)

No transistorized equipment here. This was the original control room for Melbourne's 3LO.

(Picture: ABC)

Reporting on location was not always a matter of reporter and a mobile phone. 3LO's early mobile control room was a truck of equipment and a staff of at least three, plus the journalist.

(Picture: ABC)

Keeping it ethical

About the ethics of journalism, especially broadcasting.

A regard for ethics is what elevates a journalist from proficiency to professionalism. It seems an easy transition. After all, what is difficult in maintaining accuracy, honesty and good taste while avoiding obscenities and conflicts of interest?

Those who have spent long years trying to match their everyday behaviour as journalists with the spirit of the Code of Ethics of the Australian Journalists' Association (AJA) know well that it is not always as easy as it seems.

Sociologists and psychologists claim that true objectivity can never be achieved. Even the most serious of journalists are obliged to agree with them, since they are provably right. For all this, ethical journalists still believe objectivity and impartiality are worthwhile goals, even when they know that every day they fall short of achieving them.

The problem is that what is objective or impartial to one person may not be to another. Working journalists can rest easy if they know they have made an honest attempt to present stories in the most objective, impartial way.

In news programs, with the straightforward presentation of facts and clearly attributed opinions, the attempt at impartiality is obvious. It is not always so obvious in current affairs programs. There is choice, and therefore possible partiality, in what items to use or not to use, who to interview or leave out, how much time one item gets compared with another. The partiality possibilities are endless, yet these decisions are made by journalists every day in the field or at their office desks.

It is the nature of news that such decisions must be made, and the nature of broadcast news that they be made quickly.

Every decision is a subjective decision, even though made with the best of intentions and perhaps backed by years of news judgment, so it carries the taint of bias — or it will in the eyes and ears of some people.

Novice journalists seldom have to make such judgments alone. There are more senior reporters and sub-editors around to consult and there are guidelines laid down by the AJA and the Australian Broadcasting Tribunal.

Broadcasting in Australia is governed by the Broadcasting Act and the Australian Broadcasting Tribunal, established under that Act to control commercial and public broadcasting, though in late 1990 and early 1991 the continued existence of the Tribunal as a regulatory body was under attack. The tribunal grants licences, decides on their renewal, suspension or revocation and on changes in their ownership and control. It is also required to make available information about broadcasting and to make inquiries into matters referred to it by the Minister for Communications.

The Tribunal thus controls the operation and technical standards of most Australian radio and television, and to some extent its content. It has no control over the ABC.

Section 15 of the Tribunal's new Program Standards and Procedures deals specifically with news and sets out principles which broadcasting stations must follow. This section, until late 1990 Section 27, states:

> News programs (including news flashes) transmitted by a licensee must:
> (a) present news accurately, fairly and impartially;
> (b) clearly distinguish the reporting of factual material from commentary and analysis;
> (c) not present news in such a manner as to create public panic to viewers;
> (d) not present advertising matter as if it were news.

Sections (a) and (b) are virtually the same as they have been for many years but sections (c) and (d) are genuine revisions of the former Section 27 c), dropping the controversial references to taste. That section read:

> c. Good taste should guide the selection and presentation of news

and news illustrations. Morbid, sensational or alarming details not essential to factual reporting, especially in connection with stories of crime or sex, should not be used. News should be televised in such a manner as to avoid creating public panic or distress to viewers. The provisions of this sub-paragraph apply particularly to news flashes.

A further regulation under the General Program Standards provisions, section 2(a) adds:

> No program transmitted by a licencee may, when considered as a whole:
> (1) simulate news or events in such a way as to mislead or alarm viewers.

The Tribunal in this way still gives the force of law to some of the basic beliefs of Australian journalists about how their profession should be conducted, though the regulation drafters may not have seen it this way. The Tribunal's dictates are more limiting than the journalists' self-imposed professional standards and apply only to broadcasting. There are no laws, state or federal, to impose such standards outside broadcasting. Nor should there be.

If journalists are to consider themselves professionals they should be capable of maintaining the ethical standards of their own profession and reject any form of control by governments. History has too often shown that one government control opens the door for another and Australia's unguaranteed but highly prized freedom of the press may be lost by default.

The Tribunal only goes so far. The AJA Code of Ethics, which all journalists in broadcasting and print are expected to observe, goes further. It also stresses the importance of objectivity and impartiality. The code is here quoted in full:

> Respect for truth and the public's right to information are overriding principles for all journalists. In pursuance of these principles journalists commit themselves to ethical and professional standards. All members of the Australian Journalists' Association engaged in gathering, transmitting, disseminating and commenting on news and information shall observe the following Code of Ethics in their professional activities. They acknowledge the jurisdiction of their professional colleagues in AJA judiciary committees to adjudicate on issues connected with this code.

1. They shall report and interpret the news with scrupulous honesty by striving to disclose all essential facts and by not suppressing relevant, available facts or distorting by wrong or improper emphasis.

2. They shall not place unnecessary emphasis on gender, race, sexual preference, religious belief, marital status, or physical or mental disability.

3. In all circumstances they shall respect all confidences received in the course of their calling.

4. They shall not allow personal interests to influence them in their professional duties.

5. They shall not allow their professional duties to be influenced by any consideration, gift or advantage offered and, where appropriate, shall disclose any such offer.

6. They shall not allow advertising or commercial considerations to influence them in their professional duties.

7. They shall use fair and honest means to obtain news, pictures, films, tapes and documents.

8. They shall identify themselves and their employers before obtaining any interview for publication or broadcast.

9. They shall respect private grief and personal privacy and shall have the right to resist compulsion to intrude on them.

10. They shall do their utmost to correct any published or broadcast information found to be harmfully inaccurate.

Journalists' organisations around the world have similar codes of ethics. Organisations of publishers or broadcasters also have codes of ethics and on casual reading they seem to be the same. All the codes in all the organisations have the same end: to inform the public that the organisation and its members have a regard for honesty and the welfare of the people with whom they do business. In the journalists' case this means both the people they report and the people for whom they report, the public. The Code tells the public that journalists are striving to achieve an honest, impartial and accurate presentation to the public of the events of the world.

Anyone who thinks at all about ethics realises that they are associated with, though not quite the same thing as, good behaviour. They might also realise that such ethics as are common through most of the community derive from morals (some people say ethics are morals). These in turn derive from our cultural background, especially that part based on religion.

Observing a code of ethics is a principal criterion of professionalism. All callings recognised as professions have codes which members are obliged, under threat of penalty or expulsion, to observe. The ethics of journalism, while recognised by both the Australian Press Council and the Australian Broadcasting Tribunal, are not so rigidly enforceable. The "clout" of the AJA's ethics committees is not as great as that of the Australian Medical Association or the Bar Association. Penalties do exist, however, and the greatest is expulsion from the AJA.

Ethics is a recognised subject of study allied to psychology, logic and philosophy. Researchers in those areas have defined five steps in the growth of ethical behaviour. Fear of punishment is the first. Then comes fear of being caught, which is not quite the same thing. With progress the person observes the ethics code because it results in a good feeling.

The person who is ethical because it is the right way to behave is nearing ethical maturity. This is said to be the most common stage reached by most practitioners in most professions. Full maturity is reached by those to whom ethical behaviour comes naturally at all times because they live by the golden rule and do as they would be done by — a rule which occurs in one form or another in all religions.

What happens to journalists, then, when a public radio station sets as its own policy that certain political views will be favoured? In such circumstances how can news programs be objective or impartial, or make any attempt at balance? The station's management might justify this position on the grounds that they are correcting what they see as an imbalance in the media.

An ethics-conscious journalist employed by such a broadcaster faces a dilemma. How can the beliefs of the management, with which the reporter may sympathise, be squared with the AJA Code of Ethics? In one form or another such a situation is often the first realisation most journalists have that ethics are a personal matter and that often there are no absolutes—no positive rights nor wrongs.

Like objectivity, adherence to any code of ethics is an aim. Any journalist who genuinely tries to adhere to its principles will avoid trouble. It is a case of developing worthwhile standards of professional behaviour and then standing by them, even under pressure.

Because journalists are human beings they have likes and dislikes, political preferences, prejudices and beliefs absorbed since childhood. Without them realising it, any one of these inherited or developed attitudes can blur their clear appreciation of an honest report.

A responsible journalist may think, "Why should I give publicity to that mob of political ratbags?" but doesn't act on it. To do the job properly, personal opinions and feelings must be set aside so that the report is an honest account of what happened or what was said. If Australia is to have a genuinely free press (including broadcasting) there must be room on air and in print for all shades of opinion, for all sides of an issue. There is no minority so small that its opinion is not worthy of a reporter's consideration. If minorities could have no voice, the world would still be flat.

Professional ethics demand that a journalist write an accurate and impartial report, regardless of what they think of the sources of the report. The task is to inform the audience, not to make up their minds for them.

This does not mean that controversial subjects have to be avoided, only that the opposing view—and there is always one or more on most controversial matters—should also be reported. If it can't be done in the same report, the ethical journalist makes sure that the other opinion or opinions are reported adequately as soon as possible. Controversial matters make good news and it is one of the functions of the media to make sure all views are fairly expressed.

If it is impossible to get the opposing view in time for the next news bulletin, write that fact into the story. Ethics, like justice, should be seen to be done. The audience will then know why the story so far is unbalanced and partial.

If something is a matter of opinion rather than verifiable fact, make that clear too. The Tribunal stipulates that broadcasters must separate fact and opinion. This is not written into the AJA code, but it is a basic tenet of good journalism.

The first problem for novice journalists in any medium is to learn in their own minds to separate fact and opinion. People with strong opinions tend to express them as fact and may not realise what they are doing. Sometimes this conviction carries through into the news broadcast, especially in voice inserts. It is too easy for a careless or unskilled reporter to pass on as fact what is really someone's opinion. If the facts of the matter are to be written, make sure they are facts.

Truth is fairly hard to establish in some cases, even when there are several witnesses to an event. People see different things and then interpret what they see in different ways. A clear example of this is the reporting on a single incident by eight New York dailies (when there were so many in that city). The incident was an assault by a woman on Alexander Kerensky, a Russian statesman, on the stage of the Century Theatre. Here is how each paper reported the action.

World: slashed him viciously across the cheek with her gloves.
American: dropped her flowers and slapped him in the face with her gloves.
News: struck him on the left cheek with her bouquet.
Times: slapped his face vigorously three times with her gloves.
Herald Tribune: Beat him on the head and face half a dozen blows.
Evening World: struck him across the face several times.
Mirror: struck him a single blow.
Post: vigorously and accurately slapped him.

Lack of accuracy, because of slipshod reporting, appears in the most unlikely places. The next example emanated from the New York office of United Press International (UPI), a major news agency. What appears below was the entire report and only when UPI's customers protested was more complete and accurate information supplied.

NEW YORK, FEB 27 (UPI) – A MEETING OF A NUMBER OF THE MAIN BAUXITE-PRODUCING COUNTRIES SCHEDULED TENTATIVELY FOR MARCH 5 IN CONAKRY (GUINEA) HAS CAUSED UNDERSTANDABLE CONCERN IN WASHINGTON. SOME EXPERTS FEEL THAT THE CONSEQUENCE COULD BE THE FIRST STEP IN ESTABLISHING A SERIES OF INTERNATIONAL CARTELS FOR CONTROLLING RAW MATERIALS ESSENTIAL TO THE INDUSTRIALIZED NATIONS WHICH COULD SET THE UNITED STATES ECONOMY BACK MORE THAN 40 YEARS.

Possibly this originated as a handout from an American aluminium company or from a government trade office. It was obviously sent out by the agency without any checking, since the customers (newspapers, radio and television stations) asked for and soon received a more complete and more balanced story. Some of the questions which the original story should have raised are included and in parentheses.

NEW YORK, FEB 27 (UPI) – A MEETING OF A NUMBER (how many?) OF THE MAIN BAUXITE-PRODUCING COUNTRIES (which ones?) SCHEDULED TENTATIVELY FOR MARCH 5 IN CONAKRY (GUINEA) HAS CAUSED UNDERSTANDABLE (why?) CONCERN IN WASHINGTON (to whom?). SOME EXPERTS (who are they?) FEEL THAT THE CONSEQUENCE COULD BE (unsubstantiated speculation) THE FIRST STEP IN ESTABLISHING A SERIES (should give evidence) OF INTERNATIONAL CARTELS (all cartels are international) FOR CONTROLLING RAW MATERIALS (which ones and why?) ESSENTIAL (why are they essential?) TO THE INDUSTRIALIZED NATIONS (which ones?) WHICH COULD SET THE UNITED STATES ECONOMY BACK MORE THAN 40 YEARS (who says so and how was the period calculated?).

There were possibly more queries, but that is plenty for one short story. Eventually protests came from the Third World as well, as this story is a good example of the type of "biased-to-the-West" reporting about which Third World countries are so sensitive. It is a case of opinions, perhaps including the reporter's own, slipping through to appear as facts.

Once the distinction between verifiable fact and opinion is clear in the reporter's mind it is a simple matter to differentiate them clearly in the report. It is a case of attributing the opinion unambiguously to the person who has expressed it. Newspaper reporters have few problems making it obvious to their readers what words or sentences are quotes and what are not. Quotation marks are the most straightforward way, even though writing in indirect quotes is often easier to read.

In broadcasting the audience can't see quotation marks, so it is less simple to differentiate the quotes and the opinions in copy which is to be read on air. Direct quotes are so difficult for any reader to make absolutely clear that they are best avoided. This is not always possible, since some quotes become essential to the story. Always look for a means of making clear what someone said without having use quotation marks.

Attributions are easier, but they must still be clear first time without ambiguity and should be repeated as often as necessary to make sure the audience knows whose opinion is being heard.

When the opinion statement is on tape, video or audio, it ceases to be an attribution problem. The reporter simply introduces the speaker and plays the tape.

The last thing a reporter wants, in any medium, is for the audience to think that the opinion expressed is that of the writer. It means he or she has done the job of a journalist inadequately.

The obligation to provide honest, impartial reports is the first item in the AJA code, but ethical problems appear even earlier. Deciding which items to use and which to reject is a subjective choice. So is deciding which portion of a long interview will be included and which omitted.

The first consideration is in which part of the station's news programming will the segment be used: news on-the-hour, the major news bulletin, current affairs, or documentary? It may also be for an information segment in some other program, not so directly associated with the newsroom. It could, of course, be used in several areas. There is no reason why a good interview with a celebrity can't be used in the news immediately, run at slightly greater length in the next major bulletin, used as part of a current affairs program and used again in some different form as part of an information or talk show.

The ethical aspect of the problem lies in how to make every one of these uses of the same interview represent honestly what the speaker had to say. Where a whole interview is to be aired there is very little ethical problem, apart from setting the interview in context. The ethical risk of misrepresentation increases as the duration of the interview clip is reduced. That means that where only a few seconds of an interview are edited into a brief news segment the risk can be high.

The most frequent examples of these very short grabs are from politicians, most of whom are used to broadcasting so they make sure they have ready a brief statement which makes their position clear. If the person interviewed is not so used to broadcasting the reporter should listen carefully to the story, find the "grab" which will make the point or tell the story best, and then so structure the content of the introduction to put what is said in context.

Without this consideration the words used may be accurate, so there can be no question of the interviewee being misquoted, but there is an ever-present risk of mis-reporting — a lack of honest reporting, which is a breach of the code of ethics.

Current affairs programs may use material at greater length, but it is still an ethical necessity to make sure each speaker and each view expressed is given fair and balanced treatment. Each must be balanced with or against the other interviews in the same program. There must be no distortion of any opinion gathered.

The guiding rule in this type of editing is the same as it is for interviewing. If someone else had done the editing and you were the one being reported, would you be happy with the end result on air? If not, then think again.

The need for accuracy should be so obvious to all journalists it should be unnecessary to stress it again. Yet it is slipshod checking which leads to publishers having to apologise for mistakes or, even worse, ending up in court. The only sure way to avoid this is to get it right first time.

Never accept what is said at face value, even when using a direct quote. Check that the information is correct before publishing it as fact. Those giving out information may believe it to be accurate, even when it is not. There is a newsroom adage: "When in doubt, leave out." It is good advice. Once it has been broadcast it is too late to check. Check it first. There is always the next bulletin, and in radio's case it may be only half an hour away.

There are several aspects to accuracy.

- Did the person being quoted actually say what is being reported? Checking notes, or the original tape, can confirm this.
- Was it someone else who said it? In the rush of some reporting situations it is feasible that the reporter put the wrong name to some comments. A journalist working with someone else's report or tape has to be doubly careful in this regard. If it doesn't seem right, back the hunch and check it.
- What about the spelling? Is the name really spelled that way? In many cases there is an official program or an organiser who should know, but even then don't rely entirely on them. Use Who's Who?, or any other available reference (phone book, newspaper clippings, electoral roll) as a further check.
- Check all other references, such as place names and locations, as well. Sloppy reporting habits breed sloppy habits in the newsroom and mislead the audience. If a small town is unexpectedly in the news, check both its spelling and its location. Check the direction as well. A radio news bulletin in Queensland once referred to Toowoomba as east of Brisbane, thus moving it out to sea.

Too many lazy radio journalists claim that spelling doesn't matter, since no one can see it. It has alrady been explained why it matters to the person who has to read it on air, and it comes to matter ethically if the story is later used as a reference. If spelling is wrong there is no guarantee that any reference made is to the right person. In television reports the audience sees the name when it is "supered" over the interview, so both the name and the person's position must be accurate. Getting it right first time should mean it is right for posterity.

Pronunciation also has to be right. No one is insulted when asked the correct spelling and pronunciation of their name. It is part of a broadcast reporter's job to get such things right. It is ethical reporting, too, since accuracy is the first requirement in reporting honestly. In the same way, make sure of the pronunciation of the names of suburbs, towns, lakes, rivers and overseas countries, if they appear in anything for broadcast. Nothing destroys the credibility of a news service more quickly than getting pronunciations wrong.

It is the same for foreign pronunciations. There is always some way to find out which pronunciation is correct; a native speaker of the language, an embassy or consulate, a teacher of language. Just because the word or name is not in English lazy broadcasters think so few people will notice that pronunciation doesn't matter. It does. Those who know better regard the journalists as ignorant or slipshod; those who don't know better are misled and may never learn the correct pronunciation. They rely on the authority of the broadcaster to tell them.

Taste is an aspect of reporting which is now entirely up to the individual. There is no mention of taste in the AJA Code of Ethics and the brief mention in the Broadcasting Tribunal's former regulation Section 27 (c) has been ommitted in the 1990 revision. Taste is something which defies measurement, yet it is obvious when a journalist acts in poor taste.

Taste may mean not showing upsetting pictures in the early evening television news, yet it is done regularly. It may mean not showing the victims of vicious killings or showing people overcome by personal grief, yet these appear also. Basically, good taste lies in not exploiting a situation. It is about considering the feelings of others; about thinking for a moment how the reporter would feel in the "victim's" situation.

Television is the most vulnerable medium where poor taste is concerned because it is most immediately obvious on a living room screen. There is always adverse public reaction when an obviously overwrought person is shown hounded by a pack of apparently unfeeling reporters, even though they may not be from television stations.

Just what constitutes unwarranted invasion of privacy is a matter of continuing debate. The most strenuous critics claim the invasion of privacy is never warranted regardless of the circumstances. At the other extreme, some journalists claim that the public's right to know overrides all personal considerations including privacy. Personal taste can run to equal extremes.

In Perth a television cameraman and reporter were dismissed for their alleged invasion of the privacy of a mother. She was taped as she was told by a policeman that her son was dead. Journalists across the country are still divided on whether the dismissal was justified, especially since the sacked pair's editor agreed that the pictures be broadcast.

The line between genuine news, even public interest, and the right to privacy is impossible to draw. Its position changes with the individuals concerned, the circumstances, the type of news medium making the report, and the backgrounds of the journalists doing the reporting.

A regard for the feelings of others — showing compassion — doesn't detract from a reporter's ability. It enhances it.

The showing of violence on television news programs is also the subject of unsolvable argument. Long before the question is a public dilemma it is the editor's dilemma; should a picture be excised or amended because it might upset sensitive viewers, or should the audience see the world "as it is"? The public can debate the decision for months, the editor has to make the decision in minutes, perhaps seconds.

The question is obviously not whether violence should be shown on television news — too much of what happens in the world is violent, so a certain amount of it is bound to be genuinely newsworthy. As with privacy, the question is when the news value overrides the distaste level. In other words it becomes a question of taste.

Even critics who claim violence on television is causing an increase in violence in today's society, admit that there is more justification to its brief showing on news than its frequent showing in programmed entertainment. But they still claim news editors go too far and show too much. Editors tend to see such protests as attempted censorship and are suspiciously sensitive.

Across the years few problems have occasioned more discussion than that of conflict of interest. The dilemma comes in many guises. Dilemma is the right word; those cases which are clear cut are not problems at all.

If conflict of interest is one of the most insidious obstacles to telling the truth, dare journalists allow themselves to become personally interested in politics, social causes, service clubs or even school parent and teacher groups? But then again, why not? Journalists are just as much citizens as are members of the audience.

Can a reporter who is a member of a Rotary club report accurately on that club's affairs, especially if the club is involved in what it considers unwelcome publicity? He can look the other way to remain on good terms with the club members, perhaps telling himself that he is preserving his contacts for the next story. He can report the facts and lose both his friends and his contacts. If he is lucky and the staff he works for is big enough he might be able to sidestep the issue by having another staff member write the story. If he is lucky his Rotary associates will not blame him for the story which appears.

The one thing that is certain is that it is an uncomfortable situation when a reporter has to deal with people who do not share the journalist's code of ethics. That means most people. Trying to explain it to them sometimes works, but only sometimes.

The same ethical problem arises when a journalist gets too close to any source, allowing professional familiarity to become personal friendship. When the contact is a fruitful one as well as being "good company" with whom it is a pleasure to share a drink, friendship seems natural and human. It is not necessarily a trap, but it might be and journalists making friends of news contacts should know this before the friendship starts.

Of course journalists are political animals like other human beings. Their beliefs may be strong and positively expressed on polling day, but they are wise to keep their convictions to themselves in public. Political leanings which are public knowledge reduce a reporter's credibility, at least with that portion of the audience which does not lean the same way. Journalists have entered politics, as they have a right to do, but they have usually given up journalism to do so.

Similar codes to that of the AJA are recognised by journalists' unions and associations in many other countries. The Newspaper Guild of the United States, which represents journalists mainly in the northeastern states, decided a few years ago to endorse a political candidate. Members debated long and hard on their loss of credibility in the audience marketplace and the guild has never done it since.

There is a recurring debate in Australia over whether the AJA should affiliate with the Australian Council of Trade Unions. Those who favour affiliation claim that since the AJA is a union it should link itself with the larger group which may further its industrial interests. They also claim journalists should be in a position to support politicians and parties which will in turn support them, as teachers and other professional groups now do regularly. Those who oppose affiliation argue that the risks of political taint and loss of credibility outweigh all possible advantages. It is an ethical question brought to the fore again by the move for union amalgamation.

The same caution should be exercised when there are other beliefs or interests which may sway a journalist's judgment in either determining the truth or in writing it accurately. Financial journalists are discouraged — in many newspapers banned — from buying shares. Their investments could affect their judgment in writing stories, or facts they gather may tempt them to take advantage of their special knowledge by buying in advance of the facts being made public.

Unfair as this may seem to an honest reporter, it is one of the penalties imposed by observance of the code. Scrupulous observance can hurt friendships and restrain the building of loyalties, at least publicly. It can cause a journalist to turn down what might be lucrative outside work. It can mean that a welcome, perhaps deserved, gift may not be accepted because obligations may be accepted at the same time.

Just what a journalist can and can't accept is usually called "the freebie debate", a freebie being a gift or a service offered to a journalist or his newspaper/broadcasting station in return for a report in the paper or on air. If the freebie is big enough and known publicly enough, the risk is that the report will be considered biased in the giver's favour.

Put in absolute terms, freebies are bribes for which something is expected in return — small bribes for trifling returns, maybe, but still bribes. Big bribes have happened, rarely, and those involved have sometimes been exposed. It is the regularity and persistence of the little ones which make them difficult to see as bribes and thus make them an ethical problem.

Some freebies are so everyday they hardly seem like freebies at all. Some are expected — tickets for admission to sporting events which are to be reported, theatre tickets for a stage show or a film to be reviewed, meals for reporters assigned to cover gatherings or speeches. Basically all these are freebies, just the same as an all-expenses-paid trip to Europe for a reporter or television crew to report on anything in which the provider of the fare has an interest.

Freebies come in many disguises and sometimes work the other way round. Every time there is a film premiere, concert or fashion show which could do with a bit more publicity, free tickets are issued lavishly.

Sometimes it is free clothing or jewellery, or at least an offer of special reductions, for those journalists who wish to buy.

Show business people are always eager to gain publicity, especially when they are starting their careers. They are always prepared to manipulate the media if it means winning some free publicity. Yet show business people who are so publicity-hungry in their rising years can become hermit-like once they have success—but only until they have a new show for which they want more publicity.

In sport, free tickets to games are not always the only freebies. Offers can include free club memberships and more. Two sports show hosts/reporters were caught demanding huge cash freebies from sporting clubs in return for having their sports mentioned on air.

"Buying" news space or time with a freebie can be blatant at times. In the United States the Pentagon made no secret of its efforts to "sell" the Vietnam war to chosen media representatives and congressmen by providing flights to and from Saigon on a regular basis. The armed services in Australia have carried newsmen to distant areas on the grounds that it is in the interests of both parties for the public to know what is going on.

It may well be for a legitimate story with genuine news interest, but the sense of obligation remains with the journalist and with the editor who agrees to the free journey. It is all very well for the reporter to claim, probably honestly, that no free meal or football ticket has ever caused a syllable to be changed in any report. Is it really so, or have some changes been made subconsciously? And does the audience see it that way?

In theory there are two options for journalists and their organisations to take regarding freebies or any other conflict of interest. They can ensure that no conflict of interest arises, or they can be open about them and declare publicly those which either can't be avoided or which it is in the interests of the report to accept. Since the first is so impractical that it is impossible, there is really only one solution.

This is why publishers of all kinds these days make no secret of the fact that their journalist was carried to Los Angeles by such-and-such airline or to Beijing as the guest of the Chinese Government, or whoever it is who makes the journey, and the resulting report, possible.

The one-time habit of exchanging "thank you" bottles, or chocolates, or engraved pens or cuff-links at Christmas has largely been abandoned. If a journalist or his employer should not receive freebies, neither should they give them.

Some wealthy American newspaper and television interests go the whole distance in their ethics-conscious and very public rejection of freebies. They buy tickets for their theatre reviewers and sports reporters. They pay fares on planes and buses when accompanying politicians on tours. They sack reporters who accept gifts of any significance. Britain's newest quality daily newspaper, the Independent, has adopted the same policy.

It has not yet gone so far in Australia, though many news organisations avoid the apparent pressure by making sure their correspondents pay their own way while following politicians across the country.

Most media outlets in Australia, as in America and elsewhere, claim they can't afford to be so obviously ethical. Without free seats for reporters and reviewers, there will be no reports or reviews. But they deny that free admissions affect what their reporters write.

This raises the question whether news organisations should buy information. Buying news from an agency which is in the business of supplying information on a regular basis, and which observes professional ethics and standards in its gathering, is sound economics with no ethical overtones. Buying exclusive stories, often from someone made famous or infamous by chance or by crime, is another matter. It happens all over the world—which is the excuse for it happening in Australia—but is it ethical?

One of the problems which most journalists encounter sooner or later is the apparent difference in ethics between the "boss" and the staff. "I had to do it, or I would have lost my job" may be an exaggeration, but it is what many journalists feel when instructed to carry out an assignment they would rather not do for ethical reasons. Very few journalists have ever been sacked for objecting on ethical grounds, but some have suffered in their careers by not being given good assignments thereafter.

This problem is not dealt with specifically in the AJA code, nor in similar codes elsewhere, so it is a personal problem for those involved.

American journalism critic Harry J. Skornia drew a sharp response when he wrote in *Broadcast News: a trade in need of professionalizing:*

"Do newsmen, print as well as broadcast, have so little pride in their status as newsmen, in their product and in their freedoms, that they would like to be left alone to do as the boss dictates, to stay in line and to give up any further pretence of practising those qualities which characterize professionalism? If so, the public and the once-proud practice of journalism are the losers. And it has taken the media of television and radio to bring about this deterioration."

Not so, responded Pat Polillo, then news director for a group of American television stations. He claimed that radio and television journalists do in public what their print colleagues have done in the privacy of their newsrooms for decades—prepare material for publication as best they can. If the influence of the boss can occasionally be detected in television at least it is visible, is criticised and thus is not likely to happen again. If it happens in print it is not so visible. Polillo contends that broadcast journalists are winning for their colleagues ever greater freedom from managerial intrusion in the newsroom.

The management-staff ethical conflict was put succinctly by James Aubrey, CBS vice-president in charge of administration, when arguing with his equally-famous CBS vice-president in charge of news, Fred Friendly:

"In this adversary system you and I are always going to be at each other's throats. They (management) say to me 'Take your soiled hands, get the ratings and make us as much money as you can.' They say to you 'Take your lily-white hands, do your best, go the high road and bring us some prestige.'"

This shows understanding, but no resolution of the problem of what a journalist should do when an assignment conflicts with the obligation to observe the code of ethics. Reporters with the courage bring the conflict to the notice of the editor. Colleagues with courage lend support.

The major remaining ethical issue is the unsolvable one—confidentiality. The AJA Code of Ethics insists that journalists respect all confidences at all times; the law insists journalists have neither the right nor the privilege to do so when commanded by a court to tell the truth. Since all journalist so confronted have found their consciences more professionally compelling than the orders of a judge or magistrate, the problem is more properly a legal one. It is explored in the next chapter.

Even the experienced can fall foul of the law: Derrin Hinch and lawyer on the way to court. For those who don't know, the risks are even greater.

(Picture: Herald-Sun)

Know the law

Broadcasters have even more legal problems than other journalists

Journalists must know and obey the laws of the land which affect their profession. People working in the media are subject to the laws of defamation, contempt and copyright and to sundry other laws not directly associated with journalism but which affect it. There are additional controls on broadcasters imposed by the Broadcasting Act and under the regulations of the Australian Broadcasting Tribunal.

This is not a law book for journalists, nor even an attempt to explain much of the law in detail. Better and more complete texts are available. This is no more than a reminder to would-be broadcast journalists of the laws which affect them.

Ignorance of the law is no excuse. Even though a publisher pays the fine and usually keeps quiet, a defamation case, or any other law suit, seldom enhances a reporter's reputation. Defamation is a growth industry in Australia. The number of cases and the size of the judgments are increasing steadily. Only the very wealthy, supremely confident or stupidly reckless can afford to be cavalier and "Publish and be damned", a statement attributed to the Duke of Wellington. Journalists may not like the caution of their legal advisers in such matters, but it is both safer and cheaper not to end up in court.

The laws affecting journalism are so complex that most publishing concerns of any size retain legal advisers. Some have legal experts on staff. Any reporter with doubts about the legal safety of what has been written, or about what is about to be written, should consult his or her superiors immediately. It may well be referred from there to those with more legal expertise. It is too late once the report has been published. The damage is done.

On the other hand, no reporter should ignore a story because of possible legal ramifications. It is possible to "write around" a legal trap. By changing the wording, without really changing the meaning, many significant stories which might otherwise have been withheld have appeared on a front page or in a broadcast bulletin.

For the reporter without reliable legal advice at hand the axiom "when in doubt, leave out" still stands. Without knowledgeable guidance even stories in which the danger is only potential, should be set aside. There is always the next bulletin, or even the one after that if it takes that long to have the item cleared by an expert. It is no excuse to say, after the event, that there was no one around to give advice so the item was used anyway.

Defamation

Defamation is a generic as well as a legal term. At law in Australia it long ago replaced "libel" and "slander", although both are still in common use. Libel is defamation in writing, as in a newspaper, magazine or book, or any form of the printed image which is permanent. Slander is defamation by speech and thus by analogy speech on the radio or on television or on the cinema screen. At law this distinction has been abolished and printed or spoken, in any medium, the offence is defamation.

It is the initial writer of the story, usually the reporter, who is responsible for its content. In most defamation cases arising from broadcasting it is the publisher (the station), the reporter and the on-air reader (sometimes the reporter and reader are the same person) who are sued. If the offending material was first said in public by another person, or was tendered to the newsroom by a public relations organisation, they can be sued separately, but it doesn't happen very often.

Even if the offending material is passed to only one person, other than the originator and the person claiming to be defamed, it is deemed to be published and an action is possible. Anything broadcast is therefore published widely. Someone has heard it, no matter at what time of day.

Defamation laws vary from state to state, so journalists must make themselves familiar first with the laws of their own state, then with the laws of any other state in which their material may be heard, either directly or by networking. This effectively means all of them. Defamation suits which fail in one state have succeeded in others, even when the content of the report is identical. In a memorable series of cases some years ago, former Prime Minister John Gorton sued the ABC in several states over a report in "This Day Tonight". He, or his lawyers, planned to take advantage of the different laws and make sure of a win in at least one state.

Defamation is by one definition "a statement which may tend to lower the plaintiff in the estimation of right-thinking members of society generally". By another it is: "Publication without justification which is calculated to injure the reputation of another by exposing him to hatred, ridicule or contempt". Basically, defamation is anything which harms or may harm another person's reputation. It has been held to be defamatory to say that a person is a coward, dishonest or cruel.

It would be defamatory to suggest:
a) that a public figure acted in his or her public capacity to further his or her private interests;
b) to say or imply that someone has committed a criminal offence;
c) to publish anything which makes or might make a person look ridiculous—even suggesting that a policeman had smelly feet in one case.

Companies can be defamed, since in the eyes of the law they are individuals. The dead are not, so there was little legal risk in The National Times publishing revelations about former NSW Premier Sir Robert Askin after he died. But relatives of the dead can sue if they believe the report holds them up to hatred, ridicule or contempt, or damages their reputation in any way. Again, the details of this aspect of the law vary from state to state.

It is quite possible to **defame unintentionally**, even to defame someone without knowing they exist. Publishing or broadcasting that a woman has become engaged to a particular man may defame that man's wife, without the publisher knowing that the man concerned already has a wife. It has happened.

The differences in defamation law across Australian states and territories are not so much in what is held to be defamatory as in the **accepted defences** against prosecution.

- **Truth** is a complete defence in Victoria, South Australia, Western Australia and the Northern Territory.
- To be a defence in Queensland, Tasmania and the Australian Capital Territory, truth must also be for the **public benefit**.
- In New South Wales truth must be in the **public interest**.

These are vague terms open to varying interpretation, so there is still truth in the editors' complaint about defamation: "The greater the truth the greater the libel."

In all states and territories the *defendant* must begin by proving that what was published was true. In almost every other law it is up to the plaintiff to prove a case; in defamation the onus is on the defence.

Whether the statement has to be true in every minute detail or in substance also varies from state to state. It is no defence to claim that the words published did not actually constitute a defamatory statement but only seemed to do so, or that they could seem to do so in the minds of only some people. To be found guilty of **defamation by implication** is just as expensive.

Most reports about the actions of public figures, such as politicians, are usually (though not invariably) held to be "in the public interest" if the reference is to actions carried out in their capacity as public figures. Published reporting of their actions in private life, as private citizens, is much less safe, unless the publisher has legally valid "public interest/benefit" reasons for making that private life public.

Other defences against defamation are that the reports published are protected by qualified privilege or are "fair comment".

Commenting on the news, fairly or otherwise, is not a job for novices. They must report facts accurately and succinctly. When they have done that for long enough in a specific area of reporting, they may be permitted, even asked, to add comments to their interpretive writing.

Fair comment means comment on a matter of public interest — that is the essential criterion. It must be comment based on true statements, and the opinions expressed must be those "honestly held" by the writer and be reasonably based on the true statements. In other words, comments or opinions made with malice, or based on statements known to be untrue or even unchecked, will not be accepted as a "fair comment" defence. Such comments could increase the penalty.

For society to work, there must be occasions when one person can speak the truth about another without fear of being sued for defamation. In Australia this is the case in parliament, and to a large extent in courts of law. A Member of Parliament is not restrained by any law from telling the truth as he or she sees it, provided he or she speaks while Parliament is in session. The same protection applies in all Australia's parliaments, state and federal.

This is called **"absolute privilege"** and although it exists for a valid reason, like any privilege it can also be abused. When a member uses his privilege to make a personal attack he would not dare to make outside parliament for fear of the law, parliament is dubbed "cowards' castle".

This absolute privilege extends to journalists reporting the doings of parliament, but only while their reports are **"fair and accurate"**, which means they must be a balanced account of what was said or done.

There is no privilege of any kind for reports of what is said or done outside parliament, in the lobbies, offices, bar or parking lot. Anything said and reported there is subject to the same laws as anywhere else in the country, except in parliament, the highest court in the land.

Lesser courts, from the Supreme Court and Royal Commissions down to magistrates' courts, also offer privilege to those engaged in their proceedings and to those who report on them. The reason is the same: no one should be deterred from telling the truth in court for fear of defamation, or any other law. Again, to win legal protection for what is reported the report must be a fair and accurate account. It may be a greatly abbreviated account, but it must be a balanced and honest account.

It would not be "fair and accurate" to report in full from parliament the sensational aspects of a verbal attack by one member on another without also reporting the rebuttal or denial. And in court it is not fair and accurate to report the details of the case for the prosecution without also reporting the defence. "Fair" means fair to both sides, or all sides, in such reports.

When setting up Royal Commissions, governments spell out their legal standing, so those giving evidence or reporting know what level of privilege applies.

In all these circumstances the law is the same for all journalists, print or broadcast. The difference is that broadcast journalists are not permitted to take their tools of trade into parliament or the courts while they are in session. Notebooks and pencils are accepted, but not recording equipment and cameras. True, parliament is broadcast, even televised, but not by journalists seeking news items. The resulting tapes are available to journalists to help with their reports, but only at the pleasure of the Speaker.

There is no radio or television reporting from within a courtroom in session, on the grounds that such reporting may interfere with the judicial procedure and perhaps prejudice someone's fair trial. This has not yet been seriously challenged in Australia, even though broadcast reports from courts in many American States have become commonplace. Broadcast journalists are still entitled to sit at the "press" bench to make their own notes for later broadcast.

Outside parliaments and the courts, where the law of defamation applies, it differs from state to state. It pays journalists to know as much about the law as possible, and not just in their own home state. No matter in which state someone sues, the originator carries the initial responsibility.

For nearly two decades there has been a campaign for **uniform defamation laws** across Australia—an attempt to establish a new and reasonable balance between the public's right to know what is happening in their land and community, and an individual's right to privacy and the protection of his or her reputation.

In 1976, the then Federal Attorney-General, Mr Ellicott, directed the Australian Law Reform Commission (ALRC) to review the laws of defamation in the various states and to propose a uniform bill. After three years of consultation with the legal profession, the media and the public and the preparation of several discussion papers, the ALRC presented to the government in 1979 a report published as Unfair Publication: Defamation and Privacy. This was referred to the Standing Committee of Federal and State Attorneys-General which for six years tried to decide on a uniform defamation bill. When the attempt was officially abandoned in mid-1985 none of the report's recommendations had been acted upon.

As we enter the nineties, there is renewed state government interest in uniform legislation, especially in New South Wales, Victoria and Queensland. These three states have agreed that truth alone should be an absolute defence against defamation, with the only exception being an unjustified intrusion into personal lives. But at last report before this book was published the states could not agree on the details of the proposed uniform law. Queensland Attorney-General Dean Wells describes the current law as a "casino for the rich and famous".

This renewed interest in reform highlighted another problem for journalists — what is called "forum shopping", in which prospective litigants search for a court in which to get the best pay-out. Journalists and publishers hope that a uniform law will do away with this practice. An editorial in The Australian in August, 1990, noted, "It would be better if some States had good laws and others had bad laws than for all States to have uniformly bad laws".

The media, enthusiastic for reform but critical of the delays in the drawn out effort so far, lament the fact that those who must reform the present laws are those who benefit most from them — politicians. Before they formally abandoned their attempts at defamation reform in the '80s the Attorneys-General did draft a proposed bill. It varied considerably from the recommendations of the Law Reform Commission so it was attacked by lawyers and the media alike.

The draft retained the suggested "defamation of the dead" provision proposed by the legal reformers and introduced a provision for court-ordered and court-supervised corrections, which all media representatives considered obnoxious. Judges, like editors, are fallible, so under such a law a publisher in print or broadcasting could be forced to publish a correction he or she believed, or even knew, to be wrong.

The draft also included, though the recommendations from the reformers did not, new provisions for the defence of "fair report". As the new provisions related to parliament, a defence of fair report would succeed only if the publisher gave the plaintiff the right to reply, even though the same person had no such right in parliament. The media protested against this and the enforced corrections, on the grounds that the control of the content of the media would pass from editors and journalists to politicians and the courts.

Media lawyers and journalists claimed the biggest backward step in the draft bill was in the proposed defence of justification. The Law Reform Commission recommended truth alone, but the Attorneys-General proposed truth and public benefit; in the eyes of the media the worst possible option.

A further revised draft bill was put forward by the Committee of Attorneys-General in 1984 and circulated for discussion. There were changes, but not in the areas of greatest media and legal objection. Defamation of the dead and the court-ordered corrections remained. The only change was that while the court could stipulate the content, time, form, extent and manner of the published correction, it could no longer oblige the publisher to admit the error of something he or she believed to be true.

The re-draft dropped the right-of-reply pre-condition to a defence of fair report and offered a confusion of three options the defence could offer in justification: truth alone, truth and public benefit, and truth plus the protection of sensitive public facts.

The last one was new. It meant that the defence of truth would not apply where the defamatory material related to the health, private behaviour, home life or personal relationships of the person defamed, unless that information could be shown to be on record in a document available for public inspection.

Even though joint governmental attempts to attain uniform legislation were then abandoned, the reform proposals still exist, and in recent times have been revived. Many in the media believe that to gain such legislation there would have to be so many compromises that the end product would be worse than the confusion which now exists and the loser would be the public with a further restricted right to know.

Contempt

There have also been suggestions for reform of the law of **contempt of court**, but after the first few years these had progressed no further than vague suggestions.

In the case of broadcasting, contempt of court is anything mentioned on air which could obstruct the proper administration of justice — note that it is "could" not "would" — or could jeopardise the respect of the community for the administration of justice. This is strictly adhered to by the courts. An Australian newspaper was fined for contempt of court for publishing a story about the peddling of drugs during the hearing of a case about alleged drug pushers, even though no member of the jury saw the offending article.

It is permissible to comment on a crime only until someone has been charged with its commission. This is the point at which the matter becomes sub-judice, or under judicial consideration. From this point no comment may be made until the person charged is eventually acquitted or convicted and the time for lodging an appeal has expired. No comment, and only "fair and accurate" reporting, is permitted while the case is being heard or in that period between the charge being laid and the case coming to court.

The courts rebuked journalists and their editors for the plethora of reports, many of them based on rumours, published before the first Lindy Chamberlain murder trial in Darwin and between her subsequent retrial and appeal hearing. In spite of obvious contempt of court, especially of the Northern Territory Court, the matter went no further than a caution. No action was taken.

Action was taken when The National Times published information leaked from the Senate Committee of Inquiry into the Murphy affair. The committee was set up to determine whether former Attorney General Lionel Murphy, later elevated to the Bench of the High Court of Australia, had interfered with the course of justice. Publishing the leak was thus risking contempt of court should the committee decide an offence had been committed, but was also a contempt of parliament. The matter went to the Senate as a whole and it recommended that not only The National Times, but all Fairfax publications, be put on what the media described as "a good behaviour bond". The publication of the Senate Committee leak was a "first". So was the Senate's response.

Contempt of court also involves criticism of the courts or members of the judiciary made in such a way as to lower the respect of the community for the proper administration of justice. There are three main areas in which reporters must be careful:

a). Publishing material which may prejudice an impending trial. Everyone is entitled to a fair trial, so the media may publish nothing which may affect the conduct of the trial. This is why the events of a crime can be reported only until someone is charged. After that any reference made to the "facts" of the alleged offence must be limited to "facts" which can not be challenged during the trial.

This is why several New South Wales television stations found themselves in contempt of court in 1990 over the coverage of a man accused of murder in southern N. S. W. The man took his own life in gaol before the trial, but coverage of his arrest was held to be in contempt because it was held that it jeopardised his chances of a fair trial.

b). Publishing material which may bring the court into disrepute. Reporting, or even implying, that the judge lacked impartiality is contempt. To suggest that a sentence was "heavy" or "light" is commenting on the judicial system and is not permitted. If the judge says in court that he is handing down a heavy or light sentence for a particular reason this must be reported accurately. Into the early '90s this aspect was not as rigidly policed as other aspects of the law, since many of the nation's broadcasting "gurus" regularly commented on the severity of some sentences—usually the lack of severity—but did not appear in court on a contempt charge.

c). Declining to reveal the sources of information when required by a court to do so. It is contempt to withhold information in such circumstances, but it is a breach of the AJA Code of Ethics to reveal it, if the information was given to the journalist in confidence. The code states that journalists "will respect all confidences" but the courts do not accept this as a right. Many judges appreciate the dilemma for a journalist called as a witness and will try to avoid such a head-on clash between the law and the journalist's ethics. Others don't recognise the conflict, on the grounds that the law applies to everyone. But the law does not apply to lawyers, and doctors and clergy usually win immunity on the grounds of their special relationship with their "clients".

On December 11, 1989, Perth reporter Tony Barass went to gaol for refusing to reveal the source of a story. He was gaoled for seven days and fined $10,000 for refusing to disclose how he got confidential tax office files.

Contempt of Parliament, or breach of privilege, is not easy to define. Because parliament is the supreme court of the land, contempt is what sufficient members at any time deem to be contempt. It is certain that any material which may be considered as exerting improper pressure on members of parliament, which may bring the institution of parliament into disrespect or which discloses secret proceedings of parliamentary committees, is contemptuous. It should not be published.

The best-known example of "bringing the institution into disrespect" occurred in 1981 in the famous "MPs bludgers, drunks!" case in Sydney's Daily Mirror. Its then political commentator, Lawrie Oakes, wrote "the truth about the drunks and bludgers on Canberra's back benches". The front page teaser added, "It's not all hard work and stress for Australia's federal Members of Parliament. Many have little or nothing to do other than sit around the members' bar boozing and whingeing." Inside, the report made further unflattering remarks about the behaviour of members.

The Privileges Committee of the House of Representatives found that the headings and article were in contempt but that "the matter was not worthy of occupying the time of the House any further".

The penalty for Contempt of Parliament varies from state to state, but it can mean gaol for an indefinite period. This, like other aspects of the law, is again under official consideration.

In the United States where contempt, like defamation, varies from state to state, some states have introduced "shield" laws to protect journalists in "betrayal of trust" circumstances. They are far from uniformly successful. One result has been legal argument between states, and between the state and federal courts, over what journalists may or may not be obliged to divulge.

In Australia it is realistic to say that while journalists may enjoy some privileges by public acceptance—such as passes from the police and other authorities to go where the general public may not—they have no more rights than any other citizen, and even greater responsibilities. And many in the media claim this is as it should be.

All these legal problems confront print and broadcast journalists equally, but the terms of the Broadcasting Act 1942 (and subsequent amendments) and the rules and regulations devised by the Australian Broadcasting Tribunal (ABT) apply only to broadcasters.

The Tribunal is the government's regulatory authority controlling the content, operation and technical standards of Australia's commercial and public broadcasting stations in both radio and television. The ABC is by law outside the control of the Tribunal.

Section 15 of the **Tribunal's Program Standards**, as revised in 1990, has already been mentioned in connection with ethics. Since the Tribunal's stated principles have the force of law they can raise legal as well as ethical problems for broadcast journalists, who should read them again in this light. For instance, the regulations now state:

> News programs (including news flashes) transmitted by a lincesee must:
> (a) present news accurately, fairly and impartially (but who is to decide what is accurate, fair and impartial?);
> (b) clearly distinguish the reporting of factual material from commentary and analysis (but who decides whether such a distinction has been made?);
> (c) not present news in such a manner as to create public panic (but who determines what is panic?);
> (d) not present advertising matter as if it were news (but who determines what is, or appears to be, news?).

The "who" in each of these cases is the Broadcasting Tribunal, which has the power to penalise broadcasters for what it deems to be breaches of any of the above principles.

Further changes to the regulations and program standards are possible, even probable. For instance all reference to violence has been excused from the standards because it was the subject of a 1990 report on violence on TV. An inquiry on "accuracy, fairness and impartiability" was under way in 1990-1 and its outcome may again affect the wording of the regulations or standards or both. The finding may even lead to changes in the Broadcasting Act.

Obscenity, Indecency and Blasphemy

Good taste used to be mentioned in Section 27 of the Broadcasting Tribunal's Program Standards but was too vague in definition to be built into law. Not so obscenity, indecency and blasphemy. Section 118 of the Broadcasting and Television Act (since amended to the Broadcasting Act) stated that such material must not be broadcast. In reality this is not often a problem in news, though current affairs reporters sometimes have to consider whether what they want to broadcast falls into one of these categories. The problem is often one of definition.

One definition of **obscenity** declares it is anything that "tends to deprave and corrupt those whose minds are open to such immoral influences, and into whose hands a publication . . . may fall". Deciding whether what is being prepared for broadcast is likely to deprave or corrupt the audience, or any part of it, can be difficult. A broadcast may be held to be obscene if it offends "to a substantial degree the sexual modesty of the average man or woman" in the Australian community or offends similarly the "contemporary standards of decency currently accepted by the Australian community".

This seems more rigid than it is, since who can say what is "a substantial degree", let alone "an average man or woman". Also, what are the contemporary standards of decency in Australia? People frequently profess that standards are not what they used to be.

The only guideline in this area is to play safe. If the reporter thinks what is said or done borders on the obscene, he or she should not report it, or should at least report it first to the editor for a second opinion. Even journalists who know well the audience they serve soon realise that there is always a group, if only a small one, which will protest when they see or hear something they consider offensive.

Because of language change "obscene" and "indecent" have come to mean almost the same thing, though in reality they are not. A dictionary makes the distinction, though it also illustrates how the two can overlap. There is no absolute ban on the use of what might be termed obscene or indecent language and there are times when public radio, which caters to more specialised minority audiences, can use language which would never be heard on mass-audience commercial stations.

The Broadcasting Tribunal, in adjudicating on such material, takes into consideration factors such as the nature of the publication, the classes of listeners, their ages and the time of the broadcast. It also considers whether any warning is given by the broadcaster about the nature of the material about to be broadcast. News programs often issue warnings about the potentially distressing nature of some material about to be aired.

Tribunal members know that community standards have changed so that words considered obscene or indecent a decade ago may be acceptable today. Context is relevant, too. Words used in a serious discussion of a matter of social importance may not be obscene, though when used in another context they may well be. Offensive words in an interview, expressed in anger, stress or frustration, may be acceptable as long as they are natural to the person on that occasion. They are not acceptable in a reporter's script.

Blasphemy is more specific. It is blasphemous to arouse outrage or substantial resentment in Christians, though this is not intended to prevent reasoned argument or discussion about religion or the church. There are differing legal opinions on whether the prohibition is limited to Christianity, but it would be unwise to prepare a report which caused outrage or substantial resentment to the members of any other religion. Other charges could be brought, according to where the offence took place, and at the very least such a report would also be in poor taste.

Actions for blasphemy are rare, though in 1977 Gay News in Britain was prosecuted for a poem which described Christ as a practising homosexual and also as promiscuous.

The Tribunal has the power to suspend from broadcasting any people held to be responsible for the broadcast of blasphemous, obscene or indecent material. It can also suspend or cancel the broadcaster's licence. Action has been taken for indecency against two radio stations — one public and one commercial — in the past decade. In spite of this it is safe to assume that because of Section 118 of the Broadcasting Act 1942 it is risky to broadcast any material which might offend any section of the public.

Copyright

Copyright is another law which directly concerns journalists. Copyright exists in any original literary, dramatic or musical work as well as in films and sound recordings. Thus it is an infringement of copyright to publish, reproduce, adapt or perform any work without the authority of the person controlling the copyright.

But **copyright does not protect ideas or information, only their form of expression**. So there is no copyright on news, but there is on how it is expressed in any medium. Therefore there is no impediment to "stealing" the content of news published or broadcast anywhere as long as it is not republished or broadcast in the same form in which it was "stolen". You can't record material off-air and then play the recording. If it is truly worth using, either rewrite it so you are not using it in the same form, or you use it as recorded and pay the copyright fee demanded. Either way it is ethical to acknowledge where the item came from.

In most cases permission is granted willingly enough and without charge as long as an acknowledgment is made of the original source. But get the permission; don't take it for granted.

Some suppliers of news programs, especially in the international and commercial arenas, ask no acknowledgement or fee. They are happy to have their material broadcast since their motive is publicity or propaganda rather than impartial information. Journalists should be alert to such programs and make up their own minds whether to use the material or not.

If a journalist-producer elects to use music as part of a program, a detailed record must be kept of recordings used because royalties may have to be paid on them. Special licences exist which permit a station to pay an annual fee to cover much of the music used in news and information programs.

"Censorship" under the Broadcasting Act?

There are further sections of the Broadcasting Act 1942 and tribunal regulations which affect broadcast journalists at all levels and in all programs. Publishers in print are not subject to such restrictions.

The tribunal **has power to censor** material it considers objectionable, for any reason. The Broadcasting Act allows the Minister to require stations to broadcast any matter considered to be "in the national interest", though this is limited to not more than 30 minutes in any 24 hours.

The Act **prohibits any dramatisation of political matter** less than five years old, which is why no series like "The Dismissal" could be broadcast until after the end of 1980.

The objectionable censoring of political news under the election "black-out" provisions in the Act has been abolished, though political advertisements are still subject to broadcast "black-out" between midnight on the Wednesday before election day and the close of the polls.

Section 120 of the Act declares that for legal purposes broadcast programs are deemed to be publications in permanent form. Because this permanent form is not "permanent" for the listeners and viewers, radio and television stations are obliged under the Act to **keep for six weeks a taped recording of their broadcast programs** — recordings of what went to air, not what was intended for air. These tapes can be used as evidence for or against the broadcaster should a case come to court, but no station is required to make any tapes or transcripts available to anyone, unless presented with a court order to do so.

Another section of the Act **prevents anonymous political propaganda.** Any speaker on a political subject in any news or current affairs program must be identified. In news programs the speaker is identified in the normal news style, which may not comply with the letter of the law but until now has been acceptable. In all other programs the speaker must identify himself or herself, and if he or she is not the originator of the material being read, must also identify the author. This applies at all times, not just at election times.

Radio phone-in programs constantly breach this provision of the Act but there have been no prosecutions since the government announced in 1977 that it would provide an exemption for radio phone-ins. The change has never been made law, but radio stations appear to take the will for the deed and continue to ignore the provisions of the Act.

There are specific provisions in the Broadcasting Tribunal's program standards which state that

"No program broadcast by the licensee shall
1. contain any explanation of techniques of crime in such a way as to invite imitation;
2. describe in detail any form of violence or brutality;
3. incite any person to violence;
4. simulate news or events in such a way as to mislead or alarm listeners;
5. denigrate religious faiths or beliefs;
6. present as desirable the abuse of intoxicating liquor;
7. present as desirable the use of drugs or narcotics except under medical direction;
8. include the use of horror for its own sake; or
9. encourage children to enter strange places or to converse with strangers for any purpose."

In the 1990 revisions a relevant addition was
2(a)(i) simulate news or events in such a way as to mislead or alarm viewers.

These regulations apply to all programs, including news, current affairs or documentaries, but are not absolute. The tribunal also states

"these standards do not prohibit the broadcasting by the licensee in good faith, at appropriate times, and in appropriate circumstances, of:
(a) genuine works of artistic or literary merit;
(b) the serious presentation of moral and social issues; if suitable warning of the nature of the program is given, in advance publicity, at its commencement and at appropriate intervals during the program."

Under these provisions there is justification for reports on matters of social, moral or religious importance, even of violent acts, appearing in news and current affairs programs. Where such material may offend some people most stations are careful to provide the legally-required warnings.

Journalists working in radio or television should read the Act and the directions of the tribunal, not only for their application to news and current affairs programs, but also for their regulations concerning the control of contests run by broadcasting stations, simultaneous broadcasting of interviews and the broadcasting of personal messages — all of which can occasion news reports.

Confidentiality

It is fitting that this chapter should end with more about the greatest legal dilemma for print and broadcast journalists alike — respect for confidentiality. Historically it has caused few to be penalised and even fewer to be sent to gaol, yet at some stage in their careers most journalists have had to face the problem — break the Code of Ethics or break the law.

The law says that a journalist ordered by a judge to reveal the source of information must do so or be found in contempt of court. The Code of Ethics states: "in all circumstances journalists shall respect all confidences received in the course of their calling." There are good reasons on both sides.

The law claims that justice can't be done unless all information is available. A person on trial has the right to know who the accuser is and to challenge that person, or have his lawyers challenge, but this may be the information the journalist does not want to give. There have been cases where national security has been at stake, or has been said to be at stake.

Journalists claim, with equal right, that not all justice is dispensed in court. Sources of certain information will dry up if informants fear their names will be revealed in court, or anywhere else.

There is no solution for the journalist called as a witness. On the witness stand, or in the dock for contempt, it is too late to start thinking of ways out. That should have been done before confidentiality was promised.

Lawyer-client relationships are deemed private. Police are expected to protect their informers. Tolerance is shown to clergymen reluctant to tell what is said in a confession and to doctors who wish to preserve the privacy of what their patients tell them.

Journalists claim the same privilege to preserve the free flow of what could be socially valuable information obtainable in no other way, but the courts seldom agree. Few journalists are sent to gaol, though the court in Western Australia in 1989 both gaoled and fined a journalist for refusing to identify his sources.

If there is a way out, it is to be found on the way in. Since self-respecting journalists never go back on their word, every precaution must be taken before that word is given in the first place. Is confidentiality necessary? Is there no way the story can be told and the important facts made known without accepting the trust of confidence?

Confidence is a dangerous trust, not to be accepted lightly. Once accepted there is no going back. Even if some way is found to expose the story from another source, the person who revealed it in confidence will think trust has been broken. Find out before making any promises and tell the confider what you intend to do.

If there is time—and there usually is—ask the editor or a more senior journalist for advice. There is no need to give any names and the experienced journalist will not ask for them, only a reassurance that the source is a reliable one.

People seek confidentiality for a variety of reasons, not all of them valid as far as a journalist is concerned. There are those who want to expose misdeeds by their superiors to advantage themselves rather than the public. Criminals may choose to talk in confidence to shift the guilt to others and leave themselves in the clear. Look for the reasons before agreeing to accept a confidence.

Is the story worth the risk? If its publication will truly benefit the public, then it probably is, but it is an unwise young reporter who makes such a decision entirely alone. Advice helps. It also spreads the anguish if the matter ever comes to court.

Traditionally, newspaper editors give full support to staff members caught in this legal-ethical situation, but they do so more readily when they are put in the picture beforehand. After all, the newspaper or broadcaster is also liable to be found in contempt, not just the reporter.

Regrettably, broadcasters are not usually as brave in this area as are newspaper publishers. They have the Broadcasting Act and the Tribunal to contend with as well and they feel their licences may be put in jeopardy. Besides, managements in broadcasting stations have seldom reached the top through experience in the newsroom, so they don't appreciate the problem as well as newspaper editors. Thus even greater responsibility devolves on the broadcast news editor to guide his or her reporters and to educate and persuade the management that the chosen course is the right one.

The best course for a reporter faced with a confidentiality problem is to avoid it. Tell the potential informer that the matter is one for the editor to decide and then seek advice. But always make sure that nothing is published through your efforts or those of any other reporter on the staff, before the situation is made clear to the confidential informer. Only if the editor knows your problem can you guarantee this. You don't know what other reporters are working on or what they may uncover, but the editor does.

It is your word, your reputation as an ethical journalist, which is at stake. Protect it by taking all possible precautions before giving your word. Once your word is given it must be kept.

Whether broadcast journalism keeps abreast of the improvement in broadcasting equipment depends on how well those in the business do their job—and on those who plan to become part of the profession. Journalism schools educate tomorrow's broadcasters to understand what they are trying to do, as well as showing them how to do it.

(Picture: Charles Sturt University)

Yet to be

Some inequalities and deficiencies still to be remedied.

All too often radio and television are considered the poor relations of the news business. It is true they are controlled by more rules and regulations than is print, but up to a point those who practise broadcast journalism have only themselves to blame. They have allowed time and custom to add to their difficulties in performing as news media. They know they should — and can — do better.

It is no excuse for deficient reporting that deadlines are tighter in broadcasting than in print, even if that is true. Nor are television's complexities of production a reasonable excuse. It is even worse to plead that history grants privileges to print journalists that radio and television journalists don't have. If it is so, it can be changed.

Take parliamentary reporting as an example. Membership of the Press Gallery is open to journalists from all media, but within the House itself working journalists may only make notes. No audio recorders or television cameras are permitted. This was the historic situation — parliamentary reporters used their Gallery seats to make notes before radio and television were invented.

This is fast changing, partly because the broadcasting industry pushed for the change. In the new Parliament House, television cameras record all speakers during question time and those pictures are available to all members of the media. But regulations state that television may not broadcast the actual video of a minister or anyone else talking; television must freeze the videotaped scene and use audio of the particular politician's words. It is better than nothing, and the pressure continues for more sensible broadcast reporting of parliament.

In 1990 the ABC began television broadcasts of question time in the Senate as a trial and parliament agreed to wider use of the parliamentary radio broadcasts, which the ABC has made for years under the terms of its charter.

Television and radio studios have been established within the precincts of parliaments across the country so that broadcasters can conduct face-to-face interviews within minutes of a reportable speech being delivered. When the reporter does his or her job well, the end result is often a more concise and clear exposition than was the original speech.

In Canberra, and in the precincts of some state parliaments, there are special areas for news conferences with ministers and major opposition figures, but these are under the control of the parliamentarians, not the journalists. Political journalists have always resorted to "door stop" confrontations to pry comments from politicians about the news of the day, but television news crews with probing cameras and the waving of dozens of microphones prompted the Federal Government to limit such reporting to a small roped-off area.

This means that those who have nothing to say need not run a media gauntlet to enter parliament, but it also means that those who should have something to say can avoid being asked about it.

State parliaments have varying attitudes to the direct recording or televising of proceedings. In South Australia, accredited journalists and camera operators may record or make videotapes provided they have permission from the Speakers who control all actions within the Assembly or Legislative Council. The restrictions on what may be covered in this manner are more strict than the few which apply to the print media. Most other states have followed suit and to varying extents eased the total ban on broadcast reporting within parliament.

Very few municipal councils allow cameras or tape recorders within council chambers while meetings are in progress. Where such things are permitted, it is usually because the radio and television stations of the town or city have persisted in demanding equal rights with reporters from the press. Councils are much more ready to consider direct broadcast reporting of their affairs, but seldom to grant it as a right. There are still occasions on which broadcast journalists would prefer to report meetings live but are prohibited from doing so.

Broadcast news editors across Australia are doing something about this disparity of privilege by explaining to mayors and councils that they are discriminating against the electronic media. They can also explain that with more portable and less obtrusive equipment and live studio links that make on-location recording unnecessary, television's handicaps are not as great as they once were. As a result some councils now hold truly open meetings — open to the public and all news media.

On the other hand, too many broadcast news editors not only condone council bans on broadcast reporting, but also fail to protest at the growing tendency of some councils to conduct much of their business in closed sessions. Many councils hold meetings which are public in name only. In reality they are assemblies to rubber stamp decisions made by committees which meet "in camera". The public's right to know how and why decisions are made at those meetings has to be won by the media — which includes the broadcast media. Councils will seldom willingly give up the cosy practice of closed committee meetings.

In the commercial world the historic reluctance of senior executives from major companies to appear on television is coming to an end. Television reaches so many people that company representatives are keen to appear to announce new projects, answer criticism or comment on developments which affect their companies and the communities in which they operate.

Show business people, demonstrators, zealots for almost any cause — anyone who sees a political or financial advantage in appearing on the broadcast media — have been so anxious to win broadcast time for so long that they can be a problem for broadcasters. No newsroom is immune from the enducements of those who wish to manipulate the media, but it is the fault of the journalists themselves when this happens.

Public relations practitioners, whose object in life is to win favourable publicity for their clients, have long made television their main target. They sought the huge audiences by pandering to television's passion for a good picture. As a result they won television time, even with items which, compared with other news of the day, should have been ignored.

Changing methods of gathering news for television should allow worthwhile editors to bring this to an end. Why screen a local psuedo-event or non-event, even if it has a good picture, when much more significant material is available by satellite from interstate or from around the world?

In spite of constantly improving equipment and techniques and increasing professionalism in broadcast journalism, the greatest impediment to the presentation of good radio and television news is still money. Newspapers pay their way with advertisements but they exist to gather and disseminate news. Entertainment is a consideration but not the main one. Radio and television (apart from the ABC) also make money from advertising but their primary task (including the ABC) is to entertain. The gathering and presentation of news and current affairs is a necessary and important part of their programming but seldom accounts for more than 15 per cent of it, perhaps more when you include the pseudo-news programs that have proliferated on radio and television in recent years.

Broadcast news editors eye their print colleagues with envy. It seems newspapers have plenty of space to fill and plenty of staff to help fill it. Journalists comprise a small percentage of the total staff in most broadcasting organisations and this is unlikely to change without a major change in the style of the business. The major networks all had financial problems in the late '80s and into the '90s. Whether their claim that they can't afford to operate an effective newsroom is valid is a matter for the Broadcasting Tribunal to determine at licence renewal time.

Those who would like to do a better job usually claim that most broadcast newsrooms are short of both staff and money, but this is partly an excuse. Small staffs have produced good news services and some stations with large news staffs have not done as well. The yardstick is staff ability as much as size.

Because most broadcast staffs are few, the overall standard of broadcast news is not as high as it should be and broadcast news is frequently criticised by the public and by print journalists. Newsrooms with small staffs offer sparse cadet training—sparse in both cadet numbers and in the training they receive. There are significant exceptions—mainly in the major network news and current affairs departments in the larger capital cities and by the ABC in all states — but not enough to raise the public or professional image of broadcast journalism to what it could and should be.

It is a fact that television is the most believed news medium. Survey after survey confirms it. Those who think seriously about journalism, including those who practise it, know such credibility is unwarranted. Television's time devoted to news is too short to deliver the news any society needs to be adequately informed, and half that time is devoted to audience-attracting picture stories, regardless of their news merit, to maintain the ratings. Even those who work in television news, and many who work in radio, know that broadcasting is not providing the news service of which it is capable.

When its news services are so often disparaged, broadcasting finds it difficult to attract and hold the quality of journalists broadcasting needs. Broadcasting has many excellent reporters and in its wealthy years persuaded more and more to make the change from print journalism, especially in the areas of politics and economics. They are concentrated in network-originating newsrooms in Sydney, Melbourne and Canberra.

In print the best journalists are spread more evenly across the state capitals, though they are less often found in the regional press. Regional radio and television newsrooms have habitually been plundered of their best staff. The demand for them is so great that as soon as a regional journalist demonstrates ability there is a better job available with a capital city station.

Good radio journalism demands special skills in such measure that some journalists love the medium and others hate it. It is certainly not, as many print journalists claim, "an easy option where reports are so short they call for no depth in reporting". Such deprecation usually comes from print journalists whose only experience of radio is having copies of their reports passed on to a local radio station. Few reporters who have worked at gathering and presenting news on radio say the same. There are lazy journalists in radio as there are in any medium, but as radio journalism becomes ever more demanding they are being weeded out.

Television shares with radio the need to fit a maximum of relevant information into a minimum of well-chosen words. It also has the added complexity of having to merge the written word with a dominant picture. This means television is the most complex and demanding form of journalism today—who knows what will happen tomorrow? Therefore it should employ the best journalists available if it is to use its limited time to the best advantage. The good journalists in Australian television will be the first to agree that they are not enough.

The continuing problem of small staff numbers, tight budgets and too few good journalists stems from the development of the two media. Early radio, as an entertainment medium—both in the United States where it began and in Australia where it followed soon after—was in the hands of enthusiasts and entrepreneurs, not journalists. Radio was not seen as a medium for news until later; even then news was always an adjunct to management's major aim of entertaining as large an audience as possible. Station managements were headed by businessmen with backgrounds in many different areas, rarely in journalism.

When television first came to Australia, many people protested that the licences were awarded to companies which already owned newspapers or radio stations or both. From a news monopoly point of view perhaps they may have been right, but in one respect they were wrong. The licence awards meant that many of Australia's first television managers entered the business with a ready appreciation of the place of news in broadcasting.

Australian television stations presented half-hour newscasts from their first days of broadcasting. It took years of frustrating persuasion by journalists in Britain, the United States and elsewhere before their managements expanded their 10 or 15-minute newscasts to 30. Only since television has been confirmed as the source of news for most Americans have hour-long newscasts become the norm in that country. Many stations run news in two-hour blocks or longer, sometimes two or three times a day. The Cable News Network (CNN) is available on cable nationwide round the clock and in the major cities there are radio stations which broadcast nothing but news, current affairs, documentaries and interviews. News has proven both popular and profitable.

In Australia, as in the United States, news programs have become television's competitive cutting edge. Managements believe that most of the audience that tunes in for the news will stay viewing all evening.

Not everything inherited from America's television experience has served Australia well. In the first round of cut-throat competition on American news airwaves, television managements were swayed by consultants who based their advice on market surveys. These consultants saw news as just another entertainment program, showed little understanding of news content and made no concessions to it. They recommended glamour in the newsroom and in front of the news cameras as well as in the presentation studio, with ultra-short news items and a liberal sprinkling of humour and chit-chat between newsreaders. There was little room for serious news. When television managements followed this advice, television journalists worthy of the name rebelled. Many resigned rather than comply with what they saw as the destruction of television as a news medium.

It took many years, and the coming of rigorous competition in the television news arena, for the aura of "gimmick news" to begin to wane in America. Some Australian stations followed the American example and chased ratings with "fun-before-facts" journalism. This seemed to have passed from Australian screens, but has been revived by the tight budgets of today's television. Gimmicks and personalities are again usurping the place of news in broadcast programming.

For years Australian television managements appointed as reporters young men (few women) with on-camera talent rather than ability as journalists. They looked and sounded good but had to have someone else plan their questions for an interview. Most of them have disappeared, replaced in more sensible times by journalists who knew what to ask and how to ask it. Luckily some of the glamour appointees turned out to be real journalists. Equally fortunately some of the good journalists were attractive enough to hold their jobs.

This ability to be both a reporter and an on-air presenter is adding another requirement to the skills of a broadcast journalist. To succeed in broadcasting today a journalist needs a good clear voice, though not necessarily a trained one, and the ability to use it fluently as well as the ability to report accurately and quickly. Increasingly mobile television equipment is reintroducing to television reporting the need for a thorough understanding of how to gather news. Common sense now dictates that television news staff be journalists first and personalities second.

This is why, when television wants news staff, it tries to poach experienced journalists from newspapers and radio. Many editors considered it easier to teach a journalist with some experience the techniques of television than to teach the basics of journalism to someone with a knowledge of television. Because broadcast journalism's professional image was not good, most of those who made the move to television were young men and women sensing a rapid rise in grading. Television newsrooms held too many over-paid and under-experienced journalists. Hard times in broadcasting mean little demand for staff and an end to poaching, and to any training by broadcasters of their own news staff.

Television can't help but flatter the egos of people who appear regularly on millions of screens, including those of journalists with more ambition than ability. Some newsrooms, and too many current affairs programs, still foster ego-trippers who are more interested in having their say than in presenting accurate and intelligent reports. There are still too many who have never learned to take notes accurately, to tell a story coherently, or to use English correctly. There are still journalists in broadcasting who misuse or mispronounce words, even names, and fail to understand the difference between fact and opinion, especially if the opinion is their own. Their reports fail to give a balanced picture and they plead the pressure of time. The real reasons are laziness and lack of basic ability as journalists.

Such reports destroy a news service's credibility. A problem for broadcasting, especially for television, is that there are many more ways in which its credibility can be damaged than there are in print. Until television has the staff to prepare a wider range of better-reported genuine news items, and the opportunity to present them as intelligently, it will continue to be a second-best news medium.

Yet in spite of public surveys television is still striving for recognition from other journalists, and from discerning viewers, as a disseminator of worthwhile news. To many, television news is an information insert in an entertainment schedule. News, and some current affairs programs, are referred to as "infotainment".

Every accurate, diligent report should help disprove this attitude, but every slipshod, inadequate report reinforces it. Every balanced news item with intelligent use of meaningful pictures demonstrates how well television can inform, but every media event with its managed visual appeal demonstrates that television news still has a long way to go.

Appendix 1

GLOSSARY

Broadcasting has built up a language of its own, as every industry or profession. Many words have been adapted and given a new or different meaning in radio or television.

The list below gives most of those in common use. In most cases the terms used are the same for both media, in which case only the one meaning is given. Where there is a second meaning which applies in television, or a word which applies to television alone (and not radio) the television meaning is shown in italics.

Access
a system by which members of the public originate radio programs of their own, in varying degree. Public radio in Australia is largely access radio.

Acoustics
the science of sound production, transmission and effects. Specifically the quality of sound reproduction.

Acoustic Feedback
(see "feedback")

Actuality
sounds (*or pictures and sounds*) recorded at the place of an event or situation.

AM
(amplitude modulation) a form of radio transmission.

Amplifier
a device to increase sound strength or volume.

Angle
a storyline, (*or the line along which a camera looks at a subject*).

Atmosphere
sounds recorded at the place of an event to identify the location, such as traffic noise, air conditioning, crowd noises, etc.

Audio
sound (*in television, as opposed to video*).

Autocue
a prompting device on which a performer is able to read a script which is projected to appear in magnified form in front of the lens of the camera. Its use eliminates the need to refer to typewritten script material or to be prompted.

Background
sound used behind dialogue; unwanted noise behind the main program (*that part of a picture behind the performer*).

Back announcement
telling the audience what has just been played or heard (*or seen*).

Boomy (audio)
a form of distortion in which the low-pitched sounds are accentuated, resonated or prolonged.

Bridge
(1) music or sound effects used to link one item to another.
(2) *a portion of script or vision used to link two otherwise ill-fitting segments.*

Bulk eraser
a machine housing a powerful magnet which removes all recorded signals from an audio tape (*or from videotape*) in one operation.

Camera
apart from its obvious meaning, this is a script instruction (video column) to indicate that this is the chosen picture source.

Cans
headphones.

Capstan
the turning spindle on a tape recorder (*or videotape recorder*) which engages the tape and pulls it forward at the correct speed.

Cardioid microphone
a microphone which picks up sound in a heart-shaped pattern, frequently used in broadcasting studios.

Cartridge
a plastic case containing an endless loop of audio tape, used for theme music, sponsorship announcements, short news items or segments. (*similarly in television, for videotape carrying both picture and sound for any short segment which is likely to be repeated such as commercials, and also where instant start and re-cue is necessary, as in news segments.*)

Cassette
a plastic case containing audio tape, often used for recording material outside the studio.

Channel
a sound signal path. In stereo there are two channels in the system.
(*the same meaning applies within a television station, but the term is also used for the number of the wavelength on which a television station broadcasts.*)

Character generator
an electronic typewriter keyboard used to present words or symbols on a television screen. It is used to "super" names, locations and other non-pictorial information over news videotapes.

Chinagraph pencil
a pencil used to write on audio tape or film in cut editing to show edit points.

Control desk
the desk which contains the mixer.

Console
the desk which contains the mixer.

Crab
a director's instruction to a move the whole camera sideways, as a crab moves. Also the action of doing this.

Crane
(1) an instruction to raise or lower a whole camera to change its point of view, or the action of doing this. Hence crane up or crane down.
(2) *the studio camera mount specifically made for this purpose.*

Crossfade
mixing from one source to another; fading one out as the other fades in (*with pictures as well as sound in television*).

Cue
(1) signal to start or finish.
(2) listening to material before playing and getting it ready to use by lining up the record or tape just before it begins.

Cued
having something ready to play.

Cue Sheet
script showing times, duration and cues for segments in a program, or for editing.

Cut
a track on a record, or a segment of tape. (*to change instantly from one picture or picture source to another as opposed to fade. Either video or audio can be cut --- derived from cut editing.*)

Cut edit
editing method of physically cutting the tape and rejoining it with splicing tape. (*similarly in television where film is edited, hence the derived meaning to cut the television picture.*)

Cutaway
a brief shot of a different subject inserted between two others which will not edit together smoothly. In an interview it is usually a shot of the interviewer between two shots of the interviewee.

Deadline
the time by which material must be prepared.

Decibel
abbreviation (dB), a measurement of level of sound. Three dB is the smallest change in sound level that the ear can detect.

Demagnetise
removal of unwanted magnetisation from the heads of tape recorders (*or video recorders*).

Dish
the dish-shape surrounding a transmission or receiving antenna for sending and receiving signals from remote locations.

Dissolve
fading out one picture as another fades in.

Dolby
a noise reduction system used when audio recording.

Dolly
(1) *the action of physically moving a camera closer or further away from what is being shot; hence dolly in, dolly out.*

(2) *the name sometimes used for the movable stand which carries a studio camera.*

Drop out
loss of sound on a tape caused by damaged or faulty metal oxide coating on the tape or the tape itself, or by a faulty edit (*also applies to both sound and picture in television*).

Dub
transferring a signal from record to tape or tape to tape (derived from the word "double").

Dub-edit
editing by transferring material from one tape to another (*the only method of editing possible with videotape*).

Dynamic Range
the difference between the softest and loudest sounds which can be recorded without distortion.

Echo
repetition of a sound.

Editing
the addition, removal and rearrangement of recorded material. This is done by cut or dub-editing.

Erase head
the head of a tape recorder which removes signals previously recorded when the recorder is set into the "record" mode.

Eye-line
(1) the line along which a person is looking.
(2) the correct positioning of eyes or other objects to ensure continuity of shots in editing.

Fade
to raise or lower the level of a signal.

Fader
a device to control the level of sound (*similarly used in television, but can also control the brightness of a picture*).

Fade in/out
to raise a video signal from black to normal level or to fade it from normal level to black.

Feedback
a howling sound caused by a microphone picking up the signal from a loudspeaker.

Flutter
distortion of a signal caused by rapid fluctuation in tape speed, usually caused by a mechanical problem in the player.

FM
(frequency modulation) a form of radio transmission.

FX
abbreviation for "sound effects", (*also for the effects generator which produces optical patterns such as wipes, expanding circles, rotating cubes etc. in television production*).

Generation of tape
the original recording is the first generation. When dubbed once it is the second generation, and so on. Each generation slightly reduces the quality of the signal (*more so in video generation*).

Head
(1) electromagnetic device over which tape passes for erasing, recording or playing of material (*similarly in video recording*).
(2) the beginning of a tape.
(3) *the name for the mount for a camera which enables it to pan or tilt.*

Headroom
the space between the top of the frame and the top of a person's head in a television picture.

Insert
live or recorded segments within a news item, or any other program.

IPS
inches per second --- the speed at which audio tape travels.

Jack
a socket or plug for a tape recorder or other audio or *video* equipment.

Key
electronically superimposing one picture, or part of a picture, over another. Words or numerals can also be keyed. Chromakey means that the keying is tied to a particular colour in the original shot, so that all portions of the original which are in that colour are replaced by the new picture.

Kill
(1) delete, take out, remove, cut.
(2) switch off equipment.

Kine
abbreviation of kine recording, which is the recording on film of a television program.

Leader tape
uncoated tape attached to audio tape for threading and identifying start and end of taped material. It is often coloured. There is usually about six seconds of leader tape on the head and tail of an audio cassette.

Lead time
time available for the preparation of a program.

Level
the strength of sound signal as measured by a VU or peak meter.

Library
storage for historic audio or video material.

Link
(1) that portion of a script written specifically to provide a cohesive flow between two separate items or disparate segments within an item; often called a bridge (*The term is more often used in television than in radio.*)
(2) *another name for the microwave equipment used to send and receive television signals between the studio and remote locations, even satellites. They are usually dishes.*

Magazine
a type of program containing many segments, such as a current affairs magazine programs, but they can also include music, interviews and comment.

Meters
instruments which provide a visual measurement of signal strength. The two main types in audio work are VU meters, which show the average level of the program material and the peak meter (PPM) which shows more accurately the peak level of the signal. The levels are usually shown by a needle moving across a scale, though some recent equipment uses a scale of coloured lights.

Mike or Mic.
abbreviation of microphone.

Mix
the blending, even briefly, of two sources of sound (or picture).

Mixer
equipment with a variety of inputs which can be selected or combined when recording, editing or broadcasting. Each input and output channel is controlled by its own fader.

Monitor
(1) a loudspeaker to listen to program or cue material.
(2) as a verb; listening to a program for a particular purpose.
(3) *a precision television set used to check the quality of the picture when broadcasting, producing or editing.*

Mono
(monaural, monophonic) sound reproduction using one sound channel only. If there are left and right channels, they are combined into one.

Monochrome
black and white, or one-colour television.

Narrowcasting
As opposed to broadcasting, where a station broadcasts to a narrow range of people — either by interest or ethnic group. The Melbourne station 3AK caters for an Italian audience (and Sky Channel broadcasts to hotels and clubs a range of programs suited for that audience in particular).

Noise
unwanted sounds such as hum or hiss, usually caused by electronic interference (*the same word applies to unwanted specks and lines on a television picture, usually for the same reason, even though the noise cannot be heard.*)

O.B.
stands for Outside Broadcast, hence an O.B.Van is the vehicle which carries the necessary equipment for an O.B to the remote location.
(*a single news camera, even with a link to the studio, is seldom called an O. B.* It usually *refers to two or more cameras with a mixer and link or recording facilities.*)

On air
(1) a sign which indicates that a studio is in use for broadcasting or recording. (2) words used to refer to anything included in the actual broadcast --- script, props, clothes.

Omni-directional Mike
a microphone which responds equally to sound from any direction.

Off air
refers to a signal received by radio or television receivers from broadcast material; thus heard off air or recorded off air.

Package
the name given a report on radio or tv which involved the inclusion of more than two segments: presenter, voice report, interview or multiples of them. It may also include music or other sound effects.

Paint box
a computerised character and shapes generator used for lettering and drawing shapes of all kinds. The name arises from the ability of the computer to add colour or colours to everything. The more complex paint boxes allow for the pictures to move as directed and for the colours to change.

Pan
physically turning the camera to left or right, so that the resulting picture appears to move slowly across a scene. From panoramic view.

Panel
mixer.

Pan pot
a control which allows a signal to pass through one channel or another or both.

Patch cord
a short cable to connect two pieces of equipment.

Peak Program Meter (PPM)
a meter used to measure the peak level of a signal.

Pedestal
(1) *control on a television signal which regulates the black level.*
(2) *a name for the movable stand on which a studio television camera stands.*

Popping
distortion in a signal caused by the consonants P, B and T by the speaker's mouth being too close to the microphone.

Pot
short for potentiometer, which is an instrument for controlling the level of signal (as in faders).

Pre-Listen
a facility on a mixer which permits the operator to listen to material before recording or broadcast, for cueing or pre-setting levels.

Promo
abbreviation for promotional announcement.

Roll
instruction to start a videotape player.

Rating
a measure of the popularity of a program arrived at by audience research.

Reverse angle
see CUTAWAY.

Rough cut
first cut of a radio program before fine editing; used to find out how the final product may fit together.

RPM
revolutions per minute (the speed of records).

Running order
the sequence of items in a program.

Running sheet
the list of items within a program, with title or identification and durations.

Sepmag
abbreviation for separate magnetic (sound), which is synchronised sound recorded on a separate tape from the picture. The camera is electronically synchronised with the tape recorder when recording.

Shot
an individual scene in a television film or tape sequence, or a description of what that individual scene shows.

Simulcast
a broadcast carried by a radio and television station simultaneously. This allows for stereo sound to accompany a television picture.

SOF
(sound on film) which means that the audio signal is recorded on the same source as the picture, now used whether that source is film or videotape.

Splicing tape
tape used to stick portions of audio tape together.

Stereo
(stereophonic) audio reproduction using two channels to provide separation of left and right sounds to create the impression of depth and spread of sound.

Storyboard
a series of drawings which show pictorial sequence in a proposed television program or commercial.

Stylus
the "needle" of a record player.

Super
the name given for superimposing one picture over another, whether keyed in or not. See KEY.

Tail
the last played portion of a tape or the blank leader appended to the end of a tape.

Take
(1) *the name for a single segment or sequence in a proposed series of shots or sequences.*
(2) *the instruction to put a source of picture or sound to air from a given point in the script.*

Talent
a person being interviewed or taking part in a program; also their ability as an entertainer or spokesperson.

Talkback
(1) a type of program in which listeners can join in the program by telephone. (2) communication between the control room and studio and vice versa.

Take-up reel
the spool on the right-hand side of a tape recorder where the recorded or played tape is collected.

Telecine (T/C)
abbreviation for television cinematograph, where films are played into television cameras to produce a television signal; hence the name for the area in which this is done. The name is also used for the television screening of slides (T/C slide) and also generically applied to the playing of videotapes.

Theme
a musical "signature" for a program, or the idea behind a program.

Throw forward file
a system or organising information about coming events.

Tighten
to change a picture so that the viewpoint appears to move closer to the subject, either by physically moving the camera closer or by zooming in.

Tilt Up/Down
physically swivelling a camera lens up or down, so that the picture appears to move up or down the scene.

Tone
a signal of a fixed frequency used to get the level of recording on broadcast equipment.

Track or Truck
physically moving a camera in or out (closer to or further from) the subject of the shot.

Transcript
a verbatim written script of a program or segment of program, usually of an interview.

TX
abbreviation for transmission.

VBU
(video broadcast unit) a format of video cassette widely used in television news.

VCR
(video cassette recorder) a piece of equipment on which video segments, complete with sound, are played and automatically re-cued (more accurately they are video cartridges).

V/O (voice over)
script written and spoken over pre-edited video material.

Vox Pop
a series of recorded comments about the same topic edited together.

VTR
videotape recording/recorder.

VU Meter
(voltage unit) meter which measures the average level of a recorded or broadcast signal. It shows the electrical strength of the signal.

Widen
instruction to include more in the picture, either by physically moving the camera back or by zooming out.

Wild Sound
background sound not needed to match or be in sync. with other sounds (or pictures), such as crowd sound at a football match.

Windshield
a cover for a microphone to reduce wind noise. Such shields also reduce popping. Sometimes called "socks".

Wipe
erase.

Wrap
a term used for a radio report containing a presenter-read section and a brief voice report, too simple to be termed "package". *Also used in tv to describe a collation of brief reports, usually received by satellite, hence "overseas wrap".*

WOW
distortion caused by incorrect or varying speed of tape or record. Sometimes the result of stretched tape.

Zoom
(1) *a lens with movable components which permit the focal length of the picture to be changed, so that the picture appears closer or further away.*
(2) the action of changing the focal length so the picture appears to come closer (zoom in) or move away (zoom out). In fact the picture area encloses less (zoom in) or more (zoom out) subject matter.

Appendix 2

Australian Broadcasting Stations

Radio

Australian Broadcasting Corporation AM Radio

* = National Radio Network

Call kHz Location

AUSTRALIAN CAPITAL TERRITORY
2CN   666   Canberra
2CY   846   Canberra*

NEW SOUTH WALES
2CR   549   Orange
2FC   576   Sydney*
      603   Nowra*
2NU   648   Tamworth
2BY   657   Byrock
2CO   675   Albury/Corowa
2KP   684   Kempsey
2BL   702   Sydney
2ML   720   Murwillumbah
2AN   720   Armidale
2NR   738   Grafton
2TR   756   Taree
2BA   810   Bega
2GL   819   Glen Innes
2NB   999   Broken Hill
2UH   1044 Muswellbrook
2GU   1098 Goulburn*
2NC   1233 Newcastle
2LG   1395 Lithgow
2WN   1431 Wollongong
2NA   1512 Newcastle*
2WA   1584 Wilcannia
2CP   1602 Cooma

VICTORIA
3WV   594   Horsham
3AR   621   Melbourne*
3MT   720   Omeo
3WA   756   Wangaratta*
3LO   774   Melbourne
3GI   828   Sale
3AB   990   Albury/Wodonga*
3WL   1602 Warrnambool

QUEENSLAND
4QL   540   Longreach
4JK   567   Julia Creek
4CH   603   Charleville
4QR   612   Brisbane
4QN   630   Townsville
4MS   639   Mossman
4QW   711   St George
4AT   720   Atherton
4QG   729   Brisbane*
4QS   747   Toowoomba
4QA   756   Mackay
4QY   801   Cairns
4RK   837   Rockhampton
4QB   855   Pialba
4QO   855   Eidsvold
4WP   1044 Weipa
4TI   1062 Thursday Island
4MI   1080 Mount Isa
4HU   1485 Hughenden
4QD   1548 Emerald
4GM   1566 Gympie
4SO   1593 Southport

SOUTH AUSTRALIA
5CK   639   Port Pirie
5SY   693   Streaky Bay
5CL   729   Adelaide*
5AN   891   Adelaide
5PA   1161 Naracoorte
5LN   1495 Port Lincoln
5MG   1584 Mount Gambier
5MW   1584 Woomera
5MV   1593 Renmark
5LC   1602 Leigh Creek

Call	MHz	Location

WESTERN AUSTRALIA
6DL	531	Dalwallinu
6WA	558	Wagin
6PU	567	Paraburdoo
6TP	567	Tom Price
6MN	567	Newman
6PN	567	Pannawonica
6PH	603	Port Hedland
6NM	612	Northam
6AL	630	Albany
6GF	648	Kalgoorlie
6KP	702	Karratha
6BE	675	Broome
6BS	684	Busselton
6WF	720	Perth
6MJ	738	Manjimup
6KW	756	Kununurra
6WN	810	Perth*
6GN	828	Geraldton
6ED	837	Esperance
6CA	846	Carnarvon
6DB	873	Derby
6WH	1017	Wyndham
6BR	1044	Bridgetown
6XM	1188	Exmouth

TASMANIA
7ZL	585	Hobart*
7QN	630	Queenstown
7NT	711	Launceston
7ZR	936	Hobart
7FG	1161	Fingal
7SH	1584	St Helens

NORTHERN TERRITORY
8DR	657	Darwin*
8KN	675	Katherine
8TC	684	Tennant Creek
8JB	747	Jabiru
8AL	783	Alice Springs
8GO	990	Gove

Australian Broadcasting Corporation FM Radio

Call	MHz	Location

AUSTRALIAN CAPITAL TERRITORY
| 2JJJ-FM | 101.5 | Canberra |
| 2ABC-FM | 102.3 | Canberra |

NEW SOUTH WALES
2ABC-FM	88.1	Khancoban
2ABC-FM	88.1	Talbingo
RN-relay	89.7	Khancoban*
RN-relay	90.5	Thredbo*
RN-relay	91.3	Talbingo*
2ABC-FM	92.9	Sydney
2ABC-FM	93.5	Dubbo
RN-relay	93.7	Lightning Rge*
RN-relay	100.9	Goodooga*
2JJJ-FM	102.1	Newcastle
2ABC-FM	102.7	Orange
2ABC-FM	103.7	Broken Hill
RN-relay	105.1	Bateman's Bay*
2ABC-FM	105.7	Bega
2JJJ-FM	105.7	Sydney
2ABC-FM	105.7	Wagga Wagga
2ABC-FM	106.1	Newcastle
RN-relay	106.1	Wilcannia
2ABC-FM	107.5	Griffith
RN-relay	107.7	Ivanhoe*
RN-relay	107.7	Walgett
2ABC-FM	107.9	Wollongong
2ABC-FM	107.9	Taree

VICTORIA
3ABC-FM	102.7	Mildura
3ABC-FM	104.1	Albury/Wodonga
3ABC-FM	105.5	Ballarat
3ABC-FM	105.9	Melbourne
3ABC-FM	105.9	Swan Hill
3ABC-FM	106.3	Bendigo
3ABC-FM	107.1	Traralgon
3ABC-FM	107.5	Hamilton
3JJJ-FM	107.5	Melbourne

QUEENSLAND
4ABC-FM	92.5	Maryborough
4ABC-FM	93.7	Rockhampton
RN-relay	93.9	Emerald*
RN-relay	97.7	Charters Towers*
RN-relay	98.9	Wandoan*
RN-relay	100.7	Longreach*
RN-relay	100.9	Nonda*
RN-relay	100.9	Springsure*
4ABC-FM	101.5	Townsville
RN-relay	101.9	Greenvale*
RN-relay	104.3	Meandarra/Tara*
4ABC-FM	104.5	Clermont
4ABC-FM	105.1	Cairns*
RN-relay	105.9	Cairns
4ABC-FM	106.1	Brisbane
RN-relay	107.3	Alpha*
RN-relay	107.3	Capella*
RN-relay	107.3	Charleville*
RN-relay	107.3	Cooktown*
RN-relay	107.3	Corfield*
RN-relay	107.3	Dirranbandi*
RN-relay	107.3	Mt Isa*
RN-relay	107.3	Normanton*
RN-relay	107.3	Roma*

RN-relay	107.3	Weipa*
RN-relay	107.5	Barcaldine*
RN-relay	107.5	Blackwater*
RN-relay	107.5	Coen*
RN-relay	107.5	Collinsville*
RN-relay	107.5	Croydon*
RN-relay	107.5	Hughenden*
RN-relay	107.5	Injune*
RN-relay	107.5	Julia Creek*
RN-relay	107.5	Morven*
RN-relay	107.5	Surat*
RN-relay	107.5	Tambo*
RN-relay	107.7	Augathella*
RN-relay	107.7	Bedourie*
RN-relay	107.7	Birdsville
RN-relay	107.7	Boulia*
RN-relay	107.7	Camooweal*
RN-relay	107.7	Clermont*
RN-relay	107.7	Cloncurry*
RN-relay	107.7	Cunnamulla*
RN-relay	107.7	Georgetown*
RN-relay	107.7	Isisford*
RN-relay	107.7	Jerico*
RN-relay	107.7	Karumba*
RN-relay	107.7	Laura*
RN-relay	107.7	Mitchell*
RN-relay	107.7	Muttaburra*
RN-relay	107.7	Pentland*
RN-relay	107.7	Quilpie*
RN-relay	107.7	Richmond*
RN-relay	107.7	St George*
RN-relay	107.7	Taroom*
RN-relay	107.7	Thursday Island*
RN-relay	107.9	Aramac*
RN-relay	107.9	Blackall*
4ABC-FM	107.9	Toowoomba
RN-relay	107.9	Winton*

SOUTH AUSTRALIA

RN-relay	101.9	Roxby Downs*
RN-relay	101.9	Tumby Bay*
5ABC-FM	103.5	Roxby Downs
5ABC-FM	103.9	Adelaide
5ABC-FM	104.1	Mt Gambier
5ABC-FM	104.3	Pt Pirie
5ABC-FM	105.1	Loxton
5JJJ-FM	105.5	Adelaide
RN-relay	105.7	Woomera*
RN-relay	106.1	Leigh Creek Sth*
RN-relay	106.7	Pt Pirie*
RN-relay	107.3	Maree*
RN-relay	107.5	Andamooka*
RN-relay	107.7	Coober Pedy*

WESTERN AUSTRALIA

RN-relay	88.1	Dampier*
6ABC-FM	93.3	Bunbury
6ABC-FM	94.5	Albany
6ABC-FM	95.1	Geraldton
6ABC-FM	95.5	Kalgoorlie
RN-relay	95.7	Pt Hedland*
6ABC-FM	97.7	Perth
6ABC-FM	98.9	Mawson
6JJJ-FM	99.3	Perth
RN-relay	100.9	Karratha*
RN-relay	100.9	Ravensthorpe*
6ABC-FM	102.5	Koolan Island
6ABC-FM	104.1	Goldsworthy
RN-relay	104.1	Mt Whaleback
6ABC-FM	104.5	Shay Gap
RN-relay	105.7	Goldsworthy*
RN-relay	106.1	Shay Gap*
RN-relay	107.3	Kunanurra*
RN-relay	107.3	Leeman*
RN-relay	107.3	Leonora*
RN-relay	107.3	Merredin*
RN-relay	107.3	Mt Magnet*
RN-relay	107.3	Norseman*
RN-relay	107.3	Tom Price*
RN-relay	107.5	Argyle*
RN-relay	107.5	Denham*
RN-relay	107.5	Derby*
RN-relay	107.5	Kaverton*
RN-relay	107.5	Marble Bar*
RN-relay	107.5	Onslow*
RN-relay	107.5	Roebourne*
RN-relay	107.7	Broome*
RN-relay	107.7	Carnarvon*
RN-relay	107.7	Cue*
RN-relay	107.7	Eneabba*
RN-relay	107.7	Exmouth*
RN-relay	107.7	Fitzroy Crossing*
RN-relay	107.7	Halls Creek*
RN-relay	107.7	Kalbarri*
RN-relay	107.7	Koolin Island*
RN-relay	107.7	Newman*
RN-relay	107.7	Pannawonica*
RN-relay	107.7	Paraburdoo*
RN-relay	107.7	Wyndham*
RN-relay	107.9	Jurien Bay*
RN-relay	107.9	Meekatharra*

TASMANIA

7ABC-FM	93.3	Launceston
7ABC-FM	93.9	Hobart

NORTHERN TERRITORY
8JJJ-FM   103.3 Darwin
8ABC-FM   107.3 Darwin
RN-relay   107.5 Galiwinku*
RN-relay   107.7 Borroloola*
RN-relay   107.7 Daly River*
RN-relay   107.7 Groote Eylandt*
RN-relay   107.7 Jabiru*
RN-relay   107.7 Mataranka*
RN-relay   107.7 Newcastle Waters*
RN-relay   107.7 Nhulunbuy*
RN-relay   107.7 Ngukurr*
RN-relay   107.7 Pine Creek*

ABC Domestic Short-wave Service

Call	kHz	Location
VLM4	4920	Brisbane
VLW6	6140	Wanneroo WA
VLR6	6150	Lyndhurst Vic
VLW9	9610	Wanneroo
VLQ9	9660	Brisbane
VLH9	9680	Lyndhurst
VLR9	9680	Lyndhurst
VLH11	11880	Lyndhurst
VLH15	15230	Lyndhurst
VLW15	15425	Wanneroo

Special Broadcasting Service (SBS) AM Stations

Call	kHz	Location
3EA	1224	Melbourne
2EA	1386	Sydney
2EA	1485	Wollongong
2EA	1584	Newcastle

Commercial (privately owned) AM Radio Stations

Call	kH	Location

AUSTRALIAN CAPITAL TERRITORY
2CA   1053 Canberra
2CC   1206 Canberra

NEW SOUTH WALES
2MC   531 Kempsey
2BH   567 Broken Hill
2CS   639 Coffs Harbour
2EC   765 Bega
       and 1584 Narooma
2KA   783 Katoomba
       and 1476 Penrith
2GO   801 Gosford
2GB   873 Sydney
2LM   900 Lismore
2LT   900 Lithgow
2XL   918 Cooma
       and 93.3 Jindabyne
       98.7 Perisher
       92.1 Thredbo
2UE   954 Sydney
2RG   963 Griffith
2MW   972 Murwillumbah
2NM   981 Muswellbrook
2ST   999 Nowra
       and 1251 Bowral/Moss Vale
       1106.1 Ulladulla
2KY   1017 Sydney
2MO   1080 Gunnedah
2GZ   1089 Orange
2UW   1107 Sydney
2AD   1134 Armidale
2HD   1143 Newcastle
2WG   1152 Wagga Wagga
2CH   1170 Sydney
2NZ   1188 Inverell
2GF   1206 Grafton
2WS   1224 Sydney/Blacktown
2DU   1251 Dubbo
       and 972 Cobar
2SM   1269 Sydney
2TM   1287 Tamworth
2WL   1314 Wollongong
2NX   1341 Newcastle
2LF   1350 Young
2GN   1368 Goulburn
2PK   1404 Parkes
2KO   1413 Newcastle
2MG   1449 Mudgee
2AY   1494 Albury
2BS   1503 Bathurst
2QN   1521 Deniliquin
2VM   1530 Moree
       and 98.3 Moree
2RE   1557 Taree
2OO   1575 Wollongong

VICTORIA
3GG   531 Warragul
3YB   882 Warrnambool
3UZ   927 Melbourne
3BO   945 Bendigo
3HA   981 Hamilton
3CV   071 Maryborough

3WM	1089 Horsham		5SE	963 Mount Gambier
3CS	1134 Colac		5CS	1044 Port Pirie
3TR	1242 Sale		5MU	1125 Murray Bridge
3SR	1260 Shepparton		5AU	1242 Port Augusta
3AW	1278 Melbourne		5AD	1323 Adelaide
3BA	1314 Ballarat		5AA	1386 Adelaide
3SH	1332 Swan Hill			
3MP	1377 Melbourne/Frankston			
3XY	1422 Melbourne			
3MA	1467 Mildura			
3AK	1503 Melbourne			
3NE	1566 Wangaratta			

WESTERN AUSTRALIA

6LN	666 Carnarvon
and	747 Exmouth
6SE	747 Esperance
6VA	783 Albany
6AM	864 Northam
6PR	882 Perth
6BY	900 Bridgetown
6NA	918 Narrogin
6TZ	963 Bunbury
and	1134 Collie
6KG	981 Kalgoorlie
6PM	990 Perth
6GE	1008 Geraldton
6NW	1026 Port Hedland
6WB	1071 Katanning
6GL	1080 Perth
6MD	1098 Merredin
6MM	1116 Mandurah
6KY	1206 Perth
6KA	1260 Karratha
and	765 Paraburdoo
	765 Tom Price

QUEENSLAND

4KZ	531 Innisfail
and	693 Tully
4AM	558 Mareeba
4GY	558 Gympie
4LM	666 Mt.Isa
and	1458 Cloncurry
4KQ	693 Brisbane
4TO	774 Townsville
4GC	828 Charters Towers
and	765 Hughenden
4SS	828 Nambour
4CA	846 Cairns
and	954 Gordonvale
4GR	864 Toowoomba
4BH	882 Brisbane
4RR	891 Townsville
4VL	918 Charleville
and	1584 Cunnamulla
4CC	927 Gladstone
and	666 Biloela
	1584 Rockhampton
4WK	963 Toowoomba/Warwick
4RO	990 Rockhampton
and	1125 Gladstone
4IP	1008 Brisbane
4MK	1026 Mackay
and	91.5 Airlie Beach
4SB	1071 Kingaroy
4LG	1098 Longreach
4BC	1116 Brisbane
4HI	1143 Emerald
and	1215 Moranbah
	945 Dysart
4MB	1161 Maryborough
4AK	1242 Toowoomba
4BK	1296 Brisbane
4BU	1332 Bundaberg
4ZR	1476 Roma

TASMANIA

7SD	540 Scottsdale
7BU	558 Burnie
7QT	837 Queenstown
and	107.1 Rosebery
7HO	864 Hobart
7AD	900 Devonport
7EX	1008 Launceston
7HT	1080 Hobart
7LA	1098 Launceston

NORTHERN TERRITORY

8HA	900 Alice Springs
8DN	1242 Darwin
and	765 Katherine

Commercial (privately owned) FM Radio Stations

Cal	MHz Location

AUSTRALIAN CAPITAL TERRITORY
2ROC-FM 104.7 Canberra
2KIX-FM 106.3 Canberra

SOUTH AUSTRALIA

5CC	765 Port Lincoln
5RM	801 Berri-Renmark

NEW SOUTH WALES
2CFM-FM 101.3 Gosford
2DAY-FM 104.1 Sydney
2MMM-FM 104.9 Sydney
2NEW-FM 105.3 Newcastle

VICTORIA
3BAY-FM 93.9 Geelong
3CAT-FM 95.5 Geelong (K-Rock)
3TT-FM 101.1 Melbourne
3FOX-FM 101.9 Melbourne
3KKZ-FM 104.3 Melbourne (KZFM)
3MMM-FM 105.1 Melbourne
3SUN-FM 107.7 Shepparton

QUEENSLAND
4SEA-FM 90.9 Gold Coast
4GGG-FM 92.5 Gold Coast
4MMM-FM 104.5 Brisbane
4BBB-FM 105.3 Brisbane
4QFM-FM 106.9 Ipswich

SOUTH AUSTRALIA
5DDN-FM 102.3 Adelaide
5KKA-FM 104.7 Adelaide (KAFM)
5SSA-FM 107.1 Adelaide

WESTERN AUSTRALIA
6NOW-FM 96.1 Perth
6FMS-FM via satellite retransmissions throughout W.A.

TASMANIA
7TTT-FM 100.9 Hobart

Public Broadcasting AM Radio Stations

Call	kHz Location
5UV	531 Adelaide/Uni.
2WEB	585 Bourke NSW
3CR	855 Melbourne
6NR	927 Perth/Curtin Uni
2XX	1008 Canberra
4EB	1053 Brisbane

Public Broadcasting FM Radio Stations

Call   MHz Location

AUSTRALIAN CAPITAL TERRITORY
2SSS 103.9 Canberra

NEW SOUTH WALES
2RDJ 88.1 Sydney/Burwood
2RRR 88.5 Sydney/Ryde
2BCR 88.7 Sydney/Bankstown
2RSR 88.9 Sydney/"Skid Row"
2GLF 89.3 Sydney/Liverpool
2RES 89.7 Sydney/Paddington
2VTR 89.7 Windsor/Colo
2NBC 90.1 Sydney/Baptist
2NSB 91.5 Sydney/Chatswood
2HAY 92.1 Hay
2ARM 92.3 Armidale
2MCE 92.3 Bathurst/CSUni.
  and 94.7 Orange
2NCR 92.5 Lismore/UNE
2MWM 93.7 Sydney/Warringah
  and 92.1 Manly
2YOU 95.5 Tamworth
2TLC 100.3 Maclean
2GLA 101.5 Forster
2MBS 102.5 Sydney/Music Soc
2CBA 103.2 Sydney/Church
2GCR 103.3 Goulburn
2NUR 103.7 Newcastle/Uni.
2CHY 104.1 Coffs Harbour
2UUU 104.5 Nowra
2BOB 104.5 Taree
2VOX 106.9 Wollongong
2AAA 107.1 Wagga Wagga
2WKT 107.1 Bowral
2BBB 107.3 Bellingen
  and 90.5 Dorrigo
2SER 107.3 Sydney/UTS
2EAR 107.5 Moruya
  and 102.9 Narooma
2TEN 107.5 Tenterfield
2REM 107.9 Albury/Wodonga
2CFM 107.9 Gosford

VICTORIA
3SCB 88.3 Moorabbin
3ZZZ 92.3 Melbourne/ethnic
3WRB 97.4 Melbourne/Footscray
3BBB 97.5 Ballarat
3RIM 97.9 Melton
3RPP 98.7 Mornington
3YYR 100.3 Geelong

3WAY	100.9 Warrnambool		5MMM	93.7 Adelaide
3RRR	102.7 Melbourne/Fitzroy		5GTR	105.7 Mt Gambier
3MBR	103.5 Murrayville		5TCB	106.1 Bordertown
3MBS	103.5 Melbourne/Music Soc		5RRR	107.3 Woomera
3CCC	103.9 Castlemaine		5YYY	107.7 Whyalla
3GCR	104.7 LaTrobe Valley			
3RPC	106.5 Portland		**WESTERN AUSTRALIA**	
3PBS	106.7 Melbourne		6NEW	92.9 Newman
3ONE	106.9 Shepparton		6EBA	95.3 Perth
3MFM	107.9 Leongatha		6SON	98.5 Perth
	and 104.5 Phillip Island		6CCR	100.1 Perth
	104.1 Foster		6RKR	101.7 Rockingham
QUEENSLAND			**TASMANIA**	
4CCR	89.1 Cairns		7THE	92.1 Hobart
4CRB	89.3 Gold Coast		7RGY	95.3 Geeveston
4YOU	98.5 Rockhampton		7HFC	103.3 Hobart
4CBL	101.1 Logan		7LTN	103.7 Launceston
4RRR	101.7 Roma		7WAY	105.3 Launceston
4ZZZ	102.1 Brisbane			
4DDB	102.7 Toowoomba		**NORTHERN TERRITORY**	
4MBS	103.7 Brisbane/Music Soc		8KIN	100.5 Alice Springs/CAAMA
4TTT	103.9 Townsville			and 103.7 Ali-Curang
				103.7 Hermannsburg
SOUTH AUSTRALIA				103.7 Santa Teresa
5PBA	89.7 Adelaide/Salisbury		8CCC	102.1 Alice Springs/TAFE
5EBI	92.9 Adelaide/ethnic			and 102.1 Tennant Creek
			8TOP	104.1 Darwin/NTUni

Television

AUSTRALIAN TELEVISION STATIONS

Australian television operates a PAL 625-line system with the following channel frequencies:

Channel MHz

Channel	MHz
0	46.25/51.75
1	57.25/62.75
2	64.25/69.75
3	86.25/91.75
4	95.25/100.75
5	102.25/107.75
5A	138.25/143.75
6	175.15/180.75
7	182.25/187.75
8	189.25/194.75
9	196.25/201.25
10	209.25/214.75
11	216.25/221.75
28	526-633
29	533-340
30	540-547
31	547-554
32	554-561
33	561-568
34	568-575
35	575-582
39	603-610
40	610-617
41	617-624
42	624-631
43	631-638
44	638-645
45	645-652
46	652-659
47	659-666
48	666-673
49	673-680
50	680-687
51	687-694
52	694-701
53	701-708
54	708-715
55	715-722
56	722-729
57	729-736
58	736-743
59	743-750
60	750-757
61	757-764
62	764-771
63	771-778
64	778-785
65	785-792
66	792-799
67	799-806
68	806-813
69	813-820

Australian Broadcasting Corporation Television Stations (VHF)

(v) vertical polarisation

Call	Channel	Location
AUSTRALIAN CAPITAL TERRITORY		
ABC	3(v)	Canberra
NEW SOUTH WALES		
ABMN	0	Wagga Wagga
ABTN	1(v)	Taree
ABCN	1(v)	Orange
ABN	2	Sydney
ABDN	2	Grafton/Kempsey
ABLN	2(v)	Broken Hill
ABHN	5A	Newcastle
ABQN	5(v)	Dubbo
ABWN	5A	Wollongong
ABRN	6	Lismore
ABUN	7	Tamworth
ABGN	7	Griffith
ABSN	8(v)	Bega/Cooma
ABMIN	10	Mungindi
VICTORIA		
ABEV	1(v)	Bendigo
ABAV	1	Albury
ABV	2	Melbourne
ABSV	2(v)	Swan Hill
ABRV	3	Ballarat
ABGV	3(v)	Shepparton
ABLV	4	Traralgon
ABMV	4	Mildura
ABWV	5A	Western Victoria

QUEENSLAND		
ABSQ	1	Warwick
ABQ	2	Brisbane
ABDQ	3	Toowoomba
ABRQ	3	Rockhampton
ABTQ	3	Townsville
ABMQ	4	Mackay
ABWQ	6(v)	Maryborough
ABRDQ	6	Richmond
ABIQ	6	Mount Isa
ABGQ	6	Goondiwindi
ABLQ	6	Longreach
ABMLQ	6	Mitchell
ABCLQ	7	Cloncurry
ABDIQ	7(v)	Dirranbandi
ABMNQ	7	Morven
ABRAQ	7	Roma
ABAQ	8	Alpha
ABSGQ	8	St George
ABWNQ	8	Winton
ABBLQ	9	Blackall
ABCEQ	9	Charleville
ABHQ	9	Hughenden
ABMKQ	9	Mary Kathleen
ABMSQ	9(v)	Miles
ABSEQ	9	Springsure
ABNQ	9	Cairns
ABBQ	10	Barcaldine
ABCAQ	10	Cunnamulla
ABCTQ	10	Clermont
ABJQ	10	Julia Creek
ABAAQ	11	Auguthella
ABEQ	11	Emerald

SOUTH AUSTRALIA		
ABGS	1	Mount Gambier
ABNS	1(v)	Port Pirie
ABS	2	Adelaide
ABRS	3(v)	Loxton
ABCS	7	Ceduna
ABWS	7	Woomera

WESTERN AUSTRALIA		
ABW	2	Perth
ABAW	2(v)	Albany
ABSW	5	Bunbury
ABSW	5A	Northam/York
ABGW	6	Geraldton
ABKW	6	Kalgoorlie
ABCNW	7	Carnarvon
ABKAW	7	Karratha
ABNW	7	Norseman
ABPHW	7	Port Hedland
ABCMW	8	Morowa
ABRBW	9	Roebourne
ABSBW	9	So.Cross/Bullfinch
ABDW	10	Dampier

ABEW	10	Esperance
ABMW	10	Moora

TASMANIA		
ABT	2	Hobart
ABNT	3	Launceston
ABKT	11	King Island

NORTHERN TERRITORY		
ABD	6	Darwin
ABAD	7	Alice Springs
ABKD	7	Katherine
ABTD	9	Tennant Creek

Special Broadcasting Service UHF Television Stations

Call	Channel	Location
SBS	28	Canberra
SBS	28	Sydney
SBS	28	Melbourne
SBS	28	Adelaide
SBS	28	Newcastle
SBS	28	Wollongong
SBS	28	Brisbane

Commercial (privately owned) Television Stations

Call	Channel	Location
AUSTRALIAN CAPITAL TERRITORY AND NEW SOUTH WALES		
RVN	2	South Western Slopes and Eastern Riverina
and	6	Young
	11	Wagga Wagga
	60	Tumut
	69	Tumbarumba
NBN	3	Newcastle/Hunter River
and	1	Murrurundi
	10	Merriwa, Scone
	39	Cassilis
	40	Gosford
	41	Bouddi, Merewether
	60	Collaroy
	61	Kotara
	69	Dungog

WIN		4 Wollongong, Southern NSW and ACT		61 Bateman's Bay/Moruya, Lithgow East
	and	3 Eden, Narooma		62 Illawarra
		6 Bega		63 Eden, Kandos, Portland/Wallerawang, Tuggeranong
		4 Illawarra		
		11 Bateman's Bay/Moruya		64 Mudgee, Young
		31 Canberra		65 Wagga Wagga
		32 Central Western Slopes, SW Slopes, East Riverina		66 Dubbo, Jindabyne
			CBN	8 Orange, Central and Southern NSW and ACT
		35 Nowra North		
		39 Bowral, Cooma, Stanwell Park, Central Tablelands	and	4 Portland/Wallerawang
				6 Central Western Slopes, Lithgow
		43 Thredbo		
		44 Lithgow		9 Mudgee
		52 Bathurst		10 Cobar, Kandos
		57 Jindabyne		11 Bathurst
		59 Illawarra		34 Canberra
		61 Bombala, Goulburn, Mudgee, Young		40 Bega
				42 Cooma/Monaro
		62 Cooma, Condoblin, Wagga Wagga		44 Narooma, Nowra North
		63 Braidwood, Dubbo		45 Bowral/Mittagong, Stanwell Park
		66 Kandos, Portland/Wallerawang, Tuggeranong		
				46 Thredbo
				47 Wollongong
ATN		7 Sydney		58 Lithgow East
	and	44 Bouddi		59 Coolah
		49 Kings Cross, Gosford		60 Dubbo, Portland/Wallerawang
		60 Wyong		63 Jindabyne
				64 Bateman's Bay/Moruya, Bombala, Goulburn
BKN		7 Broken Hill		
CTC		7 Canberra, Southern NSW and ACT		65 Cooma, Illawarra
	and	2 Bombala		66 Braidwood, Eden, Nyngan
		10 Canberra South, Cooma, Goulburn		68 Condoblin
				69 Tuggeranong
		33 Central Tablelands		
		34 Bega	RTN	8 Lismore, Richmond-Tweed
		35 Central Western Slopes, SW Slopes and Eastern Riverina		
			and	42 Currumbin
				55 Gold Coast
		40 Thredbo		58 Bonalbo
		41 Lithgow, Narooma, Nowra North		60 Kyogle
				63 Murwillumbah, Tenterfield
		42 Bowral/Mittagong, Stanwell Park		
			TCN	9 Sydney
		44 Wollongong	and	47 Bouddi
		49 Bathurst		52 Gosford, Kings Cross
		58 Captain's Flat		
		59 Condoblin		63 Wyong
		60 Braidwood		

MTN	9 Griffith, Murrumbidge Irrigation Areas and 5A Hay	and	(Traralgon) 6 Foster-Toora 7 Orbost 11 Lakes Entrance
NEN	9 Tamworth, Taree, New England/Mid-North Coast and 0 Tamworth 1 Walcha 3 Glen Innes 8 Taree 9 Upper Namoi 10 Armidale, Ashford, Inverell 11 Gloucester, Quirindi 47 Laurieton	STV GTV and ATV and	8 Mildura 9 Melbourne 45 Upwey 52 Marysville, Mt Martha, Warburton 62 Ferntree Gully 63 Selby 10 Melbourne 48 Upwey 55 Marysville, Mt Martha, Warburton 65 Ferntree Gully 66 Selby
TEN	10 Sydney and 50 Bouddi 55 Gosford, Kings Cross 66 Wyong		QUEENSLAND
		DDQ and	0 Darling Downs (Toowoomba) 5A Toowoomba 10 Miles 64 Milmerran 65 Chinchilla 66 Murgon, Tara
NRN	11 Grafton/Kempsey and 63 Coffs Harbour		
VICTORIA			
AMV	4 Albury-Wodonga, Upper Murray and 7 Khancoban 9 Myrtleford 10 Corryong-Khancoban 11 Bright 48 Tawonga South 59 Walwa-Jinjillic	SDQ and MVQ and	4 Southern Downs (Warwick) 60 Tenterfield 6 Mackay 6 Dysart 10 Middlemount 11 Moranbah-Goonyella 32 Glenden 46 Airlie Beach 58 Collinsville, Nebo, Shute Harbour 59 Clermont 65 Tieri
RTV	6 Ballarat, Shepparton and 3 Eildon 7 Nhill 8 Jerilderie 9 Warrnambool-Port Fairy 10 Deniliquin, Hamilton 11 Alexandra, Portland 48 Mansfield 57 Portland 62 Yea		
		BTQ and RTQ and	7 Brisbane 39 Currumbin 52 Gold Coast 7 Rockhampton 6 Emerald 9 Capella 10 Blackwater Bluff, Gladstone, Springsure 69 Boyne Island-Tannum Sands
HSV	7 Melbourne and 42 Upwey 49 Marysville, Mt Martha, Warburton 59 Ferntree Gully 60 Selby		
BCV	8 Bendigo and 11 Swan Hill	TNQ and	7 Townsville-Cairns, North Queensland 1 Bowen 2 Gordonvale
GLV	8 LaTrobe Valley		

	5A Cairns Nth, Herberton, Mission Beach, Townsville Nth		60 Narrogin
			66 Kojonup
		TVW	7 Perth
	6 Babinda, Mareeba	VEW	8 Kalgoorlie
	10 Cairns	and	3 Baandee, Kambalda
	11 Mossman, Ravenshoe, Tully		6 Koolyanobbing, Merredin
	53 Charters Towers		9 Esperance, Norseman
	68 Stuart		
ITQ	8 Mount Isa		10 Southern Cross
SEQ	8 Wide Bay-Burnett (Bundaberg)	STW	9 Perth
		NEW	10 Perth
and	1 Gympie	SSW	10 Albany
	5 Monto	and	9 Southern Agricultural
	60 Nambour		
QTQ	9 Brisbane		66 Gnowangerup
and	45 Currumbin		
	58 Gold Coast	GTW	11 Geraldton
		and	30 Morawa
TVQ	10 Brisbane		62 Mingenew
and	30 Currumbin		63 Mullewa
	46 Gold Coast		

SOUTH AUSTRALIA

TASMANIA

GTS	4 Spencer Gulf North (Port Pirie-Whyalla-Port Augusta)	TVT	6 Hobart
		and	8 Bicheno, Maydena, Queenstown©Zeehan, Strathgordon, Taroona
and	5 Port Lincoln		
	8 Cowell		
	35 Tumby Bay		10 Rosebery
	48 Coffin Bay	TNT	9 North-eastern Tasmania (Launceston)
	63 Port Lincoln		
RTS	5A Renmark-Loxton		
SAS	7 Adelaide	and 5A Wynyard	
and	49 Adelaide Foothills		6 Circular Head
SES	8 South East South Australia (Mt Gambier)		7 St Helens, Savage River-Luina
			8 King Island
			10 Burnie
and	32 The Gap (Naracoorte)		11 Derby, St Marys-FMingal Valley, Smithton, South Launceston, Waratah
	33 Keith		
	49 Bordertown		51 East Devonport
NWS	9 Adelaide		59 King Island
and	52 Adelaide Foothills		
ADS	10 Adelaide	**NORTHERN TERRITORY**	
and	55 Adelaide Foothills	NTD	8 Darwin

Remote Commercial Television Services

WESTERN AUSTRALIA

BTW	3 Bunbury	
and	6 Wagin	IMP CENTRAL ZONE, from Alice Springs, NT
	10 Katanning	
	11 Mawson	7 Ceduna SA, Tennant Creek,
	59 Northam	

9 Alice Springs,
   Bathurst Island,
   Bourke NSW,
   Groote Eylandt,
   Katherine, Woomera
   SA
10 Coober Pedy SA,
   Jabiru, Leigh Creek
   SA, Wilcannia NSW
63 Andamooka SA,
64 Kalkaringi
65 Cattle Creek,
   Urapunga, Wave
   Hill
66 Cook SA, Elliston
   SA, Marree SA,
   Streaky Bay SA,
   Uluru, Warrego
   Mine, Yunta SA
67 Mintabie SA
68 South Alligator,
   Umbakumba
69 Yalata SA

QQQ NORTH-EAST ZONE, from
Townsville, Queensland
   6 Cooktown, St
     George, Thursday
     Island, Wilcannia
     NSW 8 Balcaldine
   9 Cloncurry,
     Cunnamulla,
     Longreach, Roma,
     Weipa
  10 Charleville,
     Hughenden
  11 Blackall, Mitchell,
     Winton
  66 Brewarrina NSW,
     Lightning Ridge
     NSW, Walgett NSW
  69 Bourke NSW

WAW WESTERN ZONE, from
Bunbury, WA
   6 Halls Creek, Marble
     Bar, Mount Magnet,
     Roebourne
   7 Kalbarri, Kununurra,
     Laverton, Leinster,
     Menzies, Tom Price
   8 Koolan Island,
     Pannawonica,
     Ravensthorpe,
     Wyndham
   9 Goldsworthy, Mount
     Nameless, Newman,
     Shay Gap
  10 Port Hedland
  11 Exmouth, Onslow,
     Paraburdoo, Salmon
     Gums
  32 Hyden
  34 Kulin, Mukinbudin
  45 Lake Grace
  48 Green Head
  53 Nullagine
  55 Koorda
  57 Karratha, Moora
  61 Narembeen
  62 Lily Creek, Westonia
  63 Newdegate
  64 Jurien, North
     Rankin, Ongerup,
     Pingrup
  65 Gairdner, Hearson
     Cove
  66 Eucla SA, Jameison,
     Jerramungup,
     Kondinin,
     Munglinup, One
     Arm Point,
     Tjirrkarli, Trayning,
     Vlaming Head,
     Wangatjungka,
     Warburton, Wave
     Rock, Wiluna
  68 Hopetoun,
     Lombadina
  69 Lagrange, Leeman,
     Leonora,
     Oombulgurri,
     Wittenoom,
     Yandeearra

6FMS WESTERN ZONE
(monophonic), from Bunbury
   88.9 Newman
  102.5 Kununurra
  102.7 Derby
  102.9 Broome, Kalbarri
  106.9 Telfer

Appendix 3

Some useful and relevant reading

Books on radio journalism
(some also include television journalism)
ARMSTRONG, M. *Broadcasting law and policy in Australia*, Butterworth, 1981.
———*Broadcasting Act 1942* (and amendments), Australian Government Printer.
BLISS, Edward and PATTERSON, John. *Writing News for Broadcast*, Columbia University Press, New York, 1971.
BRIGGS, Asa. *Governing the BBC*, BBC, London. (no date)
BRIGGS, Susan. *Those Radio Times*, Weidenfeld, London, 1981.
BROUSSARD, E. Joseph and Jack F. HOLGATE, *Writing and Reporting Broadcast News*, Macmillan, New York, 1982.
De MAESENEER, Paul, (ed.). *Here's the News*, Asia-Pacific Institute for Broadcasting Development, Kuala Lumpur. (no date)
EBRALL, Phill. *The B.S.G. (Broadcasting Students Guidebook)*, Ebrall and Ebrall, Esperance WA, 1983. (little mention of journalism)
FANG, Irving. *Those Radio Commentators*, Iowa State University Press, Ames IO, 1977. (with recording)
FORTUNALE, Peter and MILLS, Joshua. *Radio in the television age*, Overlook Press, New York, 1980.
HALE, Julian. *Radio Power: propaganda and international broadcasting*, Paul Elek, London, 1971.
HARDING, Richard. *Outside interference: the politics of Australian broadcasting*, Sun Books, Melbourne, 1979.
HALL, Mark W. *Broadcast Journalism*, Hastings House, New York, 1978.
HEAD, Stanley W. *Broadcasting in America*, Houghton Mifflin, Boston, 1975.

HERBERT, John. *The Techniques of Radio Journalism*, A & C Black, London, 1976.
HIGGINS, C. S. and MORRIS, P. D. *Sounds Real: radio in everyday life*, University of Queensland Press, Brisbane, 1982.
HILLIARD, R. L., *Radio Broadcasting: an introduction to the sound medium*, Hastings House, New York, 1974.
LENT, John. *Broadcasting in the Pacific*, Temple University Press, Philadelphia, 1978.
MACKAY, I. *Broadcasting in America*, Melbourne University Press, 1957.
MENCHER, Melvin. *News Reporting and Writing 2nd edn*, Wm C. Brown, Dubuque IO, 1981.
MILNE, G. *The Radio Journalist (A guide to radio news)*, West Sydney Radio, Sydney, 1979.
SCHLESINGER, Philip. *Putting reality together: BBC news*, Constable, London. (Communication and Society series)
SMITH, Anthony. *The Shadow in the Cave*, Allen and Unwin, London, 1973.

Books on television journalism

ADAMS, William C. *Television coverage of the Middle East*, (Vol. 1 of the Media coverage of Public Affairs series), ABLEX, 1981.
ARMSTRONG, Mark. *Broadcasting Law and Policy in Australia*, Butterworth, 1981.
AUSTRALIAN BROADCASTING TRIBUNAL. *Television and the public: the news*, ABT, Sydney, 1978.
____*Television in Australia: its history through the ratings*, ABT, Sydney, 1980.
____*Broadcasting Act 1942* (and Amendments), Australian Government Printer.
BEILBY, Peter. *Australian TV: the first 25 years*, Nelson, Sydney, 1980. (includes several references to journalism)
BELL, Philip, BOEHRINGER, Kathe and CROFTS, Stephen. *Programmed politics: a study of Australian television*, Sable, Sydney, 1982. (much about television journalism)
BRIGGS, Asa. *Governing the BBC*, BBC, London.
____*History of Broadcasting in the UK*, Vol. 4, (*Sound & Vision*), OUP, 1979.
CHANCELLOR, John and MEARS, Walter R. *The News Business*, Harper & Row, New York, 1983.
EFFRON, Edith. *The News Twisters*, Manor Books, New York, 1972. (useful criticism of tv journalism in the US)

EPSTEIN, Edward J. *News from Nowhere*, Vintage, New York, 1973. (good criticism of US network news operations, ethics, accuracy).
____*Between Fact and Fiction*, Vintage, New York, 1975 (as above, very interesting).
FANG, Irving. *Television News*, Hastings House, New York, 1972 (was the standard text on the subject, revised and reprinted twice since).
FRIENDLY, Fred. *Due to Circumstances Beyond our Control*, Random House, New York, 1967. (excellent reading on early tv ethical problems)
____*The Good Guys, the Bad Guys and the First Amendment: free speech vs fairness in broadcasting*, Random House, New York, 1976. (American references, but also valid here)
GARVEY, Daniel E. and RIVERS, William L. *Broadcast Writing*, Longman, New York, 1982. (covers all types of writing including news)
GIBSON, Martin L. *Editing in the electronic era*, Iowa State University Press, Ames IO, 1979. (largely print, also tv)
GREEN, Timothy. *The Universal Eye: world television in the seventies*, Bodley Head, London, 1972. (international comparison, critique)
HARDING, Richard. *Outside Interference: the politics of Australian broadcasting*, Sun Books, Melbourne, 1979.
HALL, Mark. *Broadcast News*, Hastings House, New York, 1978. (since revised; still an excellent text)
HEAD, Sydney. *Broadcasting in America*, Houghton Mifflin, Boston, 1975.
HENNINGHAM, John, *Looking at Television News*, Longman Cheshire, Melbourne, 1988.
LENT, John. *Broadcasting in Asia and the Pacific*, Temple University Press, Philadelphia, 1978.
McCALLUM, Mungo. *Ten years of television*, Sun Books, Melbourne, 1968. (collection of his articles)
MILLERSON, Gerald. *Effective TV Production*, Focal, London, 1976. (excellent basic tv production book, including tv news)
SCHLESINGER, Philip. *Putting reality together: the BBC news*, Constable, London. (Communications and Society series)
SHOOK, Frederick. *The Process of Electronic News Gathering*, Morton, Englewood CO, 1982. (excellent on methods, equipment).
SKORNIA, Harry. *Television and the news: a critical appraisal*, Pacific Press, Palo Alto, 1968.(interesting but dated and too American).

SMALL, William. *To kill a messenger: television news and the real world*, Hastings House, New York, 1970. (great reading about early US tv from a journalist's point of view).
SMITH, Anthony. *Television and political life*, Macmillan, London, 1979 (more sociology than journalism).
SWALLOW, Norman. *Factual Television*, Hastings House, New York, 1966 (on documentaries, regrettably dated).
WEAVER, J. Clark. *Broadcast Newswriting as Process*, Longman, New York, 1984. (very American but perhaps the best from there)
WENHAM, Brian, (ed.). *The Third Age of Broadcasting*, Faber, London, 1982 (more about television in general, but includes journalism).
WIMER, Arthur and BRIX, Dale. *Radio and TV News Editing and Writing*, 5th edn, Wm C. Brown, Dubuque IO, 1980.
WHALE, John. *The Half-shut Eye: TV and politics in Britain and America*, Macmillan, London. (only partly about journalism as such)
YOAKAM, Richard D. and Charles F. CREMER, *ENG: Television News and the New Technology*, Southern Illinois University Press, Carbondale, 1985.
YORKE, Ivor, *The Technique of Television News*, Focal, London, 1987.

Journalism instructional books (all media)

A. J. A. Summer School of Professional Journalism series of annual publications (from 1966)
ANDERSON, Douglas A. and ITULE, Bruce D. *Documentary News Reporting*, Random House, New York, 1984.
AVIESON, John. *Applied Journalism in Australia*, Deakin University Press, 1982.
BASKETTE, Floyd and SISSORS, Jack Z. *The Art of Editing*, 2nd edn, Macmillan, New York, 1977. (excellent but expensive)
BROUSSARD, E. Joseph and HOLGATE, Jack F. *Writing & Reporting Broadcast News*, Macmillan, New York, 1982.
De MAESENEER, Paul. *Here's the News: a radio news manual*, Asia-Pacific Institute for Broadcasting Development, Kuala Lumpur.
DODGE, John and VINER, George. *The Practice of Journalism*, Heinemann, London, 1963 (was British journalists' union text).
DUNLEVY, Maurice. *Interviewing Techniques for Newspapers*, Deakin University Press, 1980.

EVANS, Harold. *Newsman's English*, Heinemann, London, 1974.
____*Handling Newspaper Text* (as above).
____*News Headlines* (as above).
____*Picture Editing* (as above).
____*Newspaper Design* (as above; probably the best series on newspaper journalism ever written).
GARVEY, Daniel E. and RIVERS, William. *Broadcast Writing*, Longman, New York, 1982.
HALL, Mark. *Broadcast Journalism*, Hastings House, New York, 1978. (revised)
HARTLEY, John. *Understanding News*, Methuen, London, 1982.
HOHENBERG, John. *The Professional Journalist*, 4th edn, Holt Rinehart & Winston, New York, 1960.
HOUGH, George A. *News Writing*, 2nd edn, Houghton Mifflin, Boston, 1980.
IZARD, Ralph, CULBERTSON, Hugh and LAMBERT, Donald. *Fundamentals of News Reporting*, Kendall Hunt, Dubuque IO, 1973 (3rd or later edn).
JERVIS, Bob. *News Sense*, Advertiser Newspapers Limited, Adelaide, 1985.
____*More News Sense*, Advertiser Newspapers Limited, Adelaide, 1988.
LEWIS, Carolyn Diana. *Reporting for Television*, Columbia University Press, New York, 1984.
LOVELL, Ron, (ed.). *Reporting, Writing and Editing: the Quill guides to Journalism*, Kendall Hunt, Dubuque IO, 1982.
LYONS, Louis M., (ed.). *Reporting the News: selections from the Nieman Reports*, Harvard University Press, Cambridge MA, 1965.
MENCHER, Melvin. *News Reporting and Writing*, 3rd edn, Wm C. Brown, Dubuque IO, 1984.
____*Basic News Writing*, Wm C. Brown, Dubuque IO, 1983.
QUINN, Hestia. *Journalism for Beginners*, Lothian, Melbourne, 1977.
SHOOK, Frederick. *The Process of Electronic News Gathering*, Morton, Englewood CO, 1982.
SMEYAK, G. Paul. *Broadcast News Writing*, Grid, Columbus OH, 1977.
SMITH, Bernard. *Industrial editing*, Pitman, London, 1961 (about house journals).
WEAVER, J. Clark. *Broadcast Newswriting as Process*, Longman, New York, 1984.

WESTLEY, Bruce H. *News Editing*, 3rd edn, Houghton Mifflin, Boston, 1972.

WULFMEYER, K. Tim. *Beginning Broadcast Newswriting*, Iowa State University Press, Ames IO, 1976.

Some broadcasting histories and biographies

ABC COMMITTEE OF REVIEW. *The ABC in Review*, Australian Government Printer, 1981.

ALLEN, Yolanda and Susan SPENCER (eds), *The Broadcasting Chronology 1809-1980*, AFTVRS, North Ryde, 1983 (with updaters)

AUSTRALIAN BROADCASTING TRIBUNAL. *Television in Australia: its history through the ratings*, ABT, Sydney, 1980.

BARNOUW, Eric, *The Tube of Plenty: the evolution of American television*, Oxford University Press, New York, 1975.

BEILBY, Peter. *Australian TV—the first 25 years*, Nelson, Sydney, 1980.

BLAINE, Ellis, *Life with Aunty: 40 years with the ABC*, Methuen, Sydney, 1977.

BLISS, Edward, (ed.). *In Search of Light: the broadcasts of Edward R. Murrow, 1938-1961*, Avon, New York, 1967.

BRIGGS, Asa. *History of Broadcasting in the UK*, Vol. 4 (Sound & Vision), OUP, 1979.

BRIGGS, Susan. *Those Radio Times*, Weidenfeld, London, 1981.

CATHCART, Rex, *The Most Contrary Region: the BBC in Northern Ireland 1924-1984*, Blackstaff Press, Belfast, 1984.

COMSTOCK, George. *Television in America*, Sage, New York, 1980.

COX, Geoffrey, *See it Happen—The Making of ITN*, London, 1983.

DIXON, Frank, *Inside the ABC: a piece of Australian history*, Hawthorn Press, Melbourne, 1975.

ETZIONI-HALEVY, E., *National Broadcasting Under Siege*, Macmillan, London, 1987.

FANG, Irving. *Those Radio Commentators*, Iowa State University Press, Ames IO, 1977.

FRIENDLY, Fred. *Due to circumstances beyond our control*, Random House, New York, 1967.

HEAD, Sydney. *Broadcasting in America*, Houghton Mifflin, Boston, 1975.

LENT, John. *Broadcasting in Asia and the Pacific*, Temple University Press, Philadelphia, 1978.

MACKAY, I. *Broadcasting in America*, Melbourne University Press, 1957.

McQUEEN, Humphrey. *Australia's Media Monopolies*, Wedescope, Melbourne, 1977.
SEMMLER, Clement, *The ABC: Aunt Sally and Sacred Cow*, Melbourne University Press, 1981.
SIEBERT, F. PETERSON, T. and SCHRAMM, W. *Four Theories of the Press*, University of Illinois Press, 1956.
THOMAS, A., *Broadcast and be Damned: the ABC's first two decades*, Melbourne University Press, 1980.
WEDLAKE, G., *SOS: the story of radio communication*, David and Charles, London, 1973.
WESTERN, J.S. and HUGHES, C. A. *The Mass Media in Australia*, University of Queensland Press, St Lucia, 1982.
WHEEN, Francis, *Television*, Century Publishing, London, 1985.

Some books on sociological aspects and ethics

ADAMS, William C., (ed.). *Television coverage of the Middle East*, Vol. 1 (Media Coverage of Public Affairs series), Ablex, Norwood NJ, 1981.
ALTHEIDE, David, *Media Power*, Sage, London, 1985.
ALTHEIDE, David, *Creating Reality: How TV News Distorts Events*, Sage, London and Beverly Hills, 1974.
BARR, Trevor. *Reflections on Reality: the media in Australia*, Rigby, Adelaide, 1977.
BELL, P. BOEHRINGER, K. and CROFTS, S. *Programmed politics: a study of Australian television*, Sable, Sydney, 1982.
BLUMLER, Jay G. and McQUAIL, Denis. *Television and Politics*, Faber and Faber, London, 1968.
BONNEY, Bill and WILSON, Helen. *Australia's Commercial Media*, Macmillan, Melbourne, 1983.
DUKE, Chris. *The impact of modern communications technology in Australia*, ANU Centre for Continuing Education, Canberra, 1979.
EDGAR, Patricia. *The News in Focus*, Macmillan, Melbourne, 1980.
EFFRON, Edith. *The News Twisters*, Manor Books, New York, 1972.
ELLIOTT, Philip. *The making of a television series: a case study in the sociology of culture*, Constable, London, 1972.
EPSTEIN, Edward J. *News from Nowhere*, Vintage, New York, 1973.
———*Between Fact and Fiction*, Vintage, New York, 1975.
GOLDIE, G. W. *Facing the nation* (TV and politics 1936–76), Bodley Head, London, 1976.
GOLDING, Peter and ELLIOTT, Philip. *Making the news*, Longman, London, 1979.

HALE, Julian. *Radio Power: propaganda and international broadcasting*, Paul Elek, London, 1971.

HULTENG, John L. *The News Media: what makes them tick?* Prentice Hall, Englewood Cliffs NJ, 1979.

―― *The Messenger's Motives*, Prentice Hall, Englewood Cliffs NJ, 1976.

JOHNSON, Nicholas and ARMSTRONG, Mark. *Two reflections on Australian Broadcasting*, (News Media Centre Paper No. 6)

KUHN, R. (ed.) *The Politics of Broadcasting*, Croon Helm, Kent, 1985.

LANGLEY, A., *Radio Station*, Franklin Watts, London, 1983.

LODZIAK, Conrad, *The Power of Television*, Frances Pinter, London, 1986.

MASTERTON, Murray. *. . . .but you'll never be bored: the five Ws of Australian journalists*, SACAE, Magill SA, 1983.

MAJOR, G., (ed.). *Mass Media in Australia*, (AIPS summer school) Hodder and Stoughton, Sydney, 1976.

OAKES, L. and SOLOMON, D. *The making of an Australian prime minister*, Cheshire, Melbourne, 1973.

SAID, Edward. *Covering Islam: how the media and the experts determine how we see the rest of the world*, Routledge, Oxford, 1981.

SILVEY, Robert. *Who's Listening: the story of BBC audience research*, Allen & Unwin, London, 1974.

SMITH, Anthony. *Television and political life*, Macmillan, London, 1979.

STEIN, M. L. *Shaping the news: how the media function in today's world*, Washington Square Press, New York, 1974.

TEMPLE, John. *The Mass Media: a personal perspective*, Angus & Robertson, Sydney, 1975.

TUNSTALL, Jeremy. *Journalists at Work*, Constable, London. 1972.

TURBAYNE, David, (ed.). *The media & politics in Australia*, Public Policy Monograph, Dept of Pol.Sci., University of Tasmania, Hobart, 1981.

WHALE, John D. *Journalism and government*, Macmillan, London, 1972.

WHEELER, Michael. *Lies, Damn Lies and Statistics*, Dell, New York, 1976.

WINDSCHUTTLE, Keith and Elizabeth, (eds). *Fixing the News*, Cassell, Sydney, 1981.

WINDSCHUTTLE, Keith. *The Media: a new analysis of the Press, Television, Radio and Advertising in Australia*, Penguin, Ringwood, 1984.

Books about law for journalists

ABC LEGAL DEPARTMENT, *ABC All-media Law Handbook*, ABC, Sydney, 1990.

ARMSTRONG, Mark. *Broadcasting law and policy in Australia*, Butterworth, Sydney, 1981.

ARMSTRONG, Mark, BLAKENEY, Michael and WATTERSON, Ray. *Media law in Australia*, OUP, Melbourne, 1983.

DEAN, Joseph. *Hatred, Ridicule, or Contempt*, Deakin University Press, 1983.

DOOGUE, John. *The Writer and the Law*, Deakin University Press, 1982.

LAWRENCE, John and TIMBER, G. (eds). *Fair use and free inquiry*, Ablex, Norwood NJ, 1980.

SAWER, Geoffrey. *A Guide to Australian Law for Journalists, Authors, Printers and Publishers*, 3rd edn, Melbourne University Press, 1984.

WALKER, Sally, *The Law of Journalism in Australia*, Law Book Co, Sydney, 1990.